The Wars of the Roses and Henry VII: Turbulence, Tyranny and Tradition in England 1459–c.1513

Colin Pendrill

Series Editors
Martin Collier
Rosemary Rees

Heinemann

Heinemann is an imprint of Pearson Education Limited,
a company incorporated in England and Wales, having
its registered office at Edinburgh Gate, Harlow, Essex, CM20 2JE.
Registered company number: 872828

Heinemann is a registered trademark of Pearson Education Limited

First published 2004

ISBN 978 0 435327 42 2

08
10 9 8 7 6

Designed, illustrated and typeset by TechType, Abingdon, Oxon

Printed and bound in China (CTPS/06)

Index compiled by Ian D Crane

Dedicated to Ken Hillier and David Cannadine, two inspirational history teachers.

Photographic acknowledgements
The author and publisher should like to thank the following for permission to reproduce photographs:

Bridgeman/Bibliotheque Municipale, Arra, France p.103; Bridgeman/Corpus Christi College, Oxford, UK p.159; Bridgeman/Kunsthitorisches Museum, Vienna, Austria p.171; Bridgeman/Musee Thomas Dobree – Musee Archeologique, Nantes, France, Giraudon p.60; Bridgeman/Private Collection p.5, p.134; Bridgeman/Syon House p.68; Bridgeman/The Stapleton Collection p.44; Bridgeman/State Collection, France p.56; British Library p.27; Corbis/Angelo Hornak p.188; Corbis/Historical Picture Archive p.81; Corbis/Historical Archive p.98, p.173; Great Malvern Priory Church p.133; Mary Evans Picture Library p.29, p.54; National Portrait Gallery p.114, p.144, p.190; The picture on p.73 I reproduced by permission of the Dean and Canons of Windsor and Jarrold publishing; University of Ghent Central Library p.17, p.33; www.northamptonshire.co.uk p.14; Werner Forman Archive p.194.

Cover photograph: © Bridgeman/V&A Museum

Picture research by Sally Claxton

Written source acknowledgements
The author and publisher gratefully acknowledge the following publication from which written sources in the book are drawn.

A. Grant, *Henry VII* (Routledge 1985): p. 204

CONTENTS

HOW TO USE THIS BOOK

This book is designed for use in the study of AS examinations. Sections 1–4 cover events in chronological order between 1459 and 1485, but Sections 5–9, on the reign of Henry VII, take a thematic approach, which is more helpful for students in making an assessment of the first Tudor monarch.

Each section begins with a broad overarching key question, which helps to focus the material for students. The text of each section is divided into manageable and logical sub-sections to help students digest the material more easily. If time allows, it is useful to read the whole section through quickly to get an overview of the main ideas being made. Notes can then be made more easily and precisely on a second reading of the section. When making notes it is useful to try to tie the details and information to key ideas. Read a few pages and then try to write down the main ideas followed by examples that back up those ideas. In this way, the order of your notes will mirror the order of your essays – each paragraph should start with a main idea and then be backed up by evidence/examples. The questions at the end of each section will challenge students to use the information and ideas that have been presented to analyse, prioritise and explain important aspects of the subject.

Several chapters include contemporary sources with an assessment of their significance. It is hoped that these will help students to become confident in the understanding and analysis of such sources, which form such a critical part of the examination process.

At the end of the book there is an AS assessment section. This offers students exam-style source and essay questions based on the requirements of the three main exam boards: Edexcel, AQA and OCR. The assessment section offers detailed guidance on how to answer the different types of source questions, as well as the more familiar essay questions on the period. In particular, there is a focus on the need to plan and structure answers with care and precision.

This book is aimed at those studying the period for the first time, but there is sufficient detail and argument to interest the general reader and student alike. For most students, the reign of Henry VII will be their main concern, but it is hoped that they will also read the sections covering events before and after his reign, as this gives the essential context for the evaluation of the successes and failures of his kingship. This book has clearly argued viewpoints on the impact of the Wars of the Roses and the limited achievements of the first Tudor. Like all historical topics, this period of English history has been much debated by historians and there is no clear agreement about the nature of the Wars of the Roses or whether they really happened! Likewise, there is a great deal of debate about the nature and the scale of the achievements of Henry VII. For those who wish to explore other viewpoints and to deepen their understanding of the period further, there is a select bibliography at the end of the book.

INTRODUCTION

ENGLAND IN THE LATE FIFTEENTH CENTURY

The people

England in this period was a relatively prosperous place. After two centuries of plague and other devastating epidemics, including the infamous **Black Death**, the population of England was beginning to recover. By 1500, it is estimated that there were 2.25 million people in England and Wales. The vast majority of those people worked on the land. The fertility of much of the soil, combined with the shortage of labour after the Black Death, meant that English peasants, who rented land from their lords, were in a relatively strong position. Sir John Fortescue wrote at the time that Englishmen of all classes ate 'every kind of flesh and fish in abundance'.

Land use

The land was given over either to arable farming (ploughing and growing crops) or to pasturage (raising livestock), or to a combination of the two. In this period, an increasing number of landowners were turning to sheep farming, which led to **enclosure**. This was seen by many contemporaries as an ever-increasing problem in this period. The lawyer and writer **Sir Thomas More** commented on 'sheep devouring men', complaining that increasing sheep farming was forcing peasants off the land and into vagrancy. Nonetheless, sheep provided wool, which was a valuable commodity in itself and was also the main raw material in a growing cloth industry in England. Great fortunes could be made in wool and cloth, and their production was the key to increasing English trade with the Continent. Increasing trade and industry also meant more merchants and growing towns. London was the greatest city in the kingdom by far, but other great regional centres such as Norwich, York and Bristol grew apace in this period.

Classes of men

Above the peasants (who made up 80 per cent of the population) came a variety of landowners. There were yeomen – farmers who owned their own land – and there were gentlemen, who might be lords of the local manor and owning large estates. At the top of the tree came the greatest landowners. Most of these were lords or had other titles showing that they were of the aristocracy. The greatest members of the nobility were earls and dukes, who often held estates in several shires. They were the natural governors in the shires and were natural advisers to the greatest man in the land: the king.

Nature of monarchy

In the period 1459–1513, England was ruled by six different kings:

- Henry VI (1422–61 and 1470–1)
- Edward IV (1461–70 and 1471–83)
- Edward V (1483)
- Richard III (1483–5)
- **Henry VII (1485–1509)**
- Henry VIII (1509–47).

In theory, the country was governed by an **hereditary monarch**. Unusually, in the period 1461–1509, the three main monarchs – Edward IV, Richard III and Henry VII – were all **usurpers**. None of their fathers had been King of England. Despite this, the monarchy in this period remained strong.

- It was generally believed that the king was appointed by God to rule and protect his people.
- The king was meant to promote justice and to rule with the other great landowners (mainly the nobility).
- The hierarchy in society was ordained by God. Therefore it was a great sin for those who were ruled to rise up against their rulers.

However, English kings were not absolute (all-powerful). Sir John Fortescue called England a 'mixed monarchy'. He claimed that the king shared power with the nobility and the Church and that he ruled within the law. The common belief in England in the sixteenth century was that only continental monarchies or the Ottoman sultans in Turkey were **despotic**.

While the King of England was expected to have regard for

KEY PERSON

Henry VII (1457–1509)
As Henry, Earl of Richmond, he defeated and killed Richard III at the Battle of Bosworth in 1485. Despite many rebellions and conspiracies against him, he held the throne until his death in 1509, when his son, Henry VIII, succeeded him.

KEY TERMS

Hereditary monarch A king or queen who inherited their title from his or her parent. Until 1553, England was always ruled by a king. While Henry I's daughter, Matilda, briefly ruled the country in 1141, she was never crowned and was not recognised as queen by the Church.

Usurpers Monarchs who took the throne by violent means rather than by peaceful inheritance.

Despotic A term used to describe a ruler who governed harshly, without regard for the law.

the views and powers of his nobility, he was also meant to call **Parliament** occasionally. Parliament had developed gradually since the days of Henry III (1216–72).

- Parliament was an institution that mainly represented the aristocracy and which met in the House of Lords.
- There was also another house, the House of Commons, which was made up of Members of Parliament (MPs) elected from the shires and selected large towns.

Parliament met only when called by the monarch and its main job was to recognise the existence of a new king and to raise taxes for warfare or the country's defences. It had also become the institution the monarch would turn to for advice in times of crisis.

Crown and nobility

The history of the monarchy in England before 1450 had often been a history of conflict between the nobility and the Crown. King Stephen, King John, Henry III, Edward II and Richard II all faced serious challenges from sections of the nobility; the last two were deposed and murdered as a result. The same was true of **late fifteenth-century monarchs**. **Henry VI**, **Edward IV**, Edward V and Richard III were all deposed at one time or another. At the same time, there were a number of battles, which gave the period 1455–85 the grand title of the Wars of the Roses (see Section 1, pages 14–15). While political instability was a serious problem in this period, it is important to stress that strong monarchical government did not break down.

Henry VI, by Francois Clouet (c.1510–72)

The Church

This was an age of faith. The English Church was a crucial institution, helping to hold the country together in these troubled times. It was a religious age, where everyone was expected to go to church on a regular basis and most did. The Church provided an ideology, (a series of related ideas) which helped to keep the peace.

- It taught that this world was 'a vale of tears' and a testing ground for everyone to see if they were worthy of achieving salvation (going to heaven).
- Most people were worried about the next world after death and whether their soul would reach heaven (eternal bliss), hell (eternal torment) or, that third alternative preached by the Church, **purgatory**.

The Church in England was an **episcopal church**. The most important churchmen were the Archbishops of Canterbury and York, with the Archbishop of Canterbury claiming primacy over York. At this time, all the bishops and archbishops were appointed by the Crown and approved automatically by the **Pope** in Rome. Since the Church in England was part of the Roman Catholic Church (the only Christian church in western Europe), it technically owed allegiance to the Pope.

Church buildings

Many of the wealthy inhabitants of fifteenth-century England put their surplus cash into beautifying their churches. Spires, towers, aisles and side chapels were being built apace and testify not only to the age of faith but also to the prosperity of the times. Architecture too was becoming more refined with the advent of the **late Gothic style**. Among the men (and sometimes women) who paid for this wondrous architecture were the kings of the time. The period saw the building of King's College Chapel in Cambridge (Henry VI), Windsor Chapel (Edward IV) and the Lady Chapel in Westminster Abbey (Henry VII).

Church and society

At the same time, the Church was the centre of social life for most people. It organised rites and rituals, processions and plays, services and feasts, which marked out the passing of the year. There were many saints' days and holy days (now called holidays), where work was abandoned in favour of feasting and relaxation. Christmas, Epiphany, Candlemas, Shrovetide, Palm Sunday and Easter were just some of the main festivals in the Church year. At the same time, the Church taught obedience and deference. Most people were taught to know their place in the world and not to attempt to change it. Rebellion against authority – either secular or ecclesiastical – was a great sin. This was

KEY TERMS

Purgatory In purgatory, the soul experienced the pangs and pains of hell but only on a temporary basis. The pains and pangs washed away the person's sins, allowing the soul to move on to heaven.

Episcopal church A church run by bishops.

Pope The spiritual head of the Roman Catholic Church, based in Rome. He claimed to be the spiritual successor of the disciple St Peter, who, it was claimed, was crucified in Rome.

KEY THEME

Late Gothic style Otherwise known as the English Perpendicular style. The ornamentation of churches was often lavish; the spires soared heavenward and the brilliant fan vaulting makes one wonder, then as now, how men and masons could create something so beautiful.

not to say that society was a model of good order and decency: far from it. There was a good deal of violent crime and, of course, suitably **violent punishments** for the guilty.

The growth of guilds

In the towns, the late fifteenth century was also a time of increased prosperity and improving urban government. The increasing number of religious guilds or fraternities in many towns was an important feature of the times.

- Guilds were organisations of merchants and craftsmen, such as silversmiths or tailors, who grouped together. By organising themselves in this way, they were able to improve their economic power, regulate apprentices and look after each other in periods of economic depression.
- Guilds usually had a religious purpose. They paid for the funerals of their members and for priests to say masses for their souls in purgatory.

The growth of such guilds during this period is further evidence of increasing economic prosperity.

Increasing social mobility

While there was a natural stress on order and hierarchy, one of the healthy signs of fifteenth-century society was that there was increasing social mobility. Ever since the Black Death, which had strengthened the hand of the labouring classes, English society had become more mobile. Families like the Pastons of Norfolk could rise in just two generations from poor yeomen farmers to major landowners. The key to success was education. Education from the Church and the taking of holy orders was one method of social advancement. Most of the bishops in this period were born into families of modest yeoman stock. Otherwise men became socially mobile through education in law. Time and again, there are examples of men of lowly origins improving their fortunes by becoming lawyers to the great and the good: men like **Sir William Catesby** and **Sir Richard Ratcliffe**, who served Richard III and were well rewarded. Sir Richard Empson and Edmund Dudley did the same for Henry VII. Everywhere great landowners needed men of business. Estate managers and ambitious, educated men from the lower orders, who were unswervingly loyal to their lord, were in great demand. Social mobility is a clear sign that English society in the late fifteenth century was a healthy and prosperous society, where talent and education could receive due reward.

Intellectual advances and printing

In addition, the late fifteenth century was a period of intellectual change. Beginning in Italy, the Renaissance brought about a new critical spirit of enquiry. Education was seen as a necessary part of the upbringing of all those who exercised power. New schools and colleges were founded. Between 1440 and 1530, Cambridge University gained an array of new colleges – King's, Queen's, Jesus, Christ's and St John's – while in Oxford, Magdalen, Brasenose, Corpus Christi and Cardinal's College (now Christ Church) were founded. At the same time, English scholars travelled to Italy to find out about **humanism** and the new 'humanist scholarship' (as it was called). Giving this intellectual movement real power was the development of printing. The Englishman **William Caxton** is credited with setting up the first printing presses in 1476, in Westminster. Before this date, books were handwritten, very rare and very valuable. Printing made books available by hundreds and thousands at new low prices. Those with a little money and a little learning could buy copies of religious books and manuals of all kinds. The development of printing meant laymen as well as churchmen were now being educated. Soon, those who had the ability to read could enjoy **Thomas a Kempis's *The Imitation of Christ*** or Bishop Fisher's sermons on the penitential psalms.

Misleading views

This brief introduction to England in the fifteenth century helps to show that a study of kings and battles may give a misleading picture of the period. Despite the political upheavals of the so-called Wars of the Roses, many English men and women enjoyed relative peace and prosperity at this time. One estimate claims that an English builder's wage in the period 1500–9 brought in more food than in any decade until the 1880s.

In 1485, Henry Tudor defeated Richard III in battle and became king. This ended the rule of the **Plantagenets** and started the rule of the Tudor family. Ever since then,

KEY TERM

Humanism An intellectual movement arising from the Renaissance in Italy. Humanists were keen to improve the level of education in society and hoped to use the wisdom of the ancient world (especially Ancient Greece and Rome) to reform and improve society in their own day. In their quest for reform of Church and State, humanists were opposed to the old view that seeking change was against God's laws.

KEY PERSON

William Caxton (1422–91) The first English printer. Caxton built up a thriving textile business, operating between England and the Low Countries (the Netherlands, Belgium and Luxembourg). He spent a year in Cologne learning the art of printing and set up the first English printing press, in 1476, at Westminster.

KEY BOOK

Thomas a Kempis's *The Imitation of Christ* Thomas a Kempis (1379–1471) was an Augustinian canon and part of the Windesheim Congregation (itself part of the broader movement known as the Modern Devotion). Kempis wrote *The Imitation of Christ*, a devotional book about religion around 1418. The simplicity of his work is particularly appealing to the other (lay) component of the Modern Devotion, the Brethren of Common Life.

KEY TERM

Plantagenets The
Plantagenets were the family
that held the throne from the
coronation of Henry II, in
1154, to the death of Richard
III in 1485. One of Henry
VII's main problems was that
he was not a Plantagenet.

KEY PEOPLE

Henry V (1387–1422)
King of England from
1413–22. In that brief time,
he launched an invasion of
France and, after success at
Agincourt, married the King
of France's daughter,
Katherine de Valois, which
allowed their son to become
King of France. Shakespeare
later wrote this as Henry's
epitaph: 'Small time but in
that small most nobly lived
this star of England.'

**George, Duke of Clarence
(1449–78)** Richard of York's
third son. He allied with
Warwick and deserted his
older brother, Edward IV, but
changed sides when Edward
returned from exile in 1471.
He was executed by Edward
in 1478 by being drowned in
a large barrel of wine in the
Tower of London. The exact
reasons for his murder have
never been fully explained.

**Richard, Earl of Warwick
(1428–71)** Richard Neville,
son of the Earl of Salisbury
and nephew of York's wife,
Cecily. He backed Edward IV
for the throne in 1461 but
became disillusioned and
swapped to the Lancastrians
in 1470, helping to bring
back Henry VI in that year.
Known as the Kingmaker, he
was not a successful general
and was killed at the Battle of
Barnet in 1471.

historians have argued that the year 1485 was a decisive
turning point in English history. It has often been claimed
that 1485 was the end of the medieval period of English
history and the beginning of the early modern period.
Contemporaries would have recognised neither name (nor
indeed did they know about the Wars of the Roses!).
Instead, life for most people carried on much as it had done
before – Plantagenet or Tudor made little difference to
them.

Political overview

Nonetheless, this change of dynasty (ruling family), the
reasons why it happened and its impact on government are
the major themes of this book.

- In 1450, England was ruled by Henry VI, who was the
  son of **Henry V**, victor against the French at the Battle
  of Agincourt in 1415. Henry VI, however, was not a
  soldier like his father. He was a quiet scholar who lacked
  the character to rule well. He became influenced by
  favourites, which led to opposition from other
  noblemen, who were missing out on royal favours.
- In 1461, Henry VI was deposed by the Earl of March,
  who took the throne as Edward IV.
- In 1470, Edward IV was overthrown by his former allies
  – **George, Duke of Clarence** and **Richard, Earl of
  Warwick** – and replaced by Henry VI. Just a few
  months later, Edward IV regained the throne and had
  Henry VI murdered. Edward then ruled peacefully
  enough until he died suddenly and unexpectedly at the
  age of 40 in 1483.
- Edward IV's son, Edward V, who was aged twelve in
  1483, was overthrown and murdered, probably by his
  uncle (Edward IV's younger brother), who now became
  king and called himself Richard III.
- Two years later, Richard, in his turn, was overthrown by
  an unknown Welshman, Henry Tudor, after a brief
  battle at Bosworth in Leicestershire. Henry VII, as the
  new king called himself, ruled until his death from
  natural causes in 1509. He was succeeded by his son,
  Henry VIII, in what was the first peaceful accession to
  the English throne since 1422.

This book will explain this complex series of events.

SECTION 1

THE WARS OF THE ROSES, 1459–61: THE LIMITS OF POLITICAL INSTABILITY

> **How serious was the political instability of the period 1459–61?**

KEY POINTS
- Henry VI's weaknesses in the 1450s led to serious divisions within the nobility.
- Richard, Duke of York, who was allied to the Neville family, engaged in a series of battles after 1459 against what he called the king's 'evil advisers'.
- Though York was killed in the struggles, Henry VI was overthrown by York's son, Edward, Earl of March, in 1461. Edward was crowned in London and then defeated Henry VI's forces at the Battle of Towton. The new king styled himself King Edward IV.

TIMELINE
1453   Henry VI suffers a mental collapse.

1455   First Battle of St Albans – York defeats the Lancastrians.

1459   Battle of Ludlow – York defeated and flees to Ireland.

1460   Battle of Northampton – Lancastrians defeated by Yorkists. Act of Accord – Parliament agrees that York is now Henry VI's heir. York killed at Battle of Wakefield.

1461   York's son declares himself king as Edward IV. Battle of Towton – Edward IV defeated the Lancastrians to secure the throne.

Fate of the Yorkists

In 1476, the same year as William Caxton began operating the first English printing press in Westminster, King Edward IV organised a bizarre and moving ceremony in the **church at Fotheringhay** in Northamptonshire. Although

KEY PLACE

Church at Fotheringhay
The collegiate church had been founded by Edmund, Duke of York, and now it was to be the family mausoleum.

KEY PERSON

Richard, Duke of York (1411–60) Richard was the founding father of the Yorkist dynasty. He was the son of the Earl of Cambridge and inherited the dukedom of York from his uncle, who was killed at Agincourt. His marriage to Cecily Neville brought him powerful political and military support from the Neville family. He became dissatisfied with the government of the Lancastrian king, Henry VI, and attempted to overthrow him in 1460. Blocked by most of his supporters as well as his enemies, he was made heir to the throne by an Act of Parliament (1460) but was killed in the Battle of Wakefield in the same year.

KEY TERM

Judicially murdered Refers to the fact that although Clarence was found guilty of treason, his execution was not carried out in public as the law demanded.

KEY PERSON

Richard, Duke of Gloucester (1452–85)
The youngest son of Richard, Duke of York. He took the throne in 1483 as Richard III on the basis that the two sons of Edward IV were illegitimate and could not, therefore, inherit the throne. Two years later, he was killed at the Battle of Bosworth.

Edward IV was a Plantagenet, he was also a Yorkist, since his father was **Richard, Duke of York**. This duke was the centre of attention at Fotheringhay on this occasion, even though he had been dead for fifteen years. Edward IV had had his father's body exhumed and the corpse carefully prepared for reburial. Also present was another corpse, the body of Edward IV's younger brother, Edmund, Earl of Rutland. Father and son had been killed in battle in Yorkshire late in 1460. They had been fighting against the Lancastrian forces of Henry VI (Henry VI's great grandfather was the Duke of Lancaster) and mistook the main Lancastrian army for a foraging party. They rushed out of the safety of Sandal Castle and were promptly killed. The Duke of York's head was cut off and sent to the city of York, where it was exhibited on a long pole and decorated with a paper crown for the benefit of passers-by.

Violent death was not unusual for the family of York. Henry V had executed York's father, Richard, Earl of Cambridge in 1415, on charges of treason. In the same year, York's uncle, Edward, Duke of York, who was a grandson of King Edward III was killed in the battle of Agincourt. He was already buried in the great collegiate church at Fotheringhay, which he had founded, and now his nephew and successor as Duke of York was to be buried alongside him.

York's surviving sons fared little better than their father. Most would meet their deaths in violent circumstances. While Edmund of Rutland had been killed in battle with his father, another son, George, Duke of Clarence, was to be **judicially murdered** by his own brother (Edward IV), and the youngest of York's sons, **Richard, Duke of Gloucester**, born in Fotheringhay Castle, would die at Bosworth in 1485; the last English king to die in battle.

The next generation of Yorkists proved to be similarly doomed. Edward IV's two sons – the '**princes in the Tower**' – were murdered there, while their cousin, **Edward, Earl of Warwick**, was to spend most of his life in prison, only to be put to death by Henry VII in 1499. The one exception to the rule that Yorkists died violent deaths was Edward IV himself, who became king at the age of eighteen. Although briefly overthrown, he went on to rule successfully and died in his bed!

The Wars of the Roses, 1459–61: the limits of political instability   11

The families of York and Lancaster

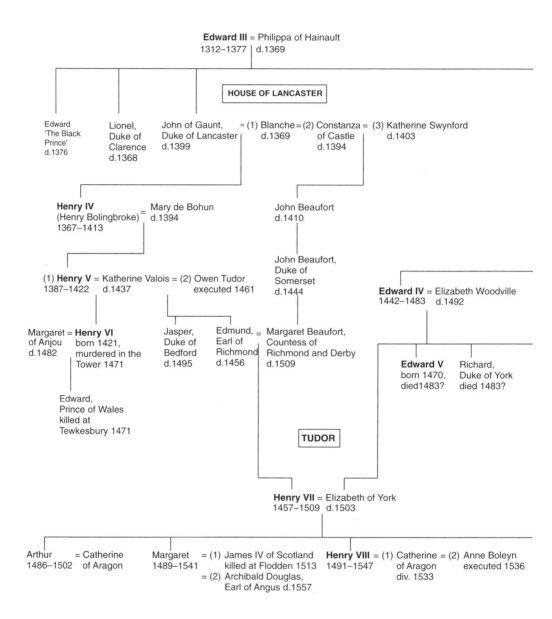

The Wars of the Roses and Henry VII: England 1459–c.1513

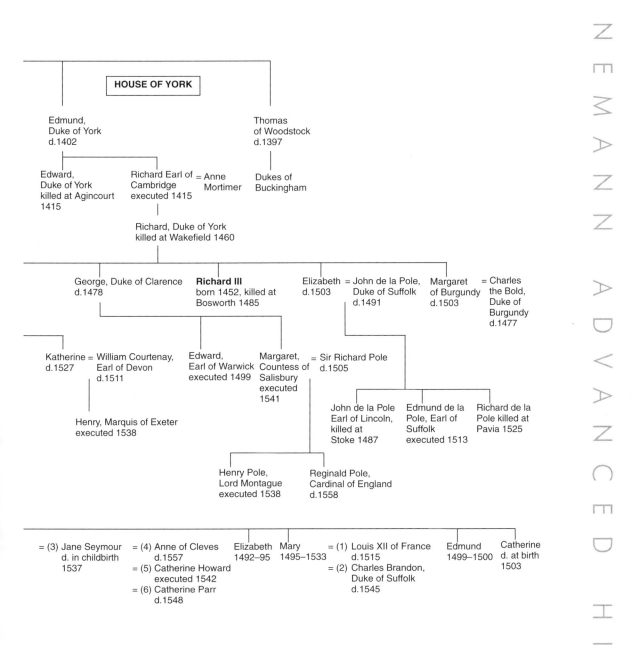

Reburial in Fotheringhay, 1476

The bodies of Richard, Duke of York and Edmund, Earl of Rutland had been buried for fifteen years in Pontefract. The corpses (or what was left of them) were dug up and transported over a five-day period from Yorkshire to the Yorkist stronghold of Fotheringhay in Northamptonshire, with its large castle and magnificent church. Clothed in cloth of gold, the two bodies reached their final destination and, amid much pomp and circumstance, were duly buried

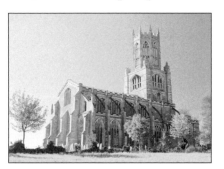

Fotheringhay Church.

in the collegiate church, with its glorious late Gothic architecture. Meanwhile, all the nobility of the realm, together with all the bishops and archbishops, acted as onlookers as the bodies were lowered into their final resting places. The proceedings were watched over by the **Duke of York's widow** and his three surviving sons, including the king of England himself. It was a massive ceremony – perhaps 5000 people attended, crowding into the church and the castle. There was feasting for the powerful men assembled there, while alms were given to the poor and needy.

It was an extraordinary ceremony by any stretch of the imagination, but what did it mean? What was Edward IV trying to prove beyond devotion to his fallen father? Why had he not done it before now – after all, he had been king for some fourteen years already? For Edward IV, the ceremony did two things, which were meant to strengthen his control of the country.

- First, it forcibly reminded the assembled notables of the disadvantages of civil war. Both the victims had fallen during a period of intense civil war, known since (but not at the time) as the **Wars of the Roses**. The red rose symbolised the family of Lancaster, while the white rose represented the family of York.
- Second, the ceremony was designed to promote the idea that the family of York had arrived on the throne and

HEINEMANN ADVANCED HISTORY

that they intended to stay. The duke was the founding father of a royal dynasty keen to establish permanence on the English throne.

By 1476, Edward had done all the things necessary to assure success. He had seen off his rivals for the throne, had led an expedition to France and would soon invade Scotland. This ceremony was designed to show the assembled notables, peers and clergy, that the conflicts which had brought the Yorkists to power were well and truly over. In this hope, Edward IV was proved right: though his father and grandfather had met violent deaths, Edward IV would not.

OVERVIEW

Looking back from the perspective of the reburial service in 1476, it would be easy to think that the conflict that preceded it had been very serious indeed. The period 1459–71 is often seen as the high point of the so-called Wars of the Roses: a series of battles, murders, betrayals and executions engaged in by the **Lancastrians** and Yorkists, which engulfed England in the middle of the fifteenth century. There was an outbreak of serious battles in the period 1459–61 and a further round of fighting in 1470 and 1471. In the ensuing carnage and confusion, kings came and went. Henry VI was deposed twice and his rival, Edward IV, once. The Earl of Warwick became known as the Kingmaker because he helped both men to the throne! Many leading noblemen were killed on both sides in scenes of carnage more concentrated and intense than any seen before in England, at least not since the troubled reign of King Stephen (1135–54).

On the other hand, the scale of the conflict should not be exaggerated. Despite the battles, English society did not descend into anarchy and confusion. Edward IV ruled without too much difficulty between 1461 and 1469 and the fighting was very much concentrated in two distinct periods before and after. Whatever the changing fortunes of the two monarchs, the institution of monarchy remained strong and respected. With the deaths of Henry VI and his only son, **Prince Edward,** in 1471, Edward IV ruled unopposed and England quickly resumed its accustomed stability.

Causes and course of the fighting

Weaknesses of Henry VI

The origins of the conflicts between the families of Lancaster and York, which are often referred to as the Wars of the Roses, went back many years and revolved around the weaknesses of King Henry VI and the ambitions of Richard, Duke of York.

- Henry VI had succeeded his father, Henry V (who had defeated the French at Agincourt in 1415), in 1422. As a small child, he was crowned king of both England and France. His **minority** proceeded surprisingly smoothly and showed the innate strength of English medieval monarchy. One of his uncles, Humphrey, Duke of Gloucester, took charge of England, while another uncle, John, Duke of Bedford, had charge of **England's French possessions**.

- Problems arose, however, after Henry came of age. He was a rather shadowy figure, a meek and pious individual, with apparently none of the military or political skills needed by a good king. Unlike his famous father, who was a warrior king and the embodiment of strong medieval kingship, Henry VI seemed to possess little will of his own, little appreciation of politics and had no apparent interest in fighting!

- Henry VI was easily dominated by favourites at his court, which annoyed powerful men excluded from favour. At the same time, his government was on the losing end of conflict in France, so that by 1453 the English had been expelled from France, except for the port of Calais. This was a terrible disaster for Henry's regime.

York's power

The man who felt most excluded from power, and a man not associated with the disasters in France, was the most powerful man in the land after the king himself. Richard, Duke of York held extensive estates in the north, south Wales and Ireland. He was linked by marriage to the powerful Neville family and together these families had the ability to raise whole armies if need be. At the same time,

KEY TERM

Minority Refers to the period when the ruler is a child or a minor.

KEY THEMES

England's French possessions Refers to the fact that ever since the Norman Conquest of 1066, kings of England held substantial lands in France. Indeed, many medieval kings of England were really French rather than English. However, by the fifteenth century, English fortunes in France were on the wane. Although Edward III (ruled 1322–77) had campaigned successfully in France, the growing strength of the French monarchy meant that English influence in France was being eroded. The end came in the reign of Henry VI. After defeat at Castillon in 1453, the port of Calais and a few forts nearby were the full extent of English possessions on the Continent.

until the birth of Henry VI's son in 1453, the Duke of York was also **heir presumptive**, since he was Henry VI's closest male relative. At first it seemed unlikely that the tension between the king and York would result in warfare and it was even more unlikely that York would dare to challenge for the throne itself.

Problems of 1453–5

In 1453, however, a series of events seriously undermined Henry VI's government.

- Quite unexpectedly, Henry VI suffered a mental collapse – now thought to be **catatonic schizophrenia** – which rendered him helpless and apparently speechless for at least fifteen months and possibly longer. This meant that some kind of protector or regent would have to be appointed to rule in the king's name. This was York's opportunity to gain power. As the king's closest adult male relative, English traditions suggested that York should be protector, in the same way as if the king were still a child. Indeed, in 1454, Parliament petitioned that York should assume this position and offered him the same limited powers as those given to the king's uncles during his minority. It was agreed that York should be protector until Henry recovered. York duly became protector and the previous favourite, **Edmund Beaufort, Duke of Somerset,** was arrested and imprisoned.
- However, York's power was uncertain and was undermined by two other developments. First, in October 1453, Henry VI's French wife, **Margaret of Anjou,** gave birth to a son, Prince Edward. If the child were indeed Henry's – and there were soon stories that he

The Duke of Somerset being executed after the Battle of Tewkesbury, 1471.

was not – then York was no longer heir to the throne.

- Queen Margaret then appealed to French traditions to claim that she, not York, should be protector while her husband was ill. Around Christmas time, 1453, she claimed that King Henry had recovered his sanity. Immediately, the Duke of Somerset was released, York was ousted from the Council and several of his enemies among the nobility were welcomed back to court.

- Stung by this sudden reversal in his fortunes, York resorted to force. Together with his ally, **Richard Neville, Earl of Salisbury**, he raised troops and marched menacingly on London. The king's advisers were taken by surprise and the royal forces were defeated at St Albans in May 1455. The battle was little more than a skirmish but the Duke of Somerset and the Earl of Northumberland were killed, leaving their heirs to plot revenge against York and his allies.

The Lancastrians seek revenge

Although York made himself protector again in November 1455, opposition from many of the nobility and from Margaret of Anjou caused him to resign his office just three months later. After that, the court party, led by the queen and the Dukes of Somerset and Buckingham, seemed determined to destroy York and his allies. The queen built up a power base in the Midlands, in the area where her young son held lands. In 1459, royal forces were again mustered to take on Yorkist troops being raised in the Ludlow area. At Ludford Bridge, Yorkist forces fled from the field when soldiers from the **Calais garrison** decided to abandon the duke and went over to the king's side. At the subsequent Parliament held in Coventry (the Yorkists nicknamed it the Parliament of Devils), York and his allies were denounced as traitors. This meant that they lived under sentence of death and all their lands were confiscated and handed over to royal stewards.

The Yorkists strike back, 1460

Faced with this desperate situation, the Yorkists had no choice but to resort to armed force. Luckily, they possessed large estates and could raise troops quite easily. In addition, they had refuges, where royal forces could not reach them.

- After the disaster at Ludlow, York had retreated to his estates in Ireland, where government by the English Crown existed in name only. His ally, Richard Neville, Earl of Warwick, slunk away to Calais, across the water, where he was Captain of the garrison.
- In June 1460, Warwick, together with his father, the Earl of Salisbury, and York's eldest son, Edward, Earl of March, sailed from Calais and landed in Kent. They brought troops and a **papal legate** called Coppini with them. As the Pope's ambassador, he gave spiritual significance to the Yorkist cause and thoughtfully **excommunicated** most of the Lancastrian nobles from the Roman Catholic Church.
- As the royal court was in the Midlands at the time, the rebels took charge of London, where the merchants supported the Yorkists, as they tended to back whoever controlled the port of Calais.

Marching north-west, the Yorkists met with unexpected success. In July 1460, they defeated a large Lancastrian force at Northampton, killing the Duke of Buckingham and the Earl of Shrewsbury in a battle that lasted barely an hour. The real bonus for the Yorkists was that they also captured the enfeebled Henry VI, who was apparently watching the battle in a state of incomprehension. With the king on their side, the Yorkists could hope to rule in his name and get rid of their enemies. They would argue that they were merely getting rid of evil men who had misled the hapless King Henry. However, York, who had played no part in the battle, took a different view.

In September, he arrived from Ireland and marched on London. When he arrived at the Parliament being held there, he strode into the House of Lords and placed his hand on the empty throne, meaning to claim it for himself. Instead of the shouts of approval and acclamation he had hoped for, he was greeted by a deafening silence. Even his closest allies had no idea that he intended to claim the throne for himself and they clearly disapproved of such a move. To rule in the name of a childlike king was one thing, but to depose an **anointed sovereign** was unthinkable, even if that king was mad. Such was the residual power of English kingship that everyone backed away from such a sacrilegious act.

York claimed the throne on the basis that Henry VI's grandfather, Henry IV (who ruled 1399–1413), had illegally taken the throne from Richard II in 1399. However, the English nobility refused to allow usurpation of the throne by York and instead would agree only to an unworkable compromise. Trying to placate both sides, the Act of Accord of 1460 declared that Henry VI would remain king for his own lifetime but on his death the Crown would pass to Richard of York or, if York had died in the meantime, to York's heir, Edward, Earl of March.

Death of the Duke of York, 1460

The Act of Accord was a recipe for more fighting. Henry's son, Edward, Prince of Wales, was hardly likely to accept being disinherited without a fight, while the Yorkists realised that they would have to continue fighting if they wished to achieve any degree of security.

- Margaret of Anjou, now in the north of England, set about recruiting troops to win back her son's inheritance. Supported by many of the great northern magnates, who disliked York and the Nevilles, they raised a great army.
- York, who may have had plans to force Henry VI to abdicate, marched north to meet them. Just after Christmas, 1460, he mistook the Lancastrian army for a foraging party, rushed out of the safety of Sandal Castle and was promptly killed by the Lancastrians, along with his second son, Edmund, Earl of Rutland.
- York's brother-in-law, Salisbury, was executed by his enemies after the battle and York's head was hacked off and sent to the city of York. There it was put on a long pike by the main bridge over the River Ouse and apparently decorated with a paper crown. Thus all those who passed along the way might mock the pretensions of a man who wished to take the Crown from the rightful king. At the same time, this grisly sight reminded everyone of the penalties for unbridled ambition.

The triumph of York's son, 1461

For York's heir, Edward, Earl of March, who was only eighteen years old, the future looked bleak indeed. The Lancastrians, under Margaret, were now free to march south and retake possession of the capital.

KEY THEME

York claimed the throne
As the Duke of York had proclaimed in 1460, 'though right for a time rest and be put to silence, yet it rotteth not, nor shall it perish'. When York's son did gain the throne in 1461, the reality of the situation was explained by Coppini, the papal legate who commented, 'In the end, my Lord of Warwick has come off best and has made a new king of the son of the Duke of York.'

Jasper Tudor (1431–95)

Henry Tudor's uncle and half-brother to Henry VI. He supported the Lancastrian cause throughout and was highly rewarded when his nephew won the throne in 1485. Created Earl of Pembroke by Henry VI, he was given a dukedom (Bedford) in 1485 by his nephew, Henry VII, after the Battle of Bosworth. Although he was married, he had no children. He was the main power in Wales during Henry VII's reign.

- Edward, Earl of March was recruiting in the Welsh Marches and hoping to come to London when he heard that **Jasper Tudor**, a keen Lancastrian, had landed in south Wales with a force of French mercenaries. Edward promptly marched his forces into Hereford and defeated Tudor's army at Mortimer's Cross. It was the biggest battle of the wars so far and it underlined young Edward's abilities as a military commander.
- Meanwhile, however, Edward's main ally in this time of crisis, his cousin, Warwick, was showing his failings as military commander. His army was now the only force that could protect the city of London from Margaret's increasingly undisciplined army. Yet Warwick's failure to track the progress of that army meant that he was taken by surprise at St Albans. Believing that the enemy was still nine miles away, he was changing the placement of his troops when they were attacked and routed.
- Warwick fled from the scene and the Lancastrian triumph seemed complete, since Margaret had now also regained the person of Henry VI. Her enfeebled husband was discovered at the rear of the Yorkist forces and reunited with his wife and supporters. The Lancastrian forces need only retake the capital and Henry VI's regime would be fully re-established, while the Yorkist faction would be doomed to exile or destruction.

However, at this point, Margaret, realising that her northern army would take great delight in sacking London and much of the rest of southern England, gave the order to march north again. In truth, the Lancastrians had neglected the city of London for many years and now they paid the price. Margaret had been keen to establish a power base in the Midlands centred on the lands of her son, the Prince of Wales. At the same time, the great London merchant companies, who dominated the city's government, tended to side with whoever controlled the port of Calais. Since 1455, of course, the Captain of Calais had been Warwick.

Queen Margaret's decision to march north gave Edward, Earl of March, a much needed breathing space. With his army fresh from victory in the west and his supporters already streaming into London, he marched on the capital and gained admittance on the basis that he was the only man likely to protect the capital from being sacked. Once there, the dangers of the situation forced Edward to take a desperate gamble and claim the throne for himself.

- In a series of stage-managed ceremonies, Edward was apparently forced to take the throne on the basis that he had a better descent from Edward III than his rival Henry VI, who was grandson of the usurper Henry IV.
- Unfortunately for Edward, this Yorkist claim to the throne via inheritance had been specifically rejected by the judges and Parliament in 1460. Furthermore there was, of course, no Parliament meeting in London at this time and so there was no important institution to recognise Edward's assumption of power.
- Edward's claim to the throne was extremely tenuous as it broke the Act of Accord of the previous year, which had proclaimed that Henry VI would be king for the rest of his natural life. In reality, a small faction of nobles and merchants had proclaimed Edward king.

The Battle of Towton

Waiting just long enough to gather further troops, Edward set off from London to meet Henry in battle. So, on 29 March 1461 – **Palm Sunday** of that year – two great armies faced each other in Yorkshire, north of the town of Pontefract. The ensuing **Battle of Towton** was certainly the greatest battle of the Wars of the Roses and probably the largest pitched battle ever on English soil. At first, the Lancastrian forces seemed to have the advantage, but the timely arrival of Yorkist reinforcements turned the long drawn out battle in their favour. After many hours of fighting, the Lancastrian forces scattered and fled, many being killed as they tried to escape. It was a decisive battle and a decisive victory for Edward, Earl of March. Three months earlier, his father, Richard, Duke of York, had been killed at the Battle of Wakefield and Edward's fortunes seemed to be at their lowest ebb. Spurred on by his father's death, Edward, still only eighteen years old, had proclaimed himself King Edward IV in London and had now secured his kingship with victory in battle. He had defeated and scattered the forces of his opponent, King Henry VI. Edward, the usurper, had made a reality of his power and would rule rather more effectively than his

KEY TERM

Palm Sunday In the Christian Church, Palm Sunday celebrates the occasion when Jesus entered Jerusalem on a donkey and was greeted by women and children welcoming him with palm leaves. It is the Sunday that starts Holy Week. Holy Week includes Good Friday, when Jesus was crucified by the Romans, and Easter Sunday, when, according to Christian belief, he rose from the dead.

KEY EVENT

Battle of Towton (1461) Chroniclers of the day embroidered it with myth and divine intervention. It was said that three suns were seen that day and the early part of the battle was fought in a snowstorm. Perhaps 50,000 men were engaged on both sides, although contemporaries almost certainly exaggerated the dead when they claimed that 28,000 had been killed.

The geography of the conflict, 1455–87

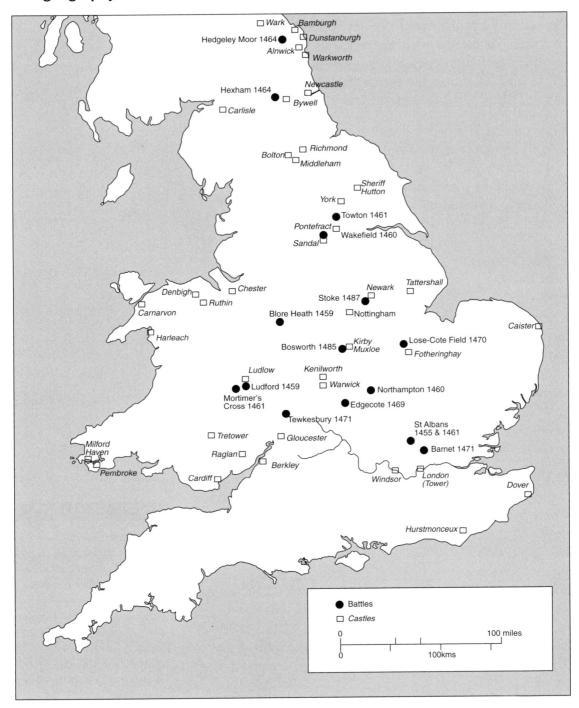

predecessor for the next nine years. When he was briefly overthrown in 1470, it was not his enemies but his friends who were responsible.

The Wars of the Roses, 1459–61: the limits of political instability   23

The scale of the fighting

Undoubtedly, the period 1459–61 witnessed a period of civil war. Thousands of troops were raised by a variety of commanders and a series of battles were fought on English soil in a way that had not happened since the days of Henry III and Simon de Montfort.

- In spite of Henry VI's feebleness, he had retained the active support of most of the nobility. Some 37 out of 60 peerage families had fought for him at some stage.
- At the same time, most of the nobility of England were actively involved in the fighting during this period. Some 56 peers (titled noblemen) had engaged in fighting on one side or the other in the years 1459–61. York's resort to warfare had sucked in the vast majority of them.
- However, 1459–61 was clearly the high point of peerage involvement in fighting. In 1471, only 31 peers were involved in the renewed conflict, and this number dropped to twelve in 1483 and ten in 1485. For the nobility, fighting was a very dangerous and chancy business. Ending up on the wrong side might mean death, but even worse was the chance of losing all your lands and thus disinheriting your heirs forever. So, after 1461, the peerage tried to avoid fighting.

At the same time, the scale of the disruption caused by these 'wars' should not be exaggerated. Most armies were fewer than 5000 men strong and existed for just a few weeks or months at a time. The historian **J.R. Lander** has calculated that the actual fighting in the period 1455–85 amounted to less than thirteen weeks in 30 years! Furthermore, there were no sieges during this first phase of the wars and no English towns were sacked. Margaret's decision to take her troops north after the second Battle of St Albans in 1461 bears witness to a sense of chivalry at the time, where civilians were not meant to get involved in the crossfire.

At the same time, the fighting was fairly limited because the struggle was not about who would be king until very late on in the period. Instead, it was about who would influence the enfeebled king and control his government. It was only late in 1460 that the struggle for the throne became the real issue, and even then this new struggle was born out of desperation rather than calculation. The fighting for the throne only lasted a few months and was ended, apparently decisively, just a few months later in March 1461. Despite Henry's obvious mental incapacity and childlike state, York and March only claimed his throne because they felt they had no alternative.

Those who stress the instability of the times naturally start the Wars of the Roses in 1455, with the first Battle of St Albans. However, this implies that there was fighting throughout the period 1455–61, when this was clearly not the case. For much of the period, leading magnates were attempting to avoid war, not promote it.

- In 1458, the Lancastrian government organised an official 'Love Day'. Here the Yorkists were reconciled with their opponents and gave money to the relatives of those Lancastrian lords killed by them in the first Battle of St Albans.
- In addition, they gave money for **masses to be said** for the souls of their victims in St Albans Abbey. The fact that warfare broke out eighteen months later should not blind us to the fact that this 'Love Day' was a genuine attempt to take the feuding out of English politics.

The English political system remained fundamentally strong in 1461 and the new king, Edward IV, could look forward to a long and prosperous reign, even though his rival, King Henry VI, was still alive (though not well) and in Lancastrian hands.

SUMMARY QUESTIONS

1 Why did Richard, Duke of York claim the throne in 1460?

2 How weak was the kingship of Henry VI?

3 Why and with what justification was Edward, Earl of March able to claim the throne in 1461?

4 How intense and serious was the armed conflict in England in the period 1459–61?

SECTION 2

THE FIRST REIGN OF EDWARD IV, 1461–71: IMPROVING STABILITY

> ## How strong was Edward IV's government in his first reign?

KEY POINTS
- Edward IV successfully ended Lancastrian opposition to his regime.
- Edward captured Henry VI in 1465 and lodged him in the Tower of London. This further strengthened his position.
- Edward faced growing opposition from Warwick the Kingmaker, which ended in his rebellion in 1469.
- Edward IV was forced to flee the country in 1470 but regained the throne in 1471.

TIMELINE
1461–5   Edward IV's campaigns to crush Lancastrian opposition.

1465   Henry VI captured by Edward IV and put in Tower.

1469   Warwick and Clarence rebel against Edward IV.

1470   Edward IV overthrown by Warwick and Clarence. Henry VI restored to the throne.

1471   Edward IV restored to throne after winning Battle of Barnet (Warwick killed) and Battle of Tewkesbury (Edward, Prince of Wales killed). Henry VI murdered in Tower. Edward IV now undisputed king.

OVERVIEW
Edward's success in establishing himself as king after the Battle of Towton in 1461 shows that monarchical government remained strong in this period. His success is all the more surprising since the previous king and his heir were still alive and since active support for Edward amounted to Warwick and not many others. Yet Edward

The coronation of Edward IV in 1461.

did establish a powerful regime and there seemed little chance of Henry VI regaining his throne. The Wars of the Roses had been short-lived and seemed to be over.

Edward IV's first reign

Edward ends Lancastrian resistance, 1461–5

Edward's first job was to deal with those peers who were still active in the Lancastrian cause. In truth, they posed only a limited threat to the new regime, as they were mainly in the north of England, far away from the capital.

- In April 1461, Edward marched to Durham and back to York, encountering little resistance. Warwick regained Alnwick Castle in Northumberland a few weeks later.
- Edward's strength in Wales also grew. Pembroke Castle was captured by the Yorkist **Sir William Herbert**, while Jasper Tudor, Henry VI's half-brother, together with the Duke of Exeter, were defeated in battle near Caernarvon in October 1461.
- Margaret of Anjou landed in the north at Bamburgh in 1462, with a small force of 800, but was quickly defeated. She and her son then left for exile in France, depriving the Lancastrians of their real leader.
- By 1464, the north of England was fully under Edward's control after easy victories for his forces at Hedgeley Moor and Hexham. In truth, these were little more than 'mopping up' operations and often the result of the continuing feud between the Percys and the Nevilles for dominance in the region.

Edward was merciful to his opponents

None of these so-called uprisings threatened Edward's kingship. He was made even more secure in July 1465, when his supporters captured the hapless Henry VI in Lancashire. Interestingly, and perhaps unwisely, Henry was not put to death, but lodged in the **Tower of London**. This surely was a mark of

Edward's confidence. This confidence and political ability were also seen in his merciful treatment of his opponents. A successful medieval king had to rule through and with the consent of the great landowners. Edward needed to win over the Lancastrian leaders with hopes of rewards rather than attempting to crush them by force. He realised that he did not have the resources to bring them to heel by force, so he employed more persuasive methods. Sir Ralph Percy, William Viscount Beaumont and **John de Vere, Earl of Oxford**, among others, were pardoned and restored to most of their lands. Many peers who had fought against either Edward or his father were not punished in the aftermath of the victory at Towton.

Edward widens his power base

As soon as he became king, Edward began to build up his power base and reward his supporters. As a result of the recent battles, Edward passed **attainders** on 113 men and confiscated their estates. It was the greatest landed windfall ever for a medieval English king. In keeping with the times, many of these lands were not kept by the Crown but granted out in order to gather political support.

- Not surprisingly, Warwick did best of all. He was made Great Chamberlain, Warden of the East and West Marches towards Scotland (confirming his control of the north at the expense of the Percys), Chief Steward of the Duchy of Lancaster and Admiral of England.
- **William, Lord Hastings** became the king's Chamberlain (controlling access to the king) and was given lands in the Midlands in order to build up an important power base there.
- Sir William Herbert became virtual viceroy (King's Deputy) in south Wales, while the south-west of England was entrusted to William Neville, the Earl of Kent and, after his death in 1463, to Humphrey Stafford, the future Earl of Devon.
- Edward's uncle, Viscount Bourchier, was made Earl of Essex and Steward of the royal household.

The Woodville marriage

By 1464, Edward was well established but it was then that he made his first major mistake. On 1 May 1464, he secretly married Elizabeth Woodville. The fact that he

kept the marriage secret until September is clear evidence that he knew that his most powerful supporter, Warwick, would be seriously upset by this move. After all, he had been negotiating with the French for a bride for Edward, only to find that Edward was already married! In addition, **Elizabeth Woodville** was hardly an ideal choice for a new king, who needed to use his marriage for political advantage – a foreign alliance was required at the very least! Elizabeth was not of aristocratic rank and she brought with her a host of brothers and sisters, who all wanted rewards for being part of the royal family. In fact, they were mainly rewarded with advantageous marriages, which meant that more peerage families were now linked to the king. Later, the Woodville marriage was seen as the start of a serious disagreement between Warwick and his youthful royal cousin, the king. However, we know that Warwick played his part in the ceremonial enthronement of the new queen, and it was only later that he would claim that Elizabeth Woodville had turned Edward against him.

Edward's disagreements with Warwick

The real reason for the growing disagreements between Warwick and the king came over foreign **policy**.

- The accession of a new French king, Louis XI, in 1461 meant that England and Edward had a choice of possible alliances. They could ally with France or with France's main enemy, the **Duke of Burgundy**. The French had, in the past, supported the Scots against England, they had recently expelled the English from their shores and they could now be a possible ally for the exiled Lancastrians. So, a French alliance seemed to be a sensible option, as a way of blocking support for the king's Lancastrian enemies.
- However, a Burgundian alliance also had advantages, since the duke ruled the **Low Countries** as well as the duchy of Burgundy proper.
- Both sides were keen to have Edward on board and the king took his time in deciding on his choice. In the end, he allied with Burgundy, sanctioning the marriage of his sister, Margaret, to Duke Charles the Bold in 1468. At the same time, he prepared for war against France, hoping that this would unite the country behind him in

the way that Henry V had used a French invasion to win the support of the nobility in 1415. Victory against France would make Edward's position unassailable.

Although Edward favoured an alliance with Burgundy against France, Warwick thought the opposite and he was engaged for long months in negotiations with the French. When Edward plumped for the Burgundian alliance, Warwick felt humiliated and isolated. The rising power of the queen's father, **Earl Rivers**, further inflamed Warwick and the feeling that his political fortunes were on the wane was made clearer to him when his brother, **George Neville**, the Archbishop of York, was dismissed from his position as Chancellor.

Warwick withdrew from court at this point, but in the next year Edward seemed to be going out of his way to conciliate the disgruntled earl. Warwick was granted the **wardship** of Francis, Lord Lovell and the king installed his youngest brother, Richard, in Warwick's household at Middleham in Yorkshire.

The rebellion of 1469

By 1469, Warwick had decided on rebellion. His plan seemed to be to build up a coalition of forces so powerful that Edward would agree to do the earl's bidding. The scheme, in fact, seemed to be similar to the Duke of York's hopes of ruling through Henry VI and it was equally doomed to failure. At first, all went well.

- Warwick encouraged a rising in Yorkshire led by his steward, Sir John Conyers, who used the name of Robin of Redesdale to encourage popular support – nothing like a Robin to rally the peasants! These forces then marched south and Edward, taken by surprise, left London to meet the threat with only limited forces.
- These forces were overwhelmed at Edgecote and the king himself was captured at Olney by none other than the ex-Chancellor, George Neville, Warwick's brother. Suddenly, Edward IV was a helpless captive, in the hands of his former foremost ally.
- At the same time, Warwick pulled off his masterstroke. He had persuaded Edward's younger brother and heir, George, Duke of Clarence, to join the plot and now, in defiance of Edward's wishes, married young George to

Earl Rivers, Richard Woodville (1416–69) was the father of Elizabeth Woodville. In 1466 Edward IV appointed him Treasurer of England and created him Earl Rivers. A year later, he became Constable of England. These moves alienated Warwick.

George Neville (1433–76) Warwick's younger brother, who was made Bishop of Exeter at the age of 23. He was moved (the technical term is translated) to the Archbishopric of York in 1465 where the celebratory feasting accounted for (among other things) 330 tuns of beer, 80 fat oxen, 3000 geese and four porpoises!

KEY TERM

Wardship This refers to the medieval custom whereby the heir of a great landowner was placed under the protection of the king (became his ward) if he was still a child when he inherited a large estate. This allowed the king to control the child's income, estates and marriage, and could therefore be very profitable. The king could sell the wardship on to another nobleman if he wished.

his own elder daughter and heir, Isobel Neville. Warwick took the pair to Calais and even had a papal legate on hand to grant a special license for the marriage of two cousins.

The failure to find powerful men to marry his two daughters had been another cause of friction between Warwick and the queen's family. With all those brothers and sisters of marriageable age, the Woodville family had dominated the marriage market. The earls of Arundel, Essex and Kent had married their heirs to Woodville wives, while Katherine Woodville had got the biggest prize of all when she won the Duke of Buckingham, much to Warwick's disappointment. All of this meant that the only great men left for Warwick's daughters were Edward IV's brothers, George and Richard, but Edward had forbidden any such marriages, fearing that where one brother had already been won over, another might follow.

Warwick's problems grow

Although his daughter, Isobel, was now married to George, Duke of Clarence, Warwick's problem was that he could not really justify the deposition or murder of the king. Though Clarence might have aspirations of taking the Crown for himself, his claim would clearly be inferior to that of his older brother. So, instead of **regicide**, Warwick issued the usual Yorkist propaganda about the evil advisers surrounding the king and hoped that Edward would be so shocked at the sudden turn of events that he would submit to the earl's direction. Sadly for Warwick, Edward was not Henry VI. Attempts were made at reconciliation but Warwick was clearly in trouble. There had been popular protests at the imprisonment of the king and, in March 1470, **Henry Percy, fourth Earl of Northumberland** – the Nevilles' main enemy in the north – was released from prison and restored to his earldom of Northumberland. The man who had to make way for him was another of Warwick's brothers, John Neville. Although he was compensated with land and titles in the south-west, it meant that Neville control of the north was at an end.

Edward now raised fresh forces to put down the remains of the Lincolnshire rising and declared Warwick and Clarence traitors. Their forces melted away and they fled in disarray.

Refused entry in Calais, the rebels took the fateful decision of seeking asylum in France. Now Edward's support for Burgundy and talk of a French invasion seriously undermined his position. **Louis XI** welcomed the rebels and prepared to help them in their struggle against the king.

Warwick's invasion of 1470

Louis' masterstroke was to bring together those long-time enemies Warwick and Margaret of Anjou. Warwick, realising that Clarence's claim to the throne, would never be strong enough to replace Edward, now reverted to his ancient allegiance to Henry VI, who, of course, was still alive and unwell in the Tower of London. Warwick pledged that he would restore Henry to the throne, but such was Margaret's hostility to the earl that she refused to lead an expedition into England until Henry had been restored. At the same time, she was seriously upset, since the price of Warwick's help was the betrothal of her son, Edward of Lancaster, to Warwick's daughter, **Anne Neville**.

Warwick's plan to get rid of Edward IV worked rather better than he could have hoped for. By stirring up yet another rising in the north of England, Warwick ensured that Edward was in that region when he landed with his own forces in Devon. Now allied to die-hard Lancastrians such as the Earl of Oxford, Warwick found he had rather more support than a year previously and many gentry came over to support the attempt to put Henry VI back on the throne. At the same time, support for Edward petered out and he decided to flee abroad rather than risk capture in England.

Edward's invasion of 1471

Luckily for Edward, his exile in Flanders (home of his sister, Margaret, Duchess of Burgundy) was short-lived.

- Finding help in the Low Countries, ruled as they were by his ally and brother-in-law, Charles the Bold, Edward was able to fit out an expeditionary force, which landed in Yorkshire in 1471.
- Edward's chances of success in regaining his throne seemed slim. He had a few ships and about 1000 men,

KEY PEOPLE

Louis XI (1423–83) King of France from 1461-83. Known as the universal spider for his skill at political intrigue and devious behaviour, Louis did much to re-establish the power of the French monarchy. He was captured by Charles the Bold of Burgundy in 1468, hence his hostility to Burgundy and Burgundy's ally, Edward IV.

Anne Neville (1456–85) Betrothed to Edward of Lancaster (son of Henry VI and Margaret of Anjou), who naturally enough still styled himself Prince of Wales. After his death at the Battle of Tewkesbury in 1471, she was married to Edward IV's younger brother, Richard, who later became Richard III. She was only briefly queen of England and died in 1485, just months before her husband's death at the Battle of Bosworth. It was rumoured that Richard had her poisoned in order to marry his niece, Elizabeth of York. Her only son, Edward of Middleham, died in 1484.

many of them Flemish mercenaries. Surely such a force could not conquer the kingdom. The speed of his return, however, caught Warwick unawares and meant that, although Henry VI had been proclaimed king again, his wife's forces had not yet arrived from France.

- Following the tradition of Henry Bolingbroke (who eventually became Henry IV), Edward claimed that he was merely returning to reclaim his duchy of York. Although he gained only limited support, none of the nobility, most notably the Earl of Northumberland, seemed prepared to fight against him – that task would be left to Warwick 'the turncoat'.
- Deserted by Clarence, who was now reconciled with his brother, Warwick's forces were not strong enough to prevent Edward's troops from entering London. There, Edward regained control of Henry VI for the last time and set out to hunt down Warwick. The two armies met at Barnet, just outside London, and Warwick's forces were decisively beaten.

Warwick was killed and thus ended one of the most extraordinary careers in English politics. He deserved his title of Kingmaker, since he had made Edward IV king and remade Henry VI. As a turncoat and political maverick, however, Warwick was the exception, not the rule. Some great men, such as the Earl of Oxford, were the opposite of Warwick. They remained actively loyal to one side or the other. Most peers merely became cautious and apolitical. Faced with renewed fighting, they now did all they could to avoid being caught up in political instability, with its attendant risks of death and forfeiture.

The Battle of Tewkesbury, 1471.

The last battle: Tewkesbury, 1471

Meanwhile, Edward raised troops once more to deal with the threat in the West Country where Margaret of Anjou and her son, Edward, Prince of Wales, had now landed. Able to face his two main opponents in separate conflicts, Edward had the good fortune to win again at the Battle of Tewkesbury on 4 May 1471. The Lancastrian forces were decisively beaten and, more significant for the future, Edward, Prince of

Wales was killed in the aftermath of the battle. While he lived, he would always be a threat to Edward, especially as he had recently reached manhood (he was seventeen at the time of his death). With his heir dead, Henry VI was doomed as well. As soon as Edward returned to London, Henry was killed, but the story was put round that he had died 'of pure melancholy' when he heard of his son's demise.

Political stability and instability 1459–71

For Edward IV, Richard III and Henry VII, it was important to put round propaganda to exaggerate the violence, chaos and evil in their predecessor's time. In that way, these three usurpers (they all took the throne by violence rather than inheritance) could justify their assumption of power as a way of bringing the '**body politic**' back to its proper order. The blessings of their new regimes would be in sharp distinction to the troubled times they inherited. Also, in an age of personal monarchy, where the power of the Crown was clearly linked to the personality of the king, it was useful to blame your predecessor directly for the evils of the day.

Historians have often endorsed the black picture of the so-called Wars of the Roses.

- They have seen the period as representing the complete breakdown of law and order as overmighty subjects (the nobility) and undermighty kings (Henry VI, Edward IV and Richard III) slugged it out for control of the kingdom.
- Some historians have gone so far as to claim that the entire social fabric was torn apart in the dark days of the fifteenth century as the old **feudal system** based on law and service broke down and was replaced by an illegitimate system – 'bastard feudalism' – where power relationships were based on money.
- Added to this was the idea that political instability was made much worse by the return of thousands of English soldiers to England after defeat in the **Hundred Years' War** against France. Flavour this mix with the

KEY TERMS

Body politic Refers to the nation or society. This term was commonly used in this period.

Feudal system A term used to describe the political and social system of the day. It centred on the ceremony of homage, whereby a fighting man swore to serve his lord and the lord offered his 'man' protection. As the king was the greatest lord, the system should provide a clearly defined power structure, which offered political stability and the ability to raise armies in case of foreign invasion. The system is thought to have been introduced by the Normans after 1066, but some historians think that there are elements of the system in Anglo-Saxon times.

KEY EVENT

Hundred Years' War (1346–1453) A series of battles between England and France, starting with Crécy and ending in 1453, when the English were defeated at the Battle of Castillon in southern France.

Paston Letters The Paston family, based in Norfolk, were a powerful, ambitious and upwardly mobile gentry family, whose letters (some 1100 items in all) of the time have survived. They reflect the uncertainties and corruption of the times but their message can easily be exaggerated. The Pastons had recently forced their way into the ranks of the gentry and were involved in a number of acrimonious legal disputes. John Paston seems to have been an abrasive character, who made enemies. Thus the conflicts that the Paston Letters portray may not have been typical of the period.

Social and political structure – Crown and nobility

So bleak a view of instability and anarchy would be very much an exaggeration of the situation in England in the period 1459–71. The so-called Wars of the Roses were serious but did not represent a breakdown in the political or social structure of the kingdom.

- English society had always been violent. The great men of the kingdom, kings and nobles, lived in fortified castles and their first duty was to fight, both to defend the kingdom and to defend their rights to land.
- All the wealthiest men of the kingdom retained other men (from knights on horseback down to peasant conscripts), who could be called upon to fight in their lord's cause if need be.
- At the same time, there was always the potential for serious fighting. On the one hand, England was engaged in a sporadic and episodic series of campaigns against France in the vain hope that English kings could retain their French possessions. On the other hand, the complexities of births, marriages and deaths meant that there was always the potential for disputes among the great men and, indeed, not-so-great men (such as John Paston) about who owned what land. Land, or rather the undisputed ownership of land, was the source of all political power at this time.
- Laws of inheritance were far from clear. Marriages among the nobility were arranged (well in advance usually) with an eye to the accumulation of further lands. Thus there could grow up great **political alliances** among the nobility based on marriages and kinship networks.

Political alliances In this period, it was the formidable alliance between the family of York and the Nevilles (symbolised by Richard of York's marriage to Cecily Neville) that caused all the trouble. Here were two great families, whose combined might was sufficient to shake the kingdom and whose forces could challenge and sometimes defeat the royal forces ranged against them.

The power of the king

The king's powers were, in fact, rather unclear and depended on personality rather than on a constitution and the law. The king was the fount of law-making but he was also, in some senses, bound by the law. He was first among equals with the peerage of titled noblemen but he was also different from them because he had been anointed as king. So kingship in the Middle Ages was what you made it and we must recognise that the real power of any individual king rested rather more on his ability to command than on the theoretical powers of the monarchy. Less able kings were those who did not share the military predispositions of their nobility or who lacked the political ability to command the support of these men.

- King Henry VI was spectacularly deficient in both areas. He was not a soldier and he did not command. Despite the historian Bertram Wolffe's attempts to portray a Henry who imposed himself on policy, it is still too easy to see the old stereotype of a feeble and enfeebled man, who could not command the respect of his peers. Henry was quiet and pious, not a military leader.
- An anonymous English chronicle, written in the days of Edward IV, may well exaggerate the scale of the problems but confirms this view of Henry VI.

In this same time, the realm of England was out of all good governance, as it had been many days before, for the king was simple and led by covetous counsellors and he owed more than he was worth ... All the possessions and lordships that belonged to the Crown, the king had given away, so that he had almost nothing to live on ... For this misgovernment, the hearts of the people were turned away from them that had the government of the realm and their blessing was turned to cursing.
(Adapted from an English chronicle written in the 1460s)

Where Henry VI's regime later gained direction and strength, it came, as we have seen, from the queen, not the king. Margaret of Anjou took charge of mustering troops to destroy the Yorkist threat. She decided to turn back after the second Battle of St Albans and she invaded England with her son in 1471, only to meet with defeat and lonely exile. Henry VI remained childlike throughout his life, a situation confirmed by his descent into some form of madness. Thus he remained prey to favourites and grasping noblemen, who could exploit the situation to their advantage; hence York's fury when these same men ensured that he had no share in royal liberality.

However, the contrast between Henry VI and his successor Edward IV could not be more marked. Edward was a soldier all his life. With the death of his father, he was the premier duke of the kingdom and won the Battle of Towton at the age of eighteen. Further military campaigns in 1469 and 1471 confirmed his natural ability as a commander and won him the respect of the nobility. At the same time, his energy and height – he was around 6ft 4 inches, very tall for those days – meant that he was automatically a commanding figure. Unlike Henry VI, Edward IV looked like a king.

Weaknesses of the monarchy

While the power of the monarchy depended very much on the character of the king, the monarchy was weakened by two other important factors, which made the problems facing any monarch potentially serious.

- First, it had been established for at least two centuries that the King of England could not tax his subjects without their consent. The day-to-day government of the realm was to be funded by the king's personal income from his own lands. If he wished to receive extraordinary revenues to fight wars at home or abroad, then he had to get the consent of his peers, usually in Parliament. Thus the monarchs of England remained, in their own eyes, seriously under-funded throughout the Middle Ages and the nobility as a body had a powerful weapon to wield against any king who might get ideas above his station.
- The second serious limitation on royal power followed from the first. The king could not afford to run a standing (permanent) army. He could not usually enforce his will on his peers by military means unless the other nobles agreed. So the Crown's military muscle also depended fatefully on the goodwill of the great men. The king needed to employ their armed men and retainers if he was to mount any kind of serious military campaign. In addition, kings like Edward IV needed to hire mercenary troops – men who fought for ready money. This, in turn, meant that the king needed ready money or at least to be credit-worthy enough to get loans from the wealthy men of the kingdom. In his first reign, the London merchants loaned Edward IV about £40,000, but overall his financial situation was often weak. As a result, his troops sometimes deserted because

the money ran out, or they refused to support the king because they were called away from their own shires.

Although **financial problems** weakened Edward's military might in his first reign, improving royal finances in the second reign, together with a big reduction in disorder and rebellion, meant that the king's position was measurably strengthened and enhanced after his restoration.

Local government

At the same time, the King of England could do little to enforce law and order in the localities. The king's government consisted of a very small bureaucracy of nobles, gentry and churchmen, who either travelled with the king or remained behind at Westminster. Though England had many laws to define right and wrong and to defend men's property and possessions, the enforcement of law and order relied on the great landowners. They still held their own courts and they could overawe the unpaid Justices of the Peace appointed by the king in each shire. In all areas, there were likely to be families competing for power and that competition might lead to violent affrays and confrontations. In this period, the families of Neville and Percy were competing for power in the north of England. Both great families controlled large kinship networks (or affinities) across the region, so conflict between the great men could have repercussions in many places. In 1469, it is clear the Warwick was able to raise those who served him in Yorkshire in a rising against the king, while York had done much the same in Henry VI's reign. Ultimately, these great men had the power to raise armies to oppose and protest about the king's advisers, those who wielded the king's patronage.

Limits to disorder

Nonetheless, though the Crown was potentially weak and the nobility potentially strong, there was enough fellow feeling between them to ensure that the realm did not descend into chaos and that the social fabric remained pretty well intact.

Both Crown and nobility saw the taking up of arms within England as a last resort. The most intense fighting came about between 1459 and 1461, when the Duke of York, his heirs and allies, had been proclaimed traitors and they fought back out of desperation. In this period, the historian

Involvement of the nobility In 1469, Warwick could only raise four peers to fight against Edward and two of those were related to him by marriage. In 1471, the year of Barnet and Tewkesbury, only ten peers fought for Henry VI and eight for Edward IV.

J.R. Lander claimed that 35 peerage families fought for the Lancastrians, while nineteen or 20 families sided with the Yorkists. However, the **involvement of the nobility** in fighting declined as the decade wore on. 'A plague on both your houses' seemed to be the message, as most noblemen tried to avoid active involvement in the conflict. In 1470–1, there was serious fighting again because, quite unusually for England, there were two alternative kings and the Earl of Warwick, fearful of losing influence with Edward IV, swapped from one side to the other. In other words, conflict turned nasty because of peculiar circumstances, not a general breakdown of law and order. A weak king (mentally and politically in the case of Henry VI) or just politically (in the case of Edward IV in his first reign), combined with one seriously overmighty subject (York or Warwick), resulted in war.

The nature of the warfare

The nature of the warfare also limited its impact. These were not wars of long campaigns, sacking of towns and sieges that would be the case in the English Civil War of the seventeenth century. This was not a long drawn out conflict for territorial gain, which would suck in most of the population, as that later conflict would do; this was a war of episodic campaigns and sporadic battles. Armies were raised, marched towards each other and fought pitched battles, lasting a few hours. Many of the so-called battles were little more than skirmishes. This was hardly peaceful but it was not a descent into chaos either. Even here it is clear that rather less than half the period saw active military campaigning.

- Between 1461 and 1470, violence was much more limited than before of after. There were a number of regional uprisings, a few military encounters but no serious pitched battles.
- However, between 1461 and 1464, Edward mopped up Lancastrian resistance fairly easily and there was no serious threat to his throne until 1470.
- The uprisings sparked off by Warwick and Clarence were very much stage-managed affairs. They were risings of particular affinities at their lord's behest, designed to put Edward under pressure. They were not popular uprisings protesting at the breakdown of good government or lack of food to eat.

At the same time, trouble usually broke out in regions a long way from the seat of government in London. An attempt by the so-called Bastard of Fauconberg (Thomas Neville, illegitimate son of William Neville, Earl of Kent) to stir up trouble against Edward in the politically sensitive areas of Kent and London in 1471 failed dismally. One of Edward's strengths was that he always retained control of and had support from London.

The size of the armies engaged also reflects the same pattern of fighting becoming much less intense as the period went on.

- Towton, in 1461, was the biggest and most decisive battle of the period. With some 50,000 men engaged, it was probably more than twice the size of any other battle of the period.
- Barnet and Tewkesbury saw armies of around 5000 on each side. This was much more typical of Wars of the Roses battles. When it comes to casualties, the impact of these encounters was also limited.

Nobles, gentry and other landowners were hard hit, but few families died out as a result. The biggest casualty was probably Warwick himself, finally killed at Barnet. But other Nevilles remained, though their power was broken. Warwick's biggest failing was not that he was killed but that he had no son to succeed him. Instead, his accumulated lands were shared between the king and the king's brothers, who happened to be the husbands of Warwick's daughters!

Certainly, the wars did not spark off a demographic disaster. The overall population of England was little affected. At the same time, the wars do not seem to have had an impact on food supplies. The campaigns were sufficiently sporadic and regional to ensure that any shortages were of limited duration. None of the contemporary or near contemporary sources, so quick to exaggerate in other areas, speak of food shortages brought on by the wars. In the same way, the economic well-being of the realm was little affected by the wars. **Trade**, both internal and external, carried on much as before, especially between London and **Calais**.

KEY THEME

Calais trade One of the reasons, after all, why the London merchants tended to support the Yorkists was because, throughout this period, the Captain of Calais was on that side! In this period, the port of Calais was still held by the English and so a garrison was needed to defend it from the French. The man in charge of the garrison was styled the Captain of the town.

Respect for the monarchy

At the same time, the institution of monarchy continued to command the respect of the nobility, even when there were two kings! After the campaigns of 1459–61, which resulted in Edward's decisive victory, most of the nobility settled down under Edward's regime. Die-hard Lancastrians were surprisingly few, given the fact that Henry VI had ruled for so long. In addition, Edward built up and extended that group of nobles who could hope to benefit from Yorkist rule and displayed mercy towards former enemies, which might at least win their grudging support. In the end, of course, many men still did not like or approve of the new regime but realised, after a year or so, that their interests would best be served by complying with the Yorkist government even if they did not give it their active support. Edward IV was safe enough until, rather unexpectedly, the greatest nobleman in the realm, together with his own brother, turned against him. Again, it was failings in particular relationships rather than a general breakdown of political rule that brought Edward low in 1469–70. Once Edward IV was firmly re-established in 1471 and his rivals were dead, it seemed that the so-called Wars of the Roses were over.

SUMMARY QUESTIONS

1 How serious was the opposition to Edward IV in the period 1461–70?

2 'In 1470, Edward IV was overthrown by his friends, not his enemies.' To what extent do you agree with this judgement?

3 Why was Edward IV able to regain the throne in 1471?

4 How useful is the term 'the Wars of the Roses' when applied to the period 1459–71?

SECTION 3

THE SECOND REIGN OF EDWARD IV, 1471–83: STABILITY ACHIEVED

> ## Why was Edward IV so much more successful during his second reign?

KEY POINTS
- Edward IV was in a much stronger position in 1471 than he had been in 1461.
- The deaths of Henry VI and his son, Edward, Prince of Wales, meant that there was no one to challenge Edward's right to the throne.
- Edward was an able politician. He acted with a mixture of mercy and firmness to win over possible opponents.
- He expanded his political power base in the country, using major noblemen to govern difficult regions of the country.
- He married and provided two sons to succeed him.
- He launched successful invasions of France and Scotland, underlining his status as a warrior king.
- There were no battles or rebellions in England during his second reign.

TIMELINE

1471 Edward IV wins Battle of Barnet (Warwick killed) and Battle of Tewkesbury (Edward, Prince of Wales killed). Henry VI murdered in Tower of London.

1472 Edward's brother, Richard, made Duke of Gloucester.

1475 Edward invades France. Signs the Treaty of Picquigny.

1478 Clarence executed in the Tower of London after being attainted.

1482 Gloucester invades Scotland successfully.

1483 Edward IV dies after a short illness.

OVERVIEW

The events of 1471 transformed Edward's fortunes for the better. All the main problems that had confronted him in his first reign now melted away, leaving him in full control of his kingdom. Never again would his position as king be challenged, either from within the realm or from outside. After 1471, the Wars of the Roses were definitely over and, unlike his predecessor and his successor, Edward IV died in his bed! How did this transformation come about?

* First, 1471 had seen the destruction of the Lancastrian threat to Edward. Henry VI was murdered in the Tower of London. This meant that there was no longer an alternative anointed sovereign to challenge Edward's position.
* Second, Henry's position was still strong as long as he lived. Even though he still had serious mental health problems, only the Duke of York and his son had challenged Henry VI's right to the throne. The vast majority of the peerage had supported the Act of Accord in 1460 because it would have seen Henry remain king for the rest of his life. This residual loyalty to Henry VI was demonstrated again when the Earl of Warwick restored him to his throne in 1470. While there were two kings in England, Edward IV's position was always under threat.

Edward IV overcomes the opposition

Death of Prince Edward

The year 1471 had also seen the death in battle at Tewkesbury of Henry VI's only son, Edward, Prince of Wales. This was possibly more significant in improving Edward's position than the death of Henry VI. Although Prince Edward was only seventeen when he died, King Edward had already shown that youth was no bar to kingship. If Prince Edward had survived Tewkesbury and gone into exile again, he would have found support in France and would have been well placed for future invasions of the kingdom. With his father dead, he would be in a position to build up his own party and proclaim himself the real Edward IV. After all, his namesake had managed to recover the kingdom in 1471, even though he arrived back in England with very few troops. With sufficient apathy from the territorial magnates, medieval kings might always face serious problems from a small-scale invasion from across the Channel.

Even better for Edward IV was the fact that Prince Edward's death ended the political ambitions of his formidable mother, Margaret of Anjou. She had been at the heart of Lancastrian resistance since the birth of her son; now she retired to a French nunnery to see out the rest of her days in religious contemplation rather than in political intrigue.

Lack of Lancastrian claimants for the throne

Furthermore, of course, Henry VI and his son had no close relatives to whom the Lancastrian torch might be passed. Neither had any brothers or sisters and the best Henry VI could muster were two half-brothers, Edmund and Jasper Tudor. They had been raised to the earldoms of Richmond and Pembroke, respectively, during the 1450s in an attempt to build up support for Henry VI from titled noblemen. These Tudors, however, did not have extensive estates and thus had very limited power. Edmund had died young, leaving a posthumous son, Henry Tudor. This lad had been kept under house arrest by the new Earl of Pembroke, William Herbert, but was then released when Herbert was executed and ended up in exile in Brittany. He hardly seemed much of threat, particularly as his Lancastrian claim to the throne was very weak indeed and came through his mother, **Margaret Beaufort** and not through his father. Jasper Tudor had been active in opposition during the first reign but, after the failure of Henry VI's readeption (return to the throne), he, too, was in exile abroad.

No more overmighty subjects

While Edward's position and power were clearly enhanced by the absence of any other **pretender to the throne**, the lack of overmighty subjects was also a key feature of the second reign. The conflicts of the previous decade had been sparked off by a combination of pretenders to the throne and overmighty noblemen. After 1471, both had disappeared from the political map of England.

KEY PERSON

Margaret Beaufort (1441–1509) A Lancastrian heiress and mother of Henry VII. She was the only child of the first Duke of Somerset, a cousin to Henry V. She had been contracted to marry John de la Pole, Duke of Suffolk, but that arrangement was broken off in favour of Edmund Tudor. She was vitally important in organising support for her son while he was a refugee and, although a woman, was a major player in her son's regime.

Margaret Beaufort (English school, 16th century).

KEY TERM

Pretender to the throne Someone who claimed the throne rather than someone who pretended to be someone else. The word 'pretender' comes from *prétendre*, the French word for 'to claim'.

- All the disruptive power of Richard, Duke of York had now been harnessed in support of the Crown, since his son was now king.
- The two noblemen who had done so much to engender political instability in the first reign had now been neutralised. Warwick the Kingmaker had been killed at Barnet and his lands taken mainly by the king's younger brothers. Clarence had married Isobel Neville in 1469, while her younger sister, Anne (once betrothed to Edward, Prince of Wales) was scooped up by the king's youngest brother, Richard, Duke of Gloucester.

Clarence neutralised

Furthermore, the threat from the other troublemaker of the 1460s, Clarence, had also been neutralised. He was reconciled with Edward in 1471 and, although he continued to cause problems and was a severe embarrassment to Edward, he would never again take up arms against his brother. His power and political ability were, in truth, slight enough and he had only gained prominence when he was egged on by the superior talents of Warwick. Thwarted of another lucrative marriage (with **Mary of Burgundy**) in 1477, Clarence seems to have lost his grip on reality.

- He judicially murdered one of his deceased wife's attendants on the basis that she had supposedly poisoned her mistress.
- Later, he accused his brother, Edward, of murdering some of his associates who had been found guilty of predicting the king's early death and of attempting to bring about the king's death through **necromancy**.

His patience finally at an end, Edward summoned Parliament in January 1478 and there accused his brother of high treason. He claimed in the Act of Attainder passed against Clarence that he was threatened by 'a much higher, much more malicious, more unnatural treason, than at any time hath been compassed, purposed and conspired'. In a final act of fraternal kindness, Edward decided to spare his brother the humiliation of a public execution. A few days after the death sentence had been proclaimed in the House of Lords by the Duke of Buckingham, Clarence was apparently quietly and privately drowned in a barrel of

KEY PERSON

Mary of Burgundy (1457–1482) Daughter and only child of Charles the Bold, Duke of Burgundy. She was one of the greatest heiresses of her day. Instead of marrying the ineffectual Clarence, she married the future German emperor, Maximilian von Habsburg. She died prematurely when she fell from her horse.

KEY TERM

Necromancy The use of magic to bring about someone's death.

Malmsey wine. The removal of Clarence, leaving behind an infant son (Edward, Earl of Warwick), meant there would be no threat to Edward from his own family.

At the same time, leading Lancastrians had also been neutralised. Jasper Tudor and his nephew, Henry Tudor, were in exile, while the irreconcilable Edmund Beaufort, Duke of Somerset and his brother, John, were killed at the Battle of Tewkesbury in 1471. By that date, the Beaufort family, for so long the arch-enemies of the Yorkists, had died out in the male line. Most of the rest of the nobility now threw in their lot with Edward, thus putting him in a much stronger position than before. The key point was that there was no nobleman or coalition of noble families sufficiently powerful to challenge the king's authority over the kingdom.

Regional magnates

Gloucester in the north

Edward's ability to govern the country, as opposed to being a mere figurehead like Henry VI, was also enhanced by his building up a group of powerful magnates, who effectively controlled large areas of the kingdom in the king's name. In the north of England, the frequent problems and uprisings were largely sorted out by the establishment there of the king's youngest brother, Richard, Duke of Gloucester. Unlike Clarence, Gloucester had proved to be Edward's loyal brother. When Clarence rebelled in 1469, Gloucester remained loyal and went into Flemish exile with Edward in 1470. Consequently, Edward lavishly rewarded him after 1471. He was now given a highly advantageous marriage to Anne Neville and extensive estates. The north of England had been his home for a number of years, so he was the natural choice to take charge there. He had also distinguished himself as a soldier, being in the thick of the fighting at both Barnet and Tewkesbury. On the whole, Richard did a good job in the north. The earls of Northumberland would scarcely be his friends but the current earl (Henry Percy, fourth Earl of Northumberland) did homage to Gloucester and was retained by him. This ensured that Northumberland could not act independently of royal authority, though the Percy

KEY PEOPLE

Thomas, Lord Stanley (1435–1504) Margaret Beaufort's fourth husband and thus Henry Tudor's third stepfather! He eventually threw in his lot with Henry Tudor at the Battle of Bosworth in 1485, delaying his intervention until the last minute because his son, George Stanley (Lord Strange), was being held as a hostage by Richard III at the time. Lord Stanley was rewarded for his support by being made first Earl of Derby. He was not really trusted by Henry VII, especially after his brother, Sir William Stanley, was executed for high treason in 1495.

Richard, Duke of York (1473–83) Not to be confused with his grandfather, who had the same name and title, Richard was the second son of Edward IV and the younger of the princes in the Tower. His uncle, Richard III, probably had him murdered in 1483.

family were allowed to retain a lot of their power in the north of Yorkshire.

By an Act of Parliament, Gloucester was granted most of Warwick's northern estates and was later granted a special palatinate in Cumberland, which gave him the power to raise troops without the king's authority. Gloucester's palatinate meant that he was effectively king in that area and did not need to consult Edward IV about what to do. The establishment of such a palatinate demonstrated Edward's complete trust in his youngest brother. In addition, Gloucester was allowed to keep any parts of Scotland that he might conquer.

At the same time, Gloucester acted as a buffer between the Percys and the Stanley family, who were the great family in southern Lancashire and Cheshire. They were notorious '**trimmers**' who had retained their power by not supporting either side with any real enthusiasm. During Edward's second reign, however, **Thomas, Lord Stanley** had married Lady Margaret Beaufort, who was the mother of the Lancastrian claimant, Henry Tudor. So Edward had especial need of Richard and his great household, centred on Middleham and York, to keep an eye on Stanley. Edward's delegation of authority over the north to his brother, Richard, was clearly successful. The Percys and the Stanleys did nothing to undermine the regime throughout the second reign.

Hastings and York in the Midlands

In the Midlands, Edward's control was at first less clear-cut, as Clarence proved politically rather unreliable. However, Edward then entrusted power to his faithful servant, William, Lord Hastings. The king's Chamberlain and notable loyalist in the first reign, Hastings was well rewarded in the second reign. In 1474, he was given estates confiscated from Clarence, including the vast honour of Tutbury spanning Derbyshire and Staffordshire. He was also given large estates in Leicestershire and Warwickshire and helped to oversee the build-up of a territorial base for Edward's infant second son, **Richard, Duke of York**. As a boy of only four or five, he was married to an heiress of the Mowbray estates of the dukes of Norfolk in East Anglia and the king then thoughtfully disinherited her co-heirs!

This meant that the lands would revert to his son. Richard of York further benefited in this period from the distribution of Clarence's estates after his fall in 1478.

Edward, Prince of Wales and Earl Rivers

At the same time, Edward set up his eldest son, Edward, Prince of Wales, while still a boy, as the principal power in the Welsh Marches. Under the control of his uncle, **Anthony Woodville, Earl Rivers**, the young Edward was sent off to Ludlow to symbolise the existence of royal power in this region. In 1479, a continuation of this policy saw Edward forcing **William Herbert, Earl of Pembroke** to give up nearly all the Welsh lordships granted to his father by the king so that the Prince of Wales might reinforce his power in that region. A rather disgruntled Herbert was compensated with thirteen manors in the West Country and the title of Earl of Huntingdon. By 1476, the young prince (guided by his uncle, Earl Rivers) had been given the power to appoint special judges and to raise armed men.

Meanwhile, royal authority in the Welsh Marches was enhanced by the minorities of key noblemen, who usually held sway in that area, notably the Duke of Buckingham and the Earl of Shrewsbury.

The Grey brothers in the south-west

At the same time, Edward's second reign saw the build up of a substantial power base in the south-west of England for Queen Elizabeth's two sons by her first marriage. In this region, the power of the Courtenay family had been largely destroyed by 1471. Then, after the destruction of Clarence, Edward built up the power of his stepson, **Thomas Grey, Marquis of Dorset**, who was given estates that had belonged to the dukes of Exeter. Dorset acquired even more land in the region through marriage to Cecily Bonville, a wealthy heiress. Their son was then married to an even wealthier heiress, who had inherited vast acres from the dukes of Exeter. The queen's second son, Richard, also acquired part of the same estates at a knockdown price from his mother! Once again, Edward IV seemed to be building up regional magnates, most of whom were his relatives.

HEINEMANN ADVANCED HISTORY

The success of the system

So, in the second reign, Edward seems to have decided to enlist members of his immediate family as key regional power brokers and, to do so, he certainly alienated other landowners. It is no surprise if Edward was a little heavy handed, since he had already been overthrown once and he was determined not to repeat the experience. On the other hand, there is no evidence of open aristocratic opposition to Edward's rule. As a man brought up in an aristocratic household, Edward understood the nobility perhaps rather better than other kings (such as Henry VI and, later, Henry VII), who did not have this advantage. He was generally merciful to those noblemen who opposed him by fighting for Henry VI (he was, after all, an anointed king), but this should not blind us to the fact that he expected loyal service in return. The important thing was that, for the rest of his reign, Edward's handling of the nobility worked.

Increasing royal power

Edward used his own family and his own determination to be more of an authority in those areas where he held royal lands. He intervened more directly and more often in local politics than his predecessors had done.

- Edward employed trusted agents to carry out his will in the shires, holding commissions (oyer and terminer) to hear and determine legal cases. Many of the leading gentry families in the shires, the families who often filled the posts of **sheriff** and **JP**, were enmeshed quite deliberately in the **royal affinity**.
- The man who continued writing *The Croyland Chronicle* (known as the Croyland Continuator) claimed that Edward placed 'the most trustworthy of his servants throughout all parts of the kingdom as keepers of castles, forests, manors and parks'.

Clearly, deposition had concentrated the king's mind. The government of the kingdom had to be taken seriously because Edward did not wish to go into exile again. While medieval England undoubtedly remained a violent and dangerous place, with men competing for land and patronage, there were no serious uprisings or rebellions during Edward's second reign. To that extent, at least, he had successfully reasserted and increased royal control over the kingdom.

KEY TERMS

Sheriff Literally 'shire reeve' appointed by the Crown as its chief financial and judicial officer in each shire.

JP Justice of the Peace – local men of standing appointed by the Crown in the Commissions of the Peace. They presided as judges in local law courts and were unpaid.

Royal affinity Refers to all those, including relatives, who gave direct service to the king. The royal affinity thus represented a very powerful body of men.

The Croyland Chronicle **and various Continuations thereof** Written at the Abbey of Crowland in the fens not far from Peterborough. It has extensive and probably contemporary accounts for much of the fifteenth century and is an important source for this period.

Improving royal finances

A popular rhyme about crown finances under Henry VI claimed that, 'Ye have made the king so poor, that now he beggeth from door to door.'

The achievement of political stability in England during Edward IV's second reign was enhanced by a noticeable **improvement in the state of royal finances**. Under Henry VI, royal income had been plundered by the king's favourites and royal lands, the main source of revenue for the Crown, had been sold. Not surprisingly, under Henry VI, the Crown's expenditure often exceeded royal income, leading to serious debt. However, the situation was not so serious that royal bankruptcy ensued!

With the accession of Edward IV, the financial situation for the Crown improved somewhat. Leaving aside military expenditure, Edward IV spent in the region of £50,000 each year for the maintenance of royal government. In medieval times, the normal costs of government were borne by the king and he was expected to finance these from his own income. The king's normal income came from three principal sources.

Crown lands

Most importantly, there was income from Crown lands. With the many forfeitures in 1461 and 1471, the confiscation of Clarence's estates at the time of his fall, together with Edward's own lands as Duke of York, Edward IV immediately possessed rather more land than his predecessor. Of course, many of the newly acquired lands were granted out as rewards to faithful followers, but it is estimated that Crown lands, on average, might have brought in about £30,000 a year during Edward's reign.

At the same time, there are indications that the revenue from royal lands increased during the second reign. The King appointed commissioners (agents) to inspect the collection of revenues in the duchy of Lancaster. Following this initiative, Crown revenues collected in Lancashire by Thomas, Lord Stanley increased dramatically. Lands yielding £347 a year for the Crown in 1476 brought in £800 two years later and £885 a year by the end of the reign.

Improvement in the state of royal finances The historian Professor Ross estimates that by 1475 the Crown was clearly solvent, earning more than it spent. B.P. Wolffe has written about the 'Yorkist land revenue experiment' whereby the Crown took a more personal interest and oversight in the receiving and spending of its revenues.

Customs revenue

At the same time, the king received extensive funding from customs revenue – in the region of £25,000 a year at the start of the reign – from taxes on the import and export of goods.

- He was personally active as both importer and exporter of goods such as wool, tin and cloth.
- In 1483, he granted a special licence to John de Salvo and Antonio Spinola, two naturalised Italians, allowing them to bring in foreign craftsmen to instruct the English in new methods of dyeing cloth. Clearly the king hoped to profit from this.
- As early as 1466, Edward appointed special commissioners to investigate the collection of customs revenues at the main ports and to report abuses. Further commissions followed in 1473 and 1474.
- During Edward's reign, the collectors of customs were paid more, and more cases of fraud were brought before the courts.
- Edward's entrepreneurial spirit is especially marked during his second reign. Trade treaties with the Hanseatic League in Germany (1473–4), France (1475) and Burgundy (1478), together with a general upturn in European trade in the 1470s after the depression of the previous decade, all meant that Edward's income from customs rose to about £35,000 a year during his second reign. Representing a 40 per cent increase since the start of the reign, this was a solid achievement by Edward's government.

The king's prerogative rights

The other main source of normal revenue was the exploitation of the king's special or 'prerogative' rights. These were traditional rights that the king enjoyed because he was king. Sir Robert Somerville claimed that after 1478 there was 'an intense activity over feudal dues', which fits in with the idea that Edward became more grasping in the later years of his reign.

- Wardship was the king's right, as feudal overlord, to enjoy the income of a landowner who was a child until he came of age. When he did come of age, the Crown could charge a large 'entry fine' before he could enjoy his own income. In addition, the king could sell his ward's marriage to the highest bidder, provided the child had not already been betrothed to someone else. The most valuable wardships during the reign were those of Henry, Duke of Buckingham, who was married to Katherine Woodville, and George Talbot, Earl of Shrewsbury who married Hastings' daughter Anne.

- The Crown also took the ordinary revenue from **bishoprics** when there was a vacancy. As a vacancy could only be filled by the king's nominee, it was useful for the king, in time-honoured fashion, to delay the appointment of a new bishop for months or even years.
- The king, as the fount of justice, also enjoyed income from the implementation of that justice. He took fines where royal rights had been breached as well as a range of other judicial fees.

KEY TERM

Bishopric The area governed by a bishop. It is also known as the bishop's see or diocese.

Extraordinary income for the Crown

In addition to regular or 'ordinary' revenues, there was a range of extraordinary sources of income that Edward could and did call upon, usually to defray the cost of military action. In order to pacify the realm in the first reign and to invade France in the second reign, Edward called on Parliament to grant him taxes to fund the defence of the realm.

KEY TERM

Fifteenths and Tenths The normal form of parliamentary taxation on land. Townsmen paid a tenth, while countrymen paid a fifteenth. By this time, the taxes had become fixed in value and so did not increase as land became more valuable.

- As well as regular **Fifteenths and Tenths** granted by Parliament, Edward also collected benevolences (occasional one-off goodwill payments). In the second reign alone, Edward collected about £100,000 from the laity and £77,000 from the clergy in the form of extra taxes.
- Between 1472 and 1475, he gathered more taxes each year than any king since Henry V. Most of these taxes went to fund the French expedition of 1475. As this resulted in a peace treaty and no fighting, Edward had effectively defrauded the taxpayers! He got their money but failed to deliver the war they had given their money to support. Edward's French invasion in 1475 also brought in more cash. In order to pay off the English, Louis XI paid Edward an annual pension, which amounted in total to an extra £85,000 in the last seven years of the reign.

Furthermore, as the financial situation improved, so Edward was able to borrow more on the strength of his financial acumen. During the reign, he received extensive loans from merchants and other wealthy men. Although a little 'hand-to-mouth', it was symptomatic of the way in which royal finances were organised. We must not expect to see anything by way of bureaucratic efficiency in any area of royal government in the fifteenth century. Nor should we hope to see clear accounting and an attempt always to balance the books.

Conclusion

Clearly, then, Edward's regime did much to improve the state of royal finances, especially during the second reign. He still needed extra taxes to mount the invasion of France but it is notable that Edward felt wealthy enough to attempt an expedition into Scotland, later in the reign, without recourse to Parliament. Given the weak state of royal finances that he inherited in 1461, and the rising cost and scale of military activity during his reigns, Edward's improving financial situation was a great asset in stabilising and strengthening royal authority and a powerful legacy for future kings such as Henry VII.

In one important area, Edward IV's financial experiments are seen to anticipate the methods used by Henry VII.

- Throughout the medieval period, the Exchequer was the main agency for receiving royal revenue but, under Edward IV, an increasing part of royal income was paid directly into the **King's Chamber**.
- In times of war, it was normal for kings to divert more of their income into the Chamber so that they had ready money for the many payments associated with warfare.
- Under Edward IV, however, the transfer of income and expenditure to the Chamber became more systematic, perhaps because he did so much campaigning in his first reign. The duchy of York may have provided the inspiration for the change. The new receivers and surveyors appointed to the King's Chamber were similar in terms of their duties and functions to those appointed to supervise the king's own duchy.
- Such personal supervision of the financial comings and goings need not mean that Edward made a lot more

money, but it does attest to a personal interest in finances and an improved flexibility in the financial system, which for too long has been accredited to Henry VII alone.

By the end of the reign, aided by a revival in trade, Edward had increased revenue from regular sources to £65,000 or £70,000 a year. Given the debts he had inherited from Henry VI and the political instability of the first reign, this was a major achievement and one for which Edward should be given due credit. Though still underfunded, the monarchy's strength was bolstered in this period by its financial security.

The Church

Lack of change

The stability of the realm and regime in Edward's second reign was buttressed, as always, by the English Church, which acted as the social cement of the period. It is a tribute to the enduring strength of this institution that very little happened in church affairs during Edward's reign.

- In the early part of the century, there had been **heresy** in the shape of the **Lollards**. They and their leader **John Wycliffe** posed no fundamental threat to the Church and its beliefs but helped to inspire Sir John Oldcastle's revolt in 1414.
- In the whole of the period 1450–1520, there were few changes in religious affairs. This was because most people were religious or at least complied outwardly with the ceremonies and rituals of the Church. Those ceremonies and rituals stressed the importance of stability, continuity and respect for authority. The fallen world that man inhabited was not a particularly pleasant place but it was designed thus by God in order to punish the sins of mankind. At the same time, God's world was an essentially unchanging landscape. Heresy and rebellion were the worst of sins, to be punished with the eternal torments of hell.

The Church and government

In a more practical sense, the Church preached and enforced order. The king appointed the bishops. Most of these men

Cartoon depicting the Lollards as heretics

**John Wycliffe
(c.1330–84)** The inspiration for England's only late medieval heretical sect, Lollardy. Although his ideas were condemned, Wycliffe, who had powerful friends, was not. He was not the leader of the Lollards, as such, since the movement was founded by his pupils.

**John Morton
(1420–1500)** Born in Dorset and educated at Balliol College, Oxford. He was a Lancastrian at heart, who nonetheless found favour with Edward IV and was made Bishop of Ely in 1478. Imprisoned by Richard III, he escaped and joined Henry Tudor in exile. He was well rewarded when Henry became king: in 1486, he was made Chancellor of England and Archbishop of Canterbury. He was made a cardinal by the Pope (at the king's insistence) in 1493.

Embryonic bureaucracy
Compared to today, there was very little by way of a bureaucracy or civil service. The king could issue proclamations but he relied on local unpaid officials to carry them out.

Tithes The main tax paid by parishioners to the Church. Often paid in kind, (i.e. agricultural produce), tithes represented one tenth of the value of produce and were designed for the upkeep of the parish priest.

were lawyers and men from gentry background or lower. Relatively few aristocrats were ever appointed (George Neville, Archbishop of York was the exception rather than the rule), which ensured that the Church could not become the plaything of the mighty. In Spain and France, by contrast, the Church was a useful and wealthy refuge for the younger sons of the nobility. In this way, those Churches could often become the centres of aristocratic intrigue rather than their antidote.

In England, the great churchmen usually gained their appointments because they were already useful Crown servants running the **embryonic bureaucracy** of the period. The vast majority of the clergy then had a large vested interest in upholding the regime. The political instability of the first reign did little to ruffle their feathers. **John Morton** was fairly exceptional in being a die-hard Lancastrian, who went into exile twice with other Lancastrian leaders. Yet even he made his peace with Edward IV and was well rewarded for his trouble. The French ambassador claimed that he was one of the most influential men in the last years of the reign. Such churchmen as Morton were usually the king's closest advisers and the advice they gave was usually cautious. The bench of English bishops at this time was a pretty reputable group. While none achieved international fame as scholars and theologians, few led outwardly scandalous lives. Bishops such as John Alcock and John Fisher were conscientious royal servants, who also helped to found new colleges in Cambridge for the education of the clergy.

At a local level, too, the Church preached and brought about stability.

- All parishioners paid taxes (**tithes**) to support their parish priest.
- All were expected to attend church services on a regular basis.
- The Church at this time also possessed its own set of law courts where spiritual cases could be tried. From blasphemy to heresy, from fornication and adultery to failure to pay mortuary fees or dabbling in witchcraft, church courts regulated the spiritual life of the nation and could impose severe penalties on offenders.

The size of the Church

At the same time, there were a great many clergy to choose from. From the humble parish priest up to the Archbishop of Canterbury, there were many echelons of ecclesiastical posts and preferments among what was known as the **secular clergy**. In the regular Church, there were hundreds of religious houses (including hospitals) occupied by thousands of **regular clergy**. Whether secular or regular, the Church's position was underpinned by its great wealth. Though the richest bishopric (Winchester) was many times more profitable than the poorest see (Bangor), the Church as a whole had great wealth and thus great power, both in a spiritual and in a political way. Most of the top clergy, whether secular or regular, were appointed by the king and this gave him enormous power over the institution as a whole. The stability of the realm, and the revival of the monarchy's fortunes in Edward's second reign, owed much then to the unchanging loyalties and social doctrines of the English Church.

War and foreign policy

Reasons for invading France

At the start of his second reign, Edward IV had every reason to contemplate invading France.

- Louis XI had always provided shelter and succour for Lancastrian exiles – after all, Margaret of Anjou was French. In addition, in 1470 and 1471, he had backed and supplied a double invasion of England, by Warwick and then Margaret of Anjou, the first of which had led to Edward's speedy departure for the Low Countries. That humiliation could not be easily forgotten or forgiven and it was important for Edward to attempt to neutralise the French threat.
- Furthermore, of course, the loss of English possessions was still fresh in the memory. Just eighteen years before, the English had lost the Battle of Castillon (1453). This startling reverse in the south-west of France had seen England's continental holdings reduced to just the port of Calais and a small area of surrounding territory known as the Pale. This national disaster, which had done so much to discredit Henry VI's regime, also needed to be revenged.

Louis XI, arch enemy of Edward IV

- As an established and highly successful military commander, and a king with the insight to realise that a renewal of the Hundred Years' War would bring active support (as opposed to the grudging **acquiescence** seen so far) from England's military élite (the nobility), Edward's quest of victory in France was clearly a top priority.

Finding allies

Nonetheless, an army could not be raised overnight and the kingdom needed settling, so the great expedition of English arms did not set out until 1475. Also holding up that departure was the tricky business of finding allies for the great enterprise. At first glance, finding allies seemed to be the least of Edward's problems. The duchies of Brittany and Burgundy (which included the Low Countries, of course) had a long history of independence from France and their geographical locations on either side of France made them ideal duchies to bring a three-front war (including England) against their common enemy. However, the relationships between the duchies and France were also tinged with fear. Making actual war against their mighty neighbour might bring about the very thing they wanted to avoid – destruction at the hands of the French. So, while they might sound warlike and aggressive, both dukes also had good reason to make terms with the French, if terms were offered. It was all very well for the English; they could retreat behind the Channel when war threatened but Burgundy and Brittany had long and vulnerable land frontiers with the French.

At first, however, French aggression played into Edward's diplomatic hands. In 1472, he sent 1000 archers to Brittany as the Bretons feared invasion. When that invasion materialised, a further 2000 archers were dispatched. With the French invasion petering out, Edward moved to make a formal alliance with Brittany. The agreement was concluded at Châteaugiron in September 1472 – too late in the campaigning season to allow for fighting that year – but the treaty provided for an English invasion of Normandy (lost under Henry VI) or Gascony (revenge for Castillon) in the next year. Edward's intentions received a further boost as it became clear that an offensive alliance with Burgundy was also possible. However, as is so often the way in these things, the shifting sands of **diplomatic negotiations** soon turned Edward's plans on their head. It was really no surprise when, by November of 1472, both Brittany and Burgundy had made truces with France. Despite these setbacks, Edward persevered with his plans to invade France and much perseverance was necessary to create the right diplomatic conditions for the great enterprise. Eventually, the commercial war between England and the **German Hanseatic League** was settled by the Treaty of Utrecht in early 1474. That same year, Edward signed a formal treaty of alliance with Burgundy (the Treaty of London).

Neutralising the Scottish threat

Meanwhile, Edward had also been busy neutralising the Scottish threat. The Scots traditionally allied with the French against England, so it took some time to persuade **King James III of Scotland** that his interests would be best served by alliance, not enmity, with the 'auld' enemy.

- In October 1473, a marriage treaty was announced, which would reinforce and lengthen the existing truce between the two countries. As was normal, the marriage (or rather betrothal) announced in Edinburgh by James III and the Bishop of Durham provided for the eventual marriage between Edward IV's daughter, Cecily, then aged four, and James's son, who had not yet reached six months!
- The treaty stipulated that they would actually marry within six months of reaching marriageable age (usually fourteen) and thoughtfully provided for alternative marriage partners should either die in the meantime.
- The treaty also laid out stringent and clear financial arrangements. It was agreed that Edward IV would provide a cash sum of 20,000 crowns to be paid over a period of seventeen years and he also settled land on his daughter so that the income would go to her future husband.
- Just to ensure favourable circumstances for the expedition against France, the truce between the two countries was officially extended so that it might last until 1519!

KEY THEME

Diplomatic negotiations
The problem with diplomatic agreements from the perspective of the two French duchies was that neither could be sure that Edward IV would actually help them.

KEY TERM

German Hanseatic League A diplomatic and trading alliance of ports in north Germany, who acted together to create a powerful trading block.

KEY PERSON

King James III of Scotland (1451–88) The son of James II and Mary of Guelders. He became king at the age of eight in 1460 and married Margaret of Denmark in 1469. Part of Margaret's dowry was the islands of Orkney and Shetland. James was imprisoned briefly in 1482 by disaffected nobles led by his brother, the Duke of Albany. They were upset at the Duke of Gloucester's successful invasion of Scotland. James was killed in 1488 by an unknown assassin, possibly with the assistance of his son, James IV!

Final preparations

In addition to this agreement with the Scots, Edward made a settlement with the rulers of Spain and the King of Denmark, though neither could materially help his campaign. Finally, and potentially more useful, came an alliance with **Francis II, Duke of Brittany**, who agreed to supply 8000 troops to help with the English attack on France.

With the foreign situation more promising than for some time, Edward had also made extensive preparations at home.

- Avoiding the traditional and outmoded Fifteenths and Tenths, Parliament (Lords and Commons) voted an income tax of ten per cent to help fund the war.
- However, wary in case Edward should take the money and not go to war, Parliament decreed that the money should be kept safe in the hands of four appointed commissioners until the king should actually set sail for the Continent. In fact, the new tax proved hard to collect, especially as Edward's departure was delayed until 1475.
- Reversion to more normal forms of taxation by Parliament meant that the expedition, when it finally departed, was called by one Italian agent in Bruges, 'the finest, largest and best appointed force that ever left England.'
- At around 12,000 fighting men, the expedition was a little larger than any of the armies sent to France by the great warrior, Henry V, whose **victory at Agincourt** in 1415 had shown how much could be gained by a military expedition in France.
- Edward IV was not apparently interested in a mere show of force; he hoped to gain territory, at the very least, and, possibly, a whole kingdom! Most of the English nobility accompanied the king, leaving just a few peers and the queen to look after the kingdom – showing how secure he now felt at home. Five years before he had crossed the seas as a refugee, now he did so as a great warrior king.

The invasion of France

Once he landed at Calais, things began to go wrong for Edward. It quickly became apparent that he would actually get no help from his supposed allies. The Duke of Brittany had never ratified the recent alliance and Duke Charles of Burgundy appeared at Edward's encampment in Calais to explain that he would not, after all, be bringing an army to help the English cause. Hopes of fighting the French were largely dashed at this point. Although the English army paraded itself through Artois and Picardy, it managed to keep the River Somme between itself and Louis's army of about 6000 advancing from the south. Edward's hopes of substantial gains through fighting were in disarray and, with the campaigning season advancing, he had no desire to spend the winter months with his army in France or Burgundy. To advance further from Calais would be decidedly risky, especially as French forces were already active in disrupting his supply lines. So, instead of fighting, the English sued for peace.

Edward IV landing at Calais prior to his invasion of France in 1475 (16th century manuscript, School of Rouen).

The Treaty of Picquigny, 1475

Louis XI, who also had no wish to fight, soon agreed to the English terms and the two kings solemnly signed the **Treaty of Picquigny** on a specially constructed bridge over the River Somme. Louis agreed to pay Edward £15,000 immediately to help defray the cost of raising an army to invade France, together with an annual pension of £10,000 payable as long as they both should live. In addition, the **dauphin** would marry Edward's first or second daughter and provide her with an income of £60,000 a year. It was, in the end, all very amicable and the enmity of previous centuries was apparently at an end. A seven-year truce was declared and both countries' merchants were exempted from taxes and tolls imposed by the other side.

There is no doubt that the Treaty of Picquigny was a triumph for the English. War against France was unlikely to be productive and with peace established (and later maintained) between the two countries, Edward's security in England was further strengthened. The leading

KEY TERMS

Treaty of Picquigny (1475) Picquigny was the agreement between Edward IV and Louis XI, where the French paid off the English invasion force and granted Edward IV a pension for life. Both sides agreed not to give any support to pretenders to each other's thrones. Of course, there were those who saw the affair as a humiliation for the English and Louis later boasted that he had driven out the English with 'fine wines and venison pasties'.

Dauphin The King of France's eldest son.

magnates returned with pensions and prizes, which assuaged their disappointment, and they soon took the longer term view that peace was, all things considered, preferable to the dangerous business of war. After all, most of them had seen war's disconcerting ability to turn success into disaster at first hand. Of course, there would be future diplomatic disagreements between the two countries, but the peace with France held until Henry VII's invasion of 1492. Much credit should go to Edward for snatching diplomatic victory from the jaws of military disaster!

The defeat of the Scots

Against Scotland, Edward also experienced something akin to triumph.

- As we have seen, he first made peace with Scotland via a long-term truce and marriage alliance in 1473.
- However, with reports of truce breaking and cross-border raiding by the Scots in 1480, Edward determined to punish his faithless ally. The plan of campaign for 1481 was to involve attacks by land and sea.
- During his second reign, Edward had steadily built up England's depleted navy to a force of fifteen or sixteen warships. The plan was that these could be used to bombard the Scottish coast and perhaps sail up the Firth of Forth to attack Edinburgh itself. Meanwhile, an army would attack from the south, thus catching the Scots in a serious English pincer.
- In 1481, the attack on Scotland fizzled out, however, as Edward, determined to lead the expedition personally, dawdled in London and did not arrive in the north until too late in the campaigning season.
- Despite this setback, Edward determined to attack the Scots the next year. At Fotheringhay in 1482, he signed an alliance with James III's treacherous younger brother, Alexander, Duke of Albany (the Scottish version of Clarence). Edward promised to help him overthrow his brother and agreed that he, rather than James's son, would now marry Cecily. In return, Albany would do homage to Edward and hand over the powerful border fortress of Berwick-upon-Tweed.
- Deciding in the end not to lead the expedition of that year, Edward appointed his brother, Richard of

Gloucester, as his lieutenant. The latter advanced with ominous speed into Scotland. Capturing the town of Berwick with hardly a shot fired, he soon entered Edinburgh.

- James III had advanced to meet the English forces but his army broke up in discontent and recriminations, which saw the king virtually arrested and placed in captivity by his leading lords who disliked the king's lowborn favourites.
- The Scots were so terrified of this invading force – which may have numbered 20,000 under the redoubtable Gloucester – that they decided to take to the hills to avoid it.
- Unfortunately for Gloucester, Albany had by now made his peace with his brother, James III, so there was no prospect of installing a puppet pro-English regime in Scotland.
- Faced with the problems of an easy victory and unable to draw the Scots into battle, Gloucester made the best of things. Rather than attempt to occupy Scotland, which would have been expensive and unpopular, he wisely retreated south but kept control of Berwick, which was a very useful fruit of victory.
- A further expedition against Scotland was planned for the next year, but Edward IV's unexpected death prevented it from taking place.

Assessment of foreign policy

In terms of foreign policy, Edward's reign should be seen as a success. In the shifting alliances of continental Europe, England would always be on the peripheries because of its geographical location. Recovery of the French Crown was never a serious prospect, especially as Louis XI of France was proving to be an able and effective ruler. Conquest of Scotland was also unlikely, and the conquest of either France or Scotland would have caused a lot more problems than it solved. In this context, Edward's foreign policy was as good as it could get. France had been invaded and shown that England could be a credible military power. Scotland had been humiliated and shown that peace with England was much better than intriguing with France. A lot, of course, depended on the proclivities of particular rulers and Edward was fortunate that neither of the rulers of France and Scotland, at this time, were keen on war. At home, Edward's active foreign policy underpinned his growing power. Where Henry VI was associated with defeat and disillusionment, his successor had turned Anglo–French relations on their head and 'bashed' the Scots.

Edward's achievement

The success and stability of Edward's second reign is clear evidence that his first reign had not been desperately unstable. The essential ingredients for political stability – a compliant nobility, dutiful Church and limited foreign intervention in English affairs – were still there in the 1460s, just a little harder to spot. Thus the 1470s did not witness a transformation in English politics and society, just a quiet reassertion of the old order. Under a vigorous and young king, who had the military wherewithal to impress his nobility, Edward was well suited to deal with the many problems of kingship in the fifteenth century. Coming to the throne as an eighteen-year-old usurper and overthrown nine years later by the treachery of his foremost supporter, Edward's achievements in his second reign were all too obvious. The realm was at peace, the nobility restored to their proper place in power sharing and the threat of foreign intervention was decisively neutralised.

Where there was novelty in Edward's government, it was not about new institutions. Edward did not invent new ways of governing but made the existing methods function more effectively. By bringing his own talents to the tasks of government, Edward revived the fortunes of personal monarchy, which had seemed in such a bad way in the reign of his predecessor. In this way, Edward's second reign showed how easy it was to end the so-called Wars of the Roses and, for this, Edward himself, his family, servants and his nobility should be given due credit. In the end, the **political nation** much preferred peace to war, stability to instability. Once a king was firmly established, he was unlikely to be overthrown.

Edward's affable nature and easy charm were also in contrast to the shy and retiring Lancastrian king. Furthermore, Edward had one other natural weapon, which

KEY TERM

Political nation Refers to that relatively small group of major landowners, who wielded political power in medieval English society. Their approval or acceptance of a new king was vital.

should not be overlooked: his height. At a time when most men were probably around 5ft 6 or less, Edward was a veritable giant at something in the region of 6ft 4 – England's tallest king.

After the invasion of France, there are a number of stories claiming that Edward was getting fat and becoming indolent and too fond of wine and women. While these stories may have been exaggerated by his enemies (and it would later suit Richard III to spread anti-Edward propaganda), they perhaps indicate again the security of Edward's position in his second reign.

By Easter of 1483, Edward seemed to be at the pinnacle of success, even the last few die-hard Lancastrians in exile, such as Henry Tudor, were negotiating terms by which they might return. Twelve years after his triumphant return to England, Edward's future tenure of the throne was assured. Since he was, even now, only 40 years old, he could expect to rule for at least another 20 years. Then, at the end of March 1483, Edward was taken ill. Ten days later, he was dead.

SUMMARY QUESTIONS

1 Why was Edward IV's second reign so much less troubled than his first reign?

2 To what extent, if at all, did Edward IV strengthen the monarchy during his second reign?

3 'By 1471, the Wars of the Roses were at an end.' To what extent do the events of the period 1471–83 back up this assertion?

SECTION 4

THE RISE AND FALL OF RICHARD III, 1483–85: A YORKIST CIVIL WAR

> **Why did Richard III usurp the throne in 1483, only to lose it two years later?**

KEY POINTS
- In 1483, Edward IV died suddenly and his son, Edward V, was only twelve years old.
- Within weeks, Richard, Duke of Gloucester, Edward IV's brother, had claimed the throne for himself on the grounds that Edward V and his younger brother, Richard, Duke of York, were illegitimate because their parents had not been married properly.
- Richard's usurpation of the throne was highly unpopular and it was soon rumoured that he had murdered his nephews while they were lodged in the Tower of London.
- In 1485, Richard was overthrown and killed at the Battle of Bosworth. The man who defeated him, Henry Tudor, was then proclaimed king as Henry VII.

TIMELINE
1483	9 April	Sudden death of Edward IV.
	30 April	Gloucester and Buckingham take charge of Edward V at Stony Stratford, Buckinghamshire.
	16 June	Richard, Duke of York, brother of Edward V, handed over to Duke of Gloucester.
	13 June?	Lord Hastings executed.
	25 June	Lords and Commons petition Gloucester to take the throne.
	6 July	Richard III crowned.
	2 November	Buckingham executed after abortive rising against Richard III.
1484	January	Parliament meets.
	April	Death of Edward, Prince of Wales.
	December	Proclamation against Henry Tudor.

1485	March	Death of Queen Anne. Rumours that she has been poisoned in order to allow Richard III to marry his niece, Elizabeth of York.
	August	Henry Tudor's forces land at Milford Haven, Wales.
	22 August	Battle of Bosworth Field. Richard III killed and Henry Tudor proclaimed King Henry VII on the battlefield.

OVERVIEW

The sudden and unexpected death of Edward IV at the age of 40 in 1483 sparked off a train of events leading to the overthrow of two kings in two years.

- First, the young Edward V, aged just twelve, was overthrown and supposedly murdered by his uncle, Richard of Gloucester.
- Richard of Gloucester then had himself crowned king.
- Twenty-six months after his accession, on 22 August 1485, Richard himself (now King Richard III) was cut down in battle against a relatively unknown Welshman called Henry Tudor, who went on to style himself Henry VII.

Given this somewhat dramatic turn of events, it has been easy to claim that the Wars of the Roses had started again and that the structural weaknesses of late medieval society were once more apparent. In fact, the double overthrow has little to do with structure and everything to do with chance events. There was nothing pre-ordained about Richard of Gloucester overthrowing his nephew in 1483. Gloucester was reacting to the consequences of his brother Edward IV's sudden and unexpected death. Two years later, Richard was killed in battle, not because he was wicked and unpopular, but because he made a rash decision in the heat of battle.

Richard III's usurpation of the throne

Shakespeare and More

In his play *Richard III*, **William Shakespeare** left his audience in no doubt about why Richard of Gloucester

KEY YEAR

1483 The year 1483, like 1066 and 1936, was a year of three kings. In 1066, Edward the Confessor died, King Harold was killed at the Battle of Hastings and William the Conqueror became king. In 1936, George V died, his eldest son, Edward VIII, abdicated (gave up the throne) and Edward's younger brother, George VI, replaced him.

KEY PERSON

William Shakespeare (1564–1616) Perhaps the greatest playwright of his or any other age. His plays included many about English medieval history. His *Richard III* is not now seen as accurate history but a play about the corrupting nature of power and ambition. It also acted as Tudor propaganda to bolster the position of Elizabeth Tudor, who was Queen of England when the play was written.

took the throne from his nephew, Edward V (Edward IV's son), in 1483. According to Shakespeare, he committed this terrible deed, along with many other terrible deeds, because he was a very wicked man. Shakespeare showed how Richard planned his route to the throne from an early age and destroyed all those who stood in his way. Edward of Lancaster (Henry VI's son) was apparently killed by Richard at Tewkesbury; his own brother, Clarence, drowned by Richard in a vat of wine in the Tower of London in 1478 and, finally, his two nephews, Edward V and Richard of York, were smothered on their uncle Richard's orders in the Tower in 1483. In his opening soliloquy in Shakespeare's play, King Richard tells the audience quite openly that he is 'determined to be a villain'. To underline the depravity and cold calculation of his character and the unnatural make-up of his soul, Richard is also portrayed as a hunchback – 'foul, bunch-backed toad,' as his future wife, Anne Neville, calls him. In Shakespeare's eyes, Richard is twisted in form and twisted in nature. Sir Thomas More, in his earlier *History of Richard III,* added to the mix of evil by claiming that when Richard was born the omens were far from good. Apparently, baby Richard was untimely ripped from his mother's womb with a full head of hair and a full set of teeth – the world had been warned!

Neither Shakespeare nor More should be taken seriously as historians. Both were presenting history as a morality tale. Evil, in the form of Richard III, carries out dreadful deeds, wading through the blood of friends and family, to satisfy unnatural ambition and to achieve power. Once there, of course, everything goes terribly wrong. Power becomes a curse and brings along its own terrors for the wicked man – death, retribution and an evil reputation that will live forever. Shakespeare, in particular, was playing to the gallery. He painted Richard in lurid colours, not because he had done the research and thought that Richard really was a monster in human form, but because it would make a good character for his play. Henry Tudor, who is the agent of retribution in the play, cuts a pretty poor figure by comparison with his adversary. He does not appear until the final act of the play and seems pretty colourless and feeble compared to the bloodthirsty Richard. If Shakespeare's play is meant to be Tudor propaganda, it is certainly not an endorsement of the first Tudor but rather an exaggerated view of the evil regime that Henry Tudor destroyed.

Expectations in 1483

In reality, Richard of Gloucester was very different from the evil stereotype offered by Sir Thomas More and William Shakespeare. The key to understanding his actions in 1483 lies in the peculiar circumstances thrown up by Edward's death and Richard's earlier experiences in the conflicts of the 1460s.

Portrait of Richard III.

- When Edward IV died at short notice, there was every hope that his son, Edward, Prince of Wales (technically King Edward V), would succeed to his father's throne without difficulty. Since 1471, the realm had been at peace and the Yorkist dynasty had no apparent rivals for the throne.
- Admittedly, there was a little-known Welshman called Henry Tudor in exile in Brittany. He thought he was the real heir of Henry VI but no one took him seriously. Indeed, Henry Tudor was on the verge of throwing in the towel, making terms with Edward for a return to England as Earl of Richmond, a title inherited from his late father, Henry VI's half-brother.
- The huge surprise of 1483 was that the threat to the Yorkist dynasty and the new Yorkist king, Edward V, came from within the family and from the most loyal member of the family – Richard, Duke of Gloucester. This was to be a Yorkist civil war and not a restart to the conflict between York and Lancaster.

What were the reasons for the crisis of 1483?

The crisis emerged partly because Edward V was only twelve years old. Four years older and he could have ruled independently of any guardians in the same way that Henry VI had been pushed, albeit rather unwillingly, into assuming sole rule at that age. Five years younger and everyone would have accepted the need for a **protector** in the shape of the king's closest adult male relative, namely Richard of Gloucester. At twelve, Edward V was between the two. This problem was fatefully compounded by the accidents of geography at the time of Edward IV's sudden death.

> ### KEY TERM
>
> **Protector** Richard would assume that he should be Edward V's protector, but others, led by the new king's mother and her family (the Woodvilles), might think differently or, more to the point, Richard might think that they thought differently! Even if he did become protector, his power might still be temporary. In 1447, another protector, Humphrey, Duke of Gloucester, had been suddenly arrested, accused of treason and thrown into prison. Three days later, he was dead. Hastings, one of Edward IV's most loyal servants, clearly approved of Gloucester becoming protector but was opposed to him becoming king. His sudden and unexpected execution ended opposition to Richard's usurpation of his nephew's throne.

KEY PEOPLE

Henry Stafford, Duke of Buckingham (1454–83)
An ally of Richard of Gloucester, who may have disliked the Woodvilles after he was forced to marry the queen's sister, Katherine Woodville, rather than a wealthy heiress. He was an ambitious man with extensive estates. He was never really trusted by Edward IV and resented the power of the Woodville family. This may explain why, in 1483, he joined in the overthrow of Elizabeth Woodville's son, Edward V, and helped to bring Richard III to the throne. That same year, he rebelled against Richard, which led to his execution in Salisbury. He also had a claim to the throne, being descended from the youngest son of Edward III. This may explain why Henry VIII suddenly executed the Duke of Buckingham's son, the third duke, in 1521.

Richard Grey (d.1483)
Elizabeth Woodville's second son by her first marriage and thus younger brother of the Marquis of Dorset, who backed Henry Tudor's rebellion against Richard III. Richard Grey was in attendance on the young Edward V in 1483 as he travelled towards London. Grey was arrested and later executed by Richard of Gloucester in 1483.

Sir Thomas Vaughan (d.1483) A Welsh gentleman who acted as private treasurer to both Edward IV and Edward V. He was likewise dispatched by Gloucester.

- Edward IV died in Westminster but his heir was away in Ludlow, while his heir's would-be protector was in Yorkshire.
- As soon as news of the king's death reached them, both parties moved towards London. Edward V was accompanied by his maternal uncle, Anthony Woodville, Earl Rivers and, of course, an armed escort. Richard moved south also with armed men – his extensive powers in the north meant he could raise whole armies on his own say so.

On his way south, Richard met up with **Henry Stafford, Duke of Buckingham**. It may have been Buckingham who first sowed the seeds of doubt and danger in Richard's mind. Whatever the case, Richard and Buckingham intercepted Edward V and his companions at Stony Stratford in Buckinghamshire before they could reach London. Richard's plan at this stage was probably just to secure custody of the king, to ensure that he could control events. At the same time, however, he sowed the first seeds of fresh discord and violence when he arrested three of the king's entourage – Rivers (the queen's brother), **Richard Grey** (one of the queen's sons by her first marriage) and **Sir Thomas Vaughan** – and sent them off to imprisonment in three of his northern strongholds.

Thus the two dukes, apparently secure from what they saw as the Woodville threat, brought the new king to London. A date was set for Edward's coronation but there was then a very significant debate among leading Yorkists as to whether Edward needed a protector.

- At twelve, he was an intelligent child, so perhaps he could rule through a council of nobles, as had the young Richard II on his accession in 1377 as a boy of seven. This was the view put forward by the Woodvilles, including the new king's mother, Elizabeth Woodville, and her son by her first marriage, the Marquis of Dorset.
- On the other hand, Lord Hastings, one of Edward IV's most powerful councillors – and no friend of Dorset – claimed that a minority council should be established under Duke Richard and that Richard, not the queen, should have charge of the king's person.

This division was the essential context for Richard's usurpation of the throne. If Edward V was crowned in the next few weeks, Richard of Gloucester was in serious trouble. If he did not become protector, he might be at the mercy of the new king and his Woodville relatives, who would surely object to the arrests of Rivers, Grey and Vaughan. All his powers in the north, given to him by a grateful brother, might be taken away from him by an ungrateful nephew! All the problems associated with his childhood – treachery, betrayal and turbulence – might return to unseat him and to end the quiet of the kingdom. However, even if Richard became protector, he would be forced to give up his powers in a few years' time anyway and would then be at the mercy of his enemies. Therefore Richard chose to usurp the throne. Only as king, he thought, could he be secure.

What was Richard's claim to the throne?

To claim the throne for himself, Richard needed to bar both Edward V and his brother from the throne. Fortunately for Richard, the Bishop of Bath and Wells suddenly claimed that Edward V and his brother, Richard, were bastards – illegitimate offspring of Edward IV – and that therefore neither of them could become king. The bishop claimed that, as a child, the future Edward IV had been contracted to marry the daughter of the Earl of Shrewsbury, Dame Eleanor Butler. Since this pre-contract (or promise) of marriage was still in force when Edward suddenly and secretly married Elizabeth Woodville, it followed, according to canon law, that the children of the marriage were illegitimate.

The timing of the story, as well as its implausible nature, make it clear that it was merely a device to bring Richard to the throne. The illegitimacy claim was obviously wishful thinking on Richard's part and it was greeted as such by contemporaries. A pre-contract of marriage, after all, was not a marriage, so Edward was not committing bigamy when he married Elizabeth Woodville. At the same time, Dame Eleanor had in fact died before Edward's children were born, so she could not make either his marriage or his children illegitimate. What made the lie more blatant was the knowledge that Richard had at first thought of putting round the story that his own brother, Edward IV, was actually illegitimate!

Was Edward IV illegitimate?

The historian Michael Jones has recently claimed that Edward IV really was a bastard; the son of an English archer in the Rouen garrison, who had an affair with Cecily Neville while her husband, Richard, Duke of York, was away campaigning. The evidence for this astonishing claim is as follows.

- If the pregnancy lasted a full term of 40 weeks, the Duke of York was not with his wife at the time of conception.
- The baby, Edward, was accorded a smaller christening in Rouen cathedral than his younger brother, Edmund of Rutland.
- Cecily Neville apparently admitted that Edward was illegitimate.
- Edward IV was always at pains to explain that he really was York's son – hence the elaborate reburial service in 1476.
- Richard III claimed that Edward was a bastard in the Act of Parliament of 1483, which settled the crown on his head.
- Edward IV was rather taller than his father, unlike Richard III, who was of similar stature.

Yet these arguments amount to no more than circumstantial evidence in favour of Edward's illegitimacy. If the pregnancy lasted two weeks longer or two weeks shorter than the full term, York would have been with his wife at the time of conception. If Cecily Neville had admitted to the affair with the English bowman, this should have been at the centre of Richard III's claim to the throne in 1483, not just an unexplained subsidiary point. With his mother still alive, it should have been possible to get her to sign a written confession, which would hand Richard the throne, provided he could dispose of the claim of Clarence's son, the Earl of Warwick. After all, the idea of Edward's illegitimacy would certainly provide a much stronger claim to the throne than the one that Richard actually chose concerning the alleged illegitimacy of the two princes. But if Edward's bastard status was widely rumoured, as Jones claims, why was it not used by Clarence and Warwick the Kingmaker in 1470 when they deposed Edward? Such a claim would have made Clarence King of England.

The reality is that there may well have been rumours about Edward's parentage because he did not look like his father, but no one actually knew if it was true and the claim was not pursued during Edward's lifetime (perhaps naturally) or after his death. Richard based his claim squarely on the illegitimacy of his nephews, not the illegitimacy of his brother.

How did Richard usurp the throne?

With the story of the princes' illegitimacy circulating, Richard of Gloucester cancelled Edward V's coronation and later forced Elizabeth Woodville to hand over her other son to lodge with his brother in the Tower of London. He called a meeting of leading councillors to the Tower and, in mid-meeting, arrested Lord Hastings in the council chamber and had him decapitated on the spot. The other councillors, who witnessed this event, now thought that Richard was, after all, the rightful king. This was despite the fact that, even if the sons of Edward IV were illegitimate, their cousin, Edward, Earl of Warwick (Clarence's son), was now the real heir of Edward IV. Richard already held the unfortunate boy in captivity, so there were no objections from him! Having demonstrated his power and his cunning, Richard had himself crowned king on 6th July 1483. His title was not confirmed by parliament until the next year.

Reasons for the usurpation

Why did Richard usurp the throne? Why would he take the throne from the son of the man whom he revered and to whom he had been loyal all his life? Richard's loyalty to Edward IV can easily be proved.

- In 1470, when Edward IV had been overthrown by a disloyal brother (Clarence) and a treacherous cousin (Warwick), Richard had gone into exile with Edward.
- Richard had returned with his brother and fought alongside him at Barnet and Tewkesbury.
- Throughout the second reign, he had been Edward's most trusty lieutenant. He had ruled the problematic north and kept it quieter than it had been for decades.
- In addition, Richard had led the troops into Scotland to teach the Scots a hard lesson.

The answer to the problem may lie in the experiences of Richard's early life. He was, after all, a child of the Wars of the Roses and in the fifteenth century, children, especially the sons of the nobility, grew up quickly. When Richard was six, his father was named by an **Act of Parliament** as heir to the throne of Henry VI. A few weeks later, father and brother, Edmund, had been killed in battle and young Richard was on his way into exile in the Low Countries. A few weeks later still, his eldest brother, Edward, had been proclaimed king and won his famous victory at Towton. So it was clear to Richard that political fortunes could change very quickly indeed. The rest of the 1460s showed that nobody could trust anyone, particularly close relatives. Clarence and Warwick sided with the enemy and overthrew Edward IV in 1470, leaving Richard to endure a second spell in exile. Although Edward's second reign had been peaceful enough, Richard's political mentality was shaped by these earlier events. So, in 1483, he panicked. Despite his enormous power, he believed the rumours of Woodville plots against his person and foresaw his own downfall unless he acted decisively. And decisively was how he acted.

Richard and the Princes in the Tower

Within weeks of Richard's coronation (July 1483), it was widely rumoured that the princes had been put to death by their uncle. As a result, in the autumn of 1483, there was a widespread but rather disorganised rebellion against Richard's regime in the southern counties of England. Some demanded the restoration of Edward V, others, a little quicker off the mark, were rebelling on the basis that Richard had already murdered the princes. The new kingmaker, Buckingham, put himself at the head of the rebels. Whether as a cause or as a result of this rebellion, it is widely believed that the princes were put to death on the orders of their uncle, Richard, well before the

Wooden panel in St George's Chapel, Windsor, depicting Edward V, one of the Princes in the Tower thought to have been murdered by Richard III

end of 1483. Despite attempts to blame the Duke of Buckingham and Henry Tudor, the case against Richard is overwhelming and, indeed, the deaths of the princes were the logical and inevitable outcome of his usurpation.

Richard was, after all, the man with the biggest motive for murder. Although an Act of Parliament later declared him the true king of England on the basis of the princes' illegitimacy, no one believed that story and so if alive they would always be the focus of plots against the new king. Thus, the rebellion in the autumn of 1483 might be the first of many designed to put the rightful king on the throne. After all, during Henry VII's reign, the king faced serious rebellions from **two men who were clearly impostors**. How much more serious would be rebellions led by Edward V or his brother.

At the same time, Richard had history to guide him as to the grave reality of the threat posed by the princes.

- In 1470, his brother, Edward, had been overthrown by the true king, Henry VI, even though that monarch was mentally incapacitated. The moral of that tale for Richard III was that Edward had been overthrown by his lack of ruthlessness. He had failed to murder King Henry when he was captured in 1465. As a result, Henry became the focus of Warwick and Clarence's plots against Edward. The lesson for Richard was clear and unambiguous – 'alternative' kings had to be killed off quickly.
- In addition, Richard had shown in 1483 that he was prepared to act ruthlessly in order to gain the throne. Rivers, Grey, Vaughan and Hastings were all murdered by Richard without trial.
- Can we really believe that Richard would hold back his murderous hand because the princes were his nephews? Certainly, Queen Elizabeth Woodville believed that Richard had killed them. She now agreed that her eldest daughter, Elizabeth, would marry Henry Tudor, thus hugely enhancing his claim to the throne. Marriage of a king's daughter to a very doubtful pretender was unthinkable unless she were desperate. This was the desperation of a woman whose sons had been killed. The

KEY PEOPLE

Two men who were clearly imposters Lambert Simnel and Perkin Warbeck. Simnel claimed to be Edward, Earl of Warwick, while Warbeck adopted the persona of Richard of York, the younger of the two princes.

king, her son, was dead, so she would support anyone who might supplant his killer.

- The reaction of Richard to the charges against him spread during Buckingham's rebellion is highly instructive. If the princes were really alive, he could have produced them. This Richard failed to do. If he had killed them, why did he not blame the Duke of Buckingham after the latter's execution in 1483? After all, Richard's tenure of power would be seriously enhanced if someone else had murdered the real king and his brother and if everyone knew this to be the case. Richard's complete silence on the fate of the princes is further damning testimony of his guilt. It indicates that he feared that raising the matter of the princes' demise by producing their bodies would lead to further opposition and his own overthrow.

In short, Richard III had motive, means and opportunity for the murder of his nephews and no one else did. And it will not do to say that their murders were some kind of unfortunate political necessity amid the carnage of civil war. The cold-blooded murder of children was as abhorrent then as it is now and there was no political necessity forcing Richard's hand. The last twelve years had been notable for their political stability. Richard only had himself to blame for getting into this terrible situation. He could easily have survived the regime change or put up serious opposition as and when his power base was threatened by the new regime. However, his experiences during childhood caused him to seriously over-react. He forgot that the Wars of the Roses had been over for 20 years and that the Woodvilles were not, in fact, very powerful. This led him down the road to murder and changed, almost overnight, the loyal brother into the wicked uncle.

Strengths and weaknesses of Richard's regime

Since Richard III's reign lasted only two years and ended with his violent death, it is easy to exaggerate the problems faced by his regime or to study the reign only as a way of finding out why it came to a bloody end. It is easier still to suppose that the reign was doomed from the start. Born out of blood, it was bound to end in blood. Furthermore Henry VII's regime, had good reason to blacken the reign and reputation of its predecessor and Shakespeare had good reasons for seeing history as a morality play. The reality, however, was that Richard's government had most of the inherent strengths of his brother's second reign and was rather surprisingly overthrown by Henry Tudor. Despite his dubious claim to the throne, Richard might have ruled successfully for many years if the pretender, rather than the usurper, had been killed on Bosworth Field in 1485.

WHAT WERE THE WEAKNESSES OF THE REGIME?

Richard's claim was weak

Despite the regime's inherent strengths, the regime looked weak at first.

- Richard's claim to the throne was based on the fictitious idea that Edward IV's sons were illegitimate and ignored the fact that Clarence's son had a better blood claim to the throne.
- It was soon widely rumoured that Richard had, in fact, murdered the princes. Even in the fifteenth century, the murder of young nephews and regicide were seen as appalling and unnatural crimes against God and man.

Buckingham's rebellion

The new king seemed to owe his throne to a kingmaker in the shape of the Duke of Buckingham. He had been the main supporter of Richard's usurpation and now waited to collect his due reward. He was to be the last example of that select group of individuals known as 'overmighty' subjects, though, in reality, he was rather less mighty than his predecessors, Richard of York and Richard of Warwick.

Richard III rewarded Buckingham well, giving him control of south Wales, but Buckingham, like his predecessors, felt less than generously treated by his royal paymaster and rebelled. In the autumn of 1483, as the regime was finding its feet, he put himself at the head of a series of uprisings across the south of England. At the same time, Henry Tudor got together a few ships and attempted to invade the kingdom from Brittany. Richard's regime thus faced a

KEY TERM

'Overmighty' subjects
Nobles who had the power to challenge the Crown. From the king's point of view, such men were clearly 'overmighty'.

KEY PERSON

John de la Pole, Earl of Lincoln (1464–87) The eldest son of the Duke of Suffolk. He was Richard III's nephew since his mother was Richard's sister. He was named as his heir after the death of Richard's son, Edward of Middleham. Lincoln was killed at the Battle of Stoke supporting Lambert Simnel against Henry VII.

serious crisis and one which helped to shape the future. Support for Richard was often lukewarm at best and opposition was apparently plentiful.

Richard, a northern king?

In terms of government, Richard's weakness was that, despite his birth in Northamptonshire, he had spent his formative years and held power in the north of England. Having to leave the north to become king, Richard left something of a power vacuum there and using his nephew, **John de la Pole, Earl of Lincoln,** to head a new **Council of the North** was no substitute for the firm rule of Richard himself. At the same time, Richard, the northern noble, sought to impose himself on southern England by bringing in trusted supporters, such as Sir Richard Ratcliffe and William Catesby. Such moves may also have bred opposition and encouraged the rebellion of 1483. As the **popular rhyme** of the time put it:

*The Cat, the Rat and **Lovell** our dog,*
Rulen all England under the Hog.

WHAT WERE THE STRENGTHS OF THE REGIME?

Limited opposition, royal progresses and patronage

Despite these weaknesses, Richard's regime should not be seen as doomed from the start.

- Politically, he was in a strong position. Buckingham's rebellion was a damp squib, resulting in the duke's execution in Salisbury.
- As a bonus for Richard, the heir to his powerful duchy was a minor and thus the king's ward.
- Henry Tudor's attempted invasion of 1483, to link up with the rebellion in England, had to turn back before it could reach the English coast. Internally thereafter, there was no overt opposition to Richard's rule.
- Richard's Woodville foes were pretty powerless or in exile and there seemed no chance that the king would be overthrown, certainly not by internal revolt.

At the same time, Richard proved as active as his brother, making royal progresses through his realm in both 1483 and 1484. The first made its way through Reading,

Oxford, Gloucester and Nottingham before reaching York, where Richard's baby son, **Edward of Middleham**, was invested as Prince of Wales.

In his use of patronage, Richard proved less generous than his brother had been but made good use of the confiscations from the 1483 rebellion to bolster the royal fortune. Although a new regime always has to buy support (or at least acceptance) from the political nation, it is clear that Richard managed this skilfully, so that his position and power, by the start of 1485, seemed more like Edward IV's second reign than his first. Richard elevated his trusty supporter, **John Howard**, to the dukedom of Norfolk and his son, **Thomas Howard**, was made the Earl of Surrey. Both men repaid these rewards by fighting for the king at Bosworth.

Richard and the nobility

By the summer of 1485, nearly half of the peers of the realm were firm supporters of Richard and none of the rest offered any open opposition. Many of those who had supported Edward IV now threw in their lot with his brother. Men like Lord Ferrers, **John, Lord Audley** and Lord Dudley worked for the new regime. In fact, 26 of the 54 men who served Richard as councillors had also served Edward IV. Whatever they thought about the demise of the princes, politics and power did not revolve around sentiment and regret. Whatever the doubts about his claim to the throne, Richard looked to be there to stay.

- He was an adult male king, hardened by treachery and disloyalty; a proven fighter and military commander in times of war and a proven administrator in times of peace.
- There was no credible alternative. Apart from those already in exile (and they were not a very powerful bunch), no English peer would declare his support for Henry Tudor before battle was joined at Bosworth.
- The most powerful peer joining Henry Tudor in exile was John de Vere, Earl of Oxford. He had an ancient name but only limited lands and power.
- Only four men in 1483 might have proved troublesome but none offered a serious threat to Richard's regime. Buckingham was executed, Norfolk was loyal,

KEY TERMS

Chantries Set up by wealthy men whereby they paid one or more priests to celebrate mass daily for the souls of themselves or their relatives forever. The priests were often called cantarists. A chantry of many priests was called a college or chantry college.

Fellows Clergymen appointed to teaching posts at a college.

KEY PEOPLE

John Russell, Bishop of Lincoln (d.1494) Entered royal service under Edward IV and went on diplomatic missions to Charles the Bold of Burgundy in 1467 and 1468. He became Bishop of Rochester in 1476 and moved to the more prestigious bishopric of Lincoln in 1480. He became Chancellor of England under Richard III, apparently rather reluctantly.

Thomas Langton, Bishop of St David's A firm supporter of Richard III and raised to his bishopric early in the reign. In a private letter of September 1483, he claimed that Richard 'contents the people where he goes best that ever did Prince, for many a poor man that hath suffered wrong many days hath been relieved and helped by him and his commands in his progress'. These words have been used to support the view that Richard was in fact a popular monarch.

Northumberland was only worried about his power in the north and Lord Stanley was seriously cautious. Although he was Henry Tudor's stepfather, he did not declare for him when he invaded England in 1485. Lord Stanley's main concern was to be on the winning side. So it was only his brother William's intervention at Bosworth that brought him belatedly into the fray on Henry Tudor's side.

What was the character of the regime?

Personally, Richard III seems to have been moderate in his habits and rather religious. He founded ten **chantries** to say prayers for the dead and was a patron of Queen's College in Cambridge, where he made provision for the payment of four **fellows**. He surrounded himself with scholars such as **John Russell, Bishop of Lincoln**, who became his Chancellor. **Thomas Langton, Bishop of St David's** and John Shirwood, Bishop of Durham, who were promoted to bishoprics by Richard, were also scholars who had studied in Italy as well as at Cambridge. These men were also humanists who believed in the need for improvements in the scanty provision of education.

At the same time, Richard III was a builder. He constructed a fine new Great Hall at Nottingham and at his favourite castle of Middleham in Yorkshire, with wide windows and the latest gothic design. He also contributed generously to the completion of the chapel of King's College in Cambridge, splendidly finished with its ceiling of intricate fan vaulting.

Richard also seems to have taken the business of government seriously enough. As far as we can see, he worked closely with his secretary, John Kendall, and his Chamber Treasurer, Edmund Chadderton, carrying on some of the routine tasks of government. After all, Richard was entirely familiar with the way in which medieval government operated. As viceroy in the north during Edward's reign, his council operated very much like the royal council. His household of servants went about the routine and not-so-routine tasks of local government in just the same way as did the king's household in Westminster (or wherever else the king was). So Richard used Edward's servants and brought in gentlemen of his own northern affinity to act as royal agents in those southern counties, which he did not know and which had proved troublesome early on in the reign.

It is clear that by the beginning of 1485, despite the continuing doubts about the legitimacy of his title, most of the gentry and landowners in the south were not conspiring against the regime. Their acceptance of Richard may have been grudging but that was all that Richard needed. After all, there would always be many others who realised that the way to fame and fortune lay in eager cooperation with the regime. After two years on the throne, Richard III seemed secure. However, in terms of royal finances, Richard faced problems.

- Although Edward IV had made the Crown solvent by 1475, his wars against Scotland and France had emptied the royal coffers.
- Nonetheless, the situation was hardly desperate. Richard outlawed benevolences whereby his brother had collected 'forced gifts' for the Crown and he also refrained from asking **Parliament** for taxation. The wars against France and Scotland had ended, so there were no continuing demands on royal income.
- At the same time, Richard continued the use of the royal chamber as a financial department, which his brother had favoured, and seems to have taken a real interest in attempting to maximise his income from royal lands. This, combined with a nature that was less generous than Edward IV, meant that the financial situation was secure enough by the end of the reign.

Richard and propaganda

Richard III also showed a succinct grasp of the politics of the day, producing powerful propaganda to explain his assumption of the throne. The **Act for the Settlement of the Crown upon Richard III (1484)** painted a bleak picture of the state of the nation during the reign of Edward IV.

- At that time, the Act claimed 'the order of all politic rule was perverted, the laws of God and of God's Church and also the laws of nature and of England were broken, subverted and held in contempt against all reason'.
- Things were so bad that there were 'many inconveniences and mischiefs as murders, extortions

KEY THEME

Parliament Met only once in Richard's reign in 1484. It confirmed his title to the Crown, passed 95 attainders against men involved in Buckingham's rebellion, banned benevolences and passed several Acts relating to the regulation of commerce. Lord Campbell, a nineteenth-century Lord Chancellor, claimed that the Parliament was 'the most meritorious assembly for the protecting the liberty of the subject and putting down abuses in the administration of justice that had sat in England since the reign of Henry III'.

KEY ACT

Act for the Settlement of the Crown upon Richard III (1484) The official law passed in Parliament stating that Richard was king. Parliament did not make him king but recognised that he was, through birth, the rightful sovereign.

and oppressions, namely of poor and impotent people, so that no man was sure of his life, land or livelihood, nor of his wife, daughter or servant. Every good maiden and woman stood in dread to be ravished and defouled!'

- The cause of all this terrible behaviour was, not surprisingly, King Edward's 'ungracious and pretended marriage' to Elizabeth Woodville. Edward, we are told, delighted in 'adulation and flattery' and was led by 'sensuality and **concupiscence**', following the advice of people who were 'insolent, vicious and of inordinate **avarice**'. The Act also claimed that Edward's union with Elizabeth Woodville was unlawful, encouraged by witchcraft and solemnised without the publishing of banns.
- The outcome was clear enough. 'It appeareth evidently,' the Act concluded, 'that all the issue and children of the said King Edward been bastards and unable to inherit or to claim anything by inheritance by the law and custom of England.'

This propaganda may have been heavy-handed and may not have been entirely convincing, but it does show that Richard appreciated the need for a powerful, if lurid, justification for his assumption of power.

Meanwhile, Richard cunningly exploited the growing number of stories that miracles were happening at the tomb of Henry VI. Even though some of these miracles seemed hostile to the regime, Richard decided to harness the increasing reverence in which this late king was being held (later Henry VII tried hard to have him proclaimed a saint) by reburying his former political opponent. Amid scenes of great pomp and ceremony, which echoed the famous reburial of Richard's own father at Fotheringhay, the king moved Henry VI from Chertsey to the great St George's Chapel at Windsor built by Edward IV. Here, Henry's miracles could be seen to enhance, not blacken, Richard's reputation.

St George's Chapel, Windsor in 1819.

KEY TERMS

Concupiscence Indulging in sins of a sexual nature.

Avarice Greed for possessions, especially money. It is usually accompanied by a desire to hoard money rather than spend it.

At the same time, Richard appreciated the propaganda value of royal ceremonial. His coronation was suitably lavish and extended as it included the crowning of his queen, Anne Neville, as well as of Richard himself. The royal progress of 1483 included great ceremonial entrances to several towns and much feasting and pageantry.

- At **York**, not only was his young son invested as Prince of Wales, but Richard also distributed some 13,000 **white boars** cut out of cloth.
- Early in 1484, Richard invited the Lord Mayor and assorted London dignitaries to the White Tower for his **Epiphany feast**. There was serious feasting and the mayor was presented with a cup set with pearls and gems. As many of these dignitaries were merchants who were important moneylenders to the Crown, Richard again demonstrated his political skill and understanding.

On many occasions then, Richard III showed that he had the personality and political ability to be a successful ruler.

The threat from Henry Tudor

Henry Tudor was the son of a minor nobleman, **Edmund Tudor, Earl of Richmond**. Edmund Tudor's only claim to fame was that his mother, Katherine de Valois, was also the mother of Henry VI. Left as a poor widow on the death of her first husband, Henry V, in 1422, she then contracted a marriage to one of her servants, a Welshman named **Owen Tudor**. Together they had two sons, Edmund and Jasper. The match was frowned upon at the time but Henry VI's political weakness and **lack of close male relatives** meant that advancement for the Tudors was at hand. In 1452, the two young Tudors, King Henry's half-brothers, were given earldoms.

- Edmund, the elder brother, received the earldom of Richmond in Yorkshire. Three years later he was allowed to marry the Lancastrian heiress, Margaret Beaufort and together they produced Henry Tudor in January 1457. Margaret was thirteen at the time of Henry's birth and must have been twelve at the time of conception! Even in the days of arranged marriages, such an early age of conception was highly unusual and frowned upon.

- Jasper Tudor became Earl of Pembroke in Wales.

Henry Tudor as powerless refugee

For young Henry Tudor, the prospects did not seem bright. His father died three months before his birth and, in 1461, at the age of four, his 'uncle', Henry VI, was deposed by Edward IV. Henry Tudor, Earl of Richmond, became the ward of the new Yorkist Earl of Pembroke, William Herbert. Thus the young Lancastrian pretender was in the hands of the Yorkist who had taken his uncle Jasper's earldom. Although the restoration of Henry VI to the throne in 1470–1 saw Henry united with that same uncle, the two of them were soon forced to flee when Edward IV returned in triumph in 1471. They boarded ship in Pembroke, hoping to reach France (after all, Henry's grandmother had been a French princess) but were blown off course and alighted in the independent French duchy of Brittany.

At the age of fourteen, the life confronting Henry Tudor was one as a penniless refugee and political pawn.

- He had probably never been to England, would come to speak French rather better than English, and had had very little contact with his mother, Margaret Beaufort, who was now married to Thomas, Lord Stanley as a way of neutralising the Tudor threat to Edward IV. Lord Stanley was actually his mother's fourth husband and she was still only 28 years old!
- Although an English attempt to kidnap Henry in 1475 failed, his prospects looked bleak as the Yorkist regime in England grew ever more powerful and secure during Edward IV's second reign.
- Henry was unknown in England and his patron, Francis, Duke of Brittany, was unlikely to help him against the English king, since he wanted Edward IV as a potential ally against his main enemy – the King of France.
- So it was that Henry Tudor, a lonely and isolated young man with just a few loyal supporters, began to think of doing a deal with Edward IV so that he might return to England as a loyal supporter of the Yorkist regime.

During much of the 1470s, as Edward's second reign became more stable and peaceful, Margaret Beaufort was negotiating for the return of her son and his marriage to a suitable Yorkist heiress.

How did Tudor fortunes improve?

In 1483, everything changed. Edward IV's sudden death and Richard III's brutal usurpation of the throne transformed Henry Tudor's position. Suddenly he was joined by a group of Yorkist exiles opposed to Richard's seizure of power and was granted the right to marry the most eligible heiress in the kingdom, namely Elizabeth of York, Edward IV's eldest daughter. At a stroke, Richard's deposition of Edward V had split Edward IV's Yorkist power base and given Henry Tudor some hope of advancement to the ultimate prize – the throne of England. On Christmas Day, 1483, a group of anti-Ricardian Yorkist refugees swore to recognise Henry as king if he married Elizabeth of York. Their oath, taken in Rennes Cathedral, was echoed by Henry's own promise to marry Elizabeth and then to rule jointly with her. By extracting this promise, the Yorkist lords were indicating that their support for Henry, far from being wholehearted, was limited and conditional. What they wanted was, in the short term to see Edward IV's heir, Elizabeth of York, on the throne, and in the long term to see the throne occupied by Edward IV's grandson. The Yorkists, who were hostile to Richard III, did not really want Henry Tudor as king but Elizabeth of York as queen.

The 1483 expedition

Although the oaths taken at Rennes were a big boost to Henry's cause, there was still little chance of him unseating Richard III. His first attempt to make a landing in a few ships in the autumn of 1483 had been a fiasco. The ships turned back because of bad weather without making a landing and the rebellion in the south of England failed to spread. Buckingham was executed and King Richard seemed secure. Thomas Grey, Marquis of Dorset, judging Henry's situation hopeless, attempted to flee back to England but was overtaken by Henry's supporters and persuaded to stay.

Henry gains French support

As a measure of his newfound security, Richard reached a deal with Francis, Duke of Brittany for the handing over of young Henry Tudor in 1484. However, just before he was due to be arrested, Henry and his small band of followers were tipped off and crossed the border into France. It was the best move they could possibly have made.

- The faction fighting at the French court cleared up in the spring of 1485 and, in the face of the new offensive alliance between Richard III and the Duke of Brittany, the French government authorised the equipping of a small fleet plus mercenary troops to be put at the disposal of Henry Tudor for an invasion of England.
- For the French, this was largely a defensive rather than an offensive move. In the spring of 1485, they feared that Richard III would invade France. After all, he, as Duke of Gloucester, had accompanied Edward IV's invasion of France in 1475 and had opposed the Treaty of Picquigny because he wanted to fight the French.
- The chances of an English invasion seemed even more likely, since the death of Louis XI in 1483 had brought about a **minority government** in France. That minority government of **Charles VIII** was seriously split by internal squabbles, which threatened to leave France in chaos.

So, the French probably saw the young Tudor (still only 28 in 1485) as a useful diversion, who would at least stop Richard III from invading France and there is no evidence that they wanted or expected him to become king. Henry's French troops could look forward to some serious raiding and chances of booty before returning home. For the Yorkists in exile and for Henry himself, it was a serious gamble. They had no guaranteed support in England as none of the English nobility had declared in Henry's favour. Furthermore, unlike the young pretender, Richard III was an able soldier, veteran of his brother's campaigns in England and his own successful campaign in Scotland. As such, in the summer of 1485, Richard was not taking the threat of a Tudor invasion lightly. He stationed himself in Nottingham, the centre of the kingdom, to await developments.

KEY TERM

Minority government
This happens when a new king is still a child when his predecessor dies. Until the child comes of age, he is called a minor.

KEY PERSON

Charles VIII (1470–98)
The only son of Louis XI, who became king at the age of thirteen when his father died in 1483. The minority government was headed by his elder sister, Anne de Beaujeu, and her husband, Pierre de Bourbon. In 1491, Charles married Anne of Brittany and, on attaining his majority, he decided to invade Italy. He did this in 1494 and the next year seized the kingdom of Naples. He was crowned King of Naples in 1495 but was forced to retreat in the face of a hostile coalition of powers including the Emperor Maximilian, the Pope, Venice and Milan. He died in 1498 by hitting his head on a low doorway while riding a tall horse!

The invasion

When Henry landed, he did so in south Wales, but that meant that his forces faced a march of over a hundred miles before they could even reach England. They also faced an uncertain future, not knowing if Richard would be drawn into battle, if they would keep their discipline, and what would happen if the campaign dragged on. Henry's forces landed unopposed on 7 August at Milford Haven in just seven ships. Two weeks later he had marched into the centre of England and faced Richard's troops near the town of Market Bosworth in Leicestershire.

Even so, the prospects for Henry looked bleak.

- Richard's forces, led by the Duke of Norfolk and his son, the Earl of Surrey, were positioned on the top of Ambion Hill. Henry's forces were at the foot of the hill with woods and marshes on either side.
- Although Henry's stepfather, **Thomas, Lord Stanley**, and his brother, **Sir William Stanley**, were there, the usual Stanley caution and determination to be on the winning side meant that they were unlikely to intervene to help Henry.
- While Henry's march through Wales had been unopposed, he had not received much support. Perhaps 3000 men had joined his original force of 2000 and only two peers had joined him: Lord Welles and the Earl of Oxford.

On the other hand, Henry's forces did have a chance of success.

- Richard's army was no larger then Henry's.
- Richard was unpopular and found it hard to rouse the nobles of the land from their natural stance of self-preservation. The Earl of Northumberland appeared at the field of battle, but, like the Stanleys, he was there to witness the outcome and to help the winning side when the identity of the victor became apparent. Certainly, Northumberland was no friend to Richard, as the two had crossed swords in the north often enough.

The Battle of Bosworth, 1485

When the battle started, it looked as though Richard, eager to smash his enemies once and for all, would win.

- After the preliminary arrow exchange, the Duke of Norfolk led a charge downhill into Henry's forces.
- Some time later, however, at the top of Ambion Hill, Richard made his one fateful and fatal miscalculation of the day. The story goes that Henry Tudor himself, fearful of defeat, rode, with a small group of followers and his standard bearer, in the direction of the Stanley forces, who had not been committed on either side and were apparently merely spectators as the battle unfolded. No doubt Henry wished to persuade them to join his side. As Richard noticed Henry's movements, he abandoned the safety of the top of the hill, charging towards Henry and his exposed bodyguard. It is believed that Richard himself cut down Henry's standard-bearer and that he was within a whisker of killing his opponent. Henry had never fought in a battle before and would have stood little chance against the experienced Richard. Yet at the last minute, Henry was saved by the prompt actions of Sir William Stanley, who now threw his troops against the lightly defended king. Richard III was hacked down and killed on the spot.

The battle was over and Henry had triumphed. The events at Bosworth in 1485 had produced one of the most surprising candidates ever to get his hands on the throne. He was not really English, he had never been to England, and he had invaded with foreign troops. The lessons of Bosworth would live with him. Henry's reign would be plagued by pretenders. Henry knew that they could succeed just as he had. No amount of Tudor propaganda could change that. His reign would be lived on a knife-edge.

Richard III and the Yorkist civil war

For many historians, the Battle of Bosworth is a major turning point in English history. It brought in a new dynasty – the Tudors – that would rule for the next 118 years. In place of the strife of civil wars and baronial revolts, they brought peace, stability and a growing sense of English identity and power. Henry VII ended the Wars of the Roses and brought in a new efficient style of government that would underpin internal peace and security in the future. Henry's son, Henry VIII, created the Church of England and ended the papal (and therefore foreign) leadership of that Church. Henry VIII's daughter, **Queen Elizabeth I**, fought off threats from the Roman Catholic Church at home and abroad and, at the time of the great Armada, defeated Spain, then the most powerful nation in the world.

However, on closer inspection, 1485 does not seem to be such an important turning point.

- It did not mark the end of the Wars of the Roses. If these are taken to be the struggle for the throne between Richard of York and Henry VI, then they effectively came to an end in 1461 with Edward IV's accession. The fighting in 1470–1, after all, was sparked off by dissident Yorkists (Warwick and Clarence) who managed to put Henry VI briefly back on the throne. The instability of that period began as a Yorkist civil war, not as a new round in the conflict between York and Lancaster.

- It is clear that the Lancastrian die-hards, who were prepared to fight for Henry VI, were finished after 1461 and only had a chance of reclaiming the throne in 1470 because of the fractures among the Yorkist élite.

- The same is true of 1483. After the security and stability of Edward IV's second reign, there was renewed conflict because the Yorkist governing party was split by Richard III's usurpation. Hastings was executed for his opposition and the Marquis of Dorset (half-brother to Edward V) joined Henry Tudor in Brittany.

- This split within the Yorkist elite then caused further conflict. The Yorkist rebellion against Richard III failed dismally in 1483 but succeeded unexpectedly in 1485.

- Admittedly, the Yorkist dissidents were helped by the pretender Henry Tudor: after all, they needed someone to replace Richard. However, the Tudors would not have been able to mount a serious challenge without Yorkist support and, in particular, without Henry's willingness to marry Elizabeth of York.

- The Yorkist exiles forced Henry to swear that he would rule jointly with Elizabeth. The new regime would thus be essentially Yorkist and produce a Yorkist heir to the throne in due course. For the anti-Ricardian forces, who

Queen Elizabeth I (1533–1603) The daughter of Henry VIII and his second wife, Anne Boleyn. She became queen in 1558 on the death of her older and Catholic half-sister, Mary I, and reintroduced Protestantism.

KEY THEME

Henry Tudor himself had no real claim to the throne On his father's side, he was the son of the Earl of Richmond, who was the son of a Welsh squire. The fact that the Earl of Richmond had the same mother as Henry VI did not transmit a claim to the latter's throne. On his mother's side, Henry Tudor was the son of Margaret Beaufort, one of the heiresses of an illegitimate line from John of Gaunt, third son of Edward III.

turned to Henry Tudor in their time of crisis, he was a Yorkist, not a Lancastrian, claimant. The Yorkists wanted to use him and his prospective wife to continue the true Yorkist dynasty to take the place of Elizabeth's murdered brothers. The Yorkists could think in these terms because **Henry Tudor himself had no real claim to the throne**.

Henry Tudor – not a Lancastrian claimant

In this way, too, 1483–5 was not just another round in a long-running civil war. Henry Tudor was not the Lancastrian claimant taking up a Crown left to him by Henry VI because, after all, his claim to the throne was tenuous to say the least.

- On both his mother's side and his father's side, Henry Tudor had no real claim to the throne; and it is notable that he never argued that he had a right to the throne by bloodline.
- Henry claimed the throne through God's judgement in his favour on the battlefield.
- Henry knew that, by male descent, the Crown should rightfully have gone to Edward, Earl of Warwick, Clarence's son.
- His uncertain title to the throne meant that the first Tudor was inviting anyone else to try their luck, since successful armed rebellion was now officially seen as a proper reason for claiming and holding on to regal power.

Differing causes of instability, 1459–85

The troubles of 1483 and 1485 were not just another round in the Wars of the Roses, since they emerged from different causes.

- In 1460, Richard of York claimed the throne as the culmination of a long struggle between himself and the regime of Henry VI. Prior to 1460, he claimed that he was fighting against Henry VI's evil advisers; then he claimed that Henry VI had never been the true King of England because his grandfather had usurped the throne from Richard II. As a result, he, not Henry, was the true King of England. With the deposition of Henry VI by Edward IV in 1461, that struggle was essentially over.

- In 1483, Richard III claimed the throne on the basis that the king and his brother were bastards – it was a struggle within the Yorkist family. In 1485, Henry VII claimed the throne on the basis that Richard III was a homicidal usurper, 'murderer of his own blood and progeny,' and therefore he did not deserve to be king. He did so with the active support of powerful Yorkists such as Elizabeth Woodville, her eldest daughter and the Marquis of Dorset.

Wars of the Roses?

Furthermore, it is misleading to lump together all the bouts of political instability in the period 1459–85 and give them one overarching name – the Wars of the Roses – as this implies not only common causes but also an unbroken series of wars. In reality, there were long periods of peace and stability and contemporaries failed to spot the connection between these periods of fighting, since the term Wars of the Roses was not used at the time: Shakespeare coined it in the reign of Queen Elizabeth I. Henry VII did, of course, enhance the myth of the Wars of the Roses by inventing the Tudor rose – a hybrid of the red Lancastrian rose and the white Yorkist rose – but no one at the time talked in terms of the Wars of the Roses. His propaganda painted him as a great healer of the nation's divisions, but we must recognise that it was Tudor propaganda.

It makes more sense to realise that the instability of 1483 and 1485 emerged from largely chance events: the sudden and unexpected death of Edward IV, together with the particular age of his heir, together with the particular fears and paranoia of Richard, Duke of Gloucester. Looked at in this way, it is clear that both the rise and the fall of Richard III were not further bouts in the conflict between York and Lancaster, but products of a Yorkist civil war.

SUMMARY QUESTIONS

1 Why did Richard of Gloucester claim the throne in 1483?

2 Should Richard III be seen as a tyrant?

3 What does the reign of Richard indicate about the strengths and weaknesses of the English monarchy in this period?

4 Why did Henry Tudor win the Battle of Bosworth?

5 Every year, on 22 August, a notice appears in the 'In Memoriam' column of some newspapers. It reads, 'Richard III, King of England, treacherously slain on Bosworth Field, 1485.' How far do you agree that Richard III was treacherously slain?

INSTABILITY DURING THE REIGN OF HENRY VII: PRETENDERS, REBELLIONS AND THREATS FROM ABROAD

> ## How serious was the political instability of Henry VII's reign?

KEY POINTS

- Henry's weak claim to the throne and violent overthrow of Richard III meant that there were serious attempts to unseat him.
- Lambert Simnel, claiming to be Edward, Earl of Warwick, invaded England and was eventually defeated at the Battle of Stoke in 1487.
- Perkin Warbeck, claiming to be Richard, Duke of York (Edward V's younger brother) was a threat to Henry VII's regime from 1491 until his execution in 1499.
- There were serious tax riots in Yorkshire in 1489, which led to the lynching of the Earl of Northumberland.
- In 1497, the Cornish Rising saw thousands of rebels march from the West Country to London in protest at heavy taxation.
- Many foreign rulers conspired to overthrow Henry VII.

TIMELINE

1485   Battle of Bosworth.

1486   Francis, Lord Lovell's revolt.

1487   January - Simnel arrives in Ireland.

       June - Battle of Stoke – defeat of Simnel's forces and death of John de la Pole, Earl of Lincoln.

1489   Tax riots in the north.

1491   Margaret of Burgundy proclaims Perkin Warbeck as Richard, Duke of York. He arrives in Ireland.

1492   Warbeck welcomed in France.

1495   Warbeck attempts to land in Kent; later welcomed in Scotland.

1496   Warbeck's invasion of England with King James IV of Scotland.

1497   Cornish Revolt – Battle of Blackheath. Capture of Warbeck.

1499   Execution of Warbeck and Warwick.

1501   Edmund de la Pole flees abroad.

1502   Death of Prince Arthur.

1503   Death of Queen Elizabeth of York.

1506   Edmund de la Pole handed over to Henry VII.

OVERVIEW

Over the years, there has been a serious contradiction, or at least a serious puzzle, in the picture painted by historians of the reign of Henry VII. It has been hard to decide whether the reign was peaceful, stable and characterised by strong and equitable government, or whether it was dominated by instability, rebellion and government terror.

Ever since 1874, when J.R. Green published his short history of England, many historians have seen the reign, which lasted for 24 years (1485–1509), largely in terms of 'new monarchy' or at least the reinvigoration of the monarchy's power. If the supposedly serious and bloody Wars of the Roses ended at Bosworth in 1485, then it seemed clear that Henry VII must have governed in a rather different way from his immediate predecessors, all four of whom (Henry VI, Edward IV, Edward V and Richard III) had been violently overthrown, with one of them (Henry VI) being overthrown twice! If the Wars of the Roses had produced so much instability over a period of 30 years, Henry VII must have adopted a seriously different approach to the task of government because he was not overthrown but died in his bed. Not only this, but when he died in 1509, he also handed over to his son, Henry VIII, in a peaceful transfer of power from one king to another, the first since the accession of Henry VI nearly 100 years before.

As a result, historians such as Roger Lockyer, R.L. Storey, Stanley Chrimes and Alexander Grant tended to concern

themselves above all with the government and
administration of the reign. They concerned themselves
with how Henry Tudor governed his people. This
approach, also encouraged by the nature of the surviving
written evidence – parliamentary statutes, legal records and
financial accounts – has meant that the reign has often been
analysed mainly from the government's point of view and
in terms of what the government did. This is why Henry
VII is so often seen as a dull monarch whose reign had to
be analysed mainly in terms of government and
administration. In this way, it has been easy to think that
government under Henry VII became stronger and that
England, under the first Tudor, enjoyed a period of peace
and prosperity.

Continued political instability

However, there is an alternative interpretation of the
reign which focuses on the continuing problems of
government. It is claimed that Henry VII's reign was just
as troubled as Henry VI's reign in the 1450s. In 1497,
Henry VII faced a popular rebellion over levels of royal
taxation. The rebels marched, unhindered, several hundred
miles from Cornwall to London, only to be defeated on the
outskirts of the capital. The scale and seriousness of the
revolt was akin to **Cade's rebellion of 1450**. Edward IV,
by contrast, never faced such a serious outburst of popular
opposition.

At the same time, Henry VII's regime was confronted by a
number of pretenders to the throne. One of these raised an
army, which marched from Lancashire to Nottinghamshire,
forcing the king into a pitched battle before finally being
crushed. Another pretender would be a serious threat to
Henry for nine years, gathering support at home and more
especially abroad. No sooner was this pretender executed,
than the regime was plunged into crisis once more as
Henry's son and heir died, giving fresh hope to yet more
Yorkist claimants. These threats to the throne lasted,
without serious intermission, throughout the reign. In this
way, Henry's reign is much more troubled than Edward
IV's second reign in which there were no pretenders and no
attempts to overthrow the king.

Henry VII's government was apparently also undermined
by his chronic and paranoid suspicion of the nobility. As an

KEY EVENTS

Cade's rebellion of 1450
A serious uprising against the
corruption of local
government in Henry VI's
reign. The rising started in
Kent and the rebels took
charge of London as the king
and his court fled. Two
prominent courtiers, Lord
Saye and William Crowmer,
the sheriff of Kent, were
lynched (murdered) by the
angry mob.

Henry's son and heir died
This refers to the death of
Arthur Tudor, Prince of Wales
in 1502 at the age of fifteen.
His death, just after his
marriage to Catherine of
Aragon, meant that the
Spanish alliance was broken
and that the heir to the
throne was now a boy of ten –
the future King Henry VIII.

KEY TERMS

Tyrannical Here it is used to refer to a ruler who governed without regard for the law. In England, the tradition was that the king's powers over the lives and goods of his subjects were restricted by the laws of the land, which the king was bound to uphold. In this sense, Henry's regime in his later years can be seen as tyrannical.

Coup d'état A French term meaning the overthrow of the government. The coup of 1509 did not overthrow the new government of Henry VIII but did reverse Henry VII's method of governing.

Te Deum A religious anthem named after the first two Latin words of that anthem. In this case, the anthem claims that victory is due to God (*Te Deum*) and not the activities of mere mortals.

outsider and faced with the continuous threat of rebellion and revolt, Henry's reaction was to trust no one, least of all the nobility and peers of the realm. The problem with this approach was that Henry did more to undermine stability than to promote it. Medieval government always depended on the collaborative efforts of the king and his nobles. By undermining and periodically upsetting his nobility, Henry created a government that was suspicious and **tyrannical**. When he died in 1509, the nobility staged a **coup d'état** to recover their lost powers.

According to this version of the period, then, the regime, far from being a model of good government and harmony after the troubles of the Wars of the Roses, was, in fact always teetering on the edge of disaster.

Problems of perspective and hindsight

It will be argued here that the second model of the reign is rather nearer the mark than the first.

- Historians have too often seen Henry VII's reign as safe, strong and sanitised because they swallowed Henry Tudor's propaganda. Naturally enough, he said that his government was strong and that all was well.
- In addition, historians have over-indulged their taste for hindsight. They have looked from the perspective of 1509, when Henry died in his bed, and focused on why he was not overthrown.
- A more useful perspective is to analyse the reign and the regime as it goes along: to see it in its own terms and through the eyes of the participants, not through the eyes of the victor. In this way, we can now see a regime beset by problems and never free from the fear of sudden overthrow. This, at least, is how Henry himself would have seen things.

The Simnel rebellion, 1486–7

Apparent strength of Henry's position in 1485

At the end of the Battle of Bosworth, with Richard III safely dead, Henry was crowned on the battlefield and a *Te Deum* was sung to thank God for the victory. In some ways, the new king appeared to be in a strong position. Unlike Edward IV and Richard III, who also came to power by violent usurpation of the throne, Henry could at least make it clear that his predecessor was dead. So, **Richard III's body** was stripped naked and slung over a horse for all to see.

At the same time, Henry was strong because he did not owe his throne to an ambitious and grasping kingmaker.

- Edward IV had been overthrown by a vengeful Warwick.
- Richard III had faced rebellion from an ungrateful Buckingham.

The only possible kingmakers at Bosworth were the Stanley family. They were altogether in a lower league compared to Warwick and Buckingham and, anyway, Thomas, Lord Stanley was married to Henry's mother, Margaret Beaufort, so was unlikely to cause trouble. In addition, Henry's strength was boosted by the fact that most people who mattered did believe that **Richard III had killed his nephews** to secure his hold on the monarchy. Even in the late fifteenth century, this was a terrible crime.

How weak was Henry's position in 1485?

Henry's strength in 1485 was more apparent than real.

- He was seen as a foreigner (contemporaries would have said an alien) because of his long years in Brittany, and because he probably spoke French better than English.
- He had taken the throne by violent means, with foreign help, on his first visit to England.
- Although he had won the battle, Henry had received scant backing from the nobility and there were plenty of great men who thought he was not the rightful king. If the throne could be won so easily in one small-scale encounter on the battlefield or, even more quickly, by the sudden death of the reigning monarch, then there was real hope for a number of Yorkist pretenders.
- First and foremost, there was Edward, Earl of Warwick – son of George, Duke of Clarence. Though he became a prisoner in the Tower a few weeks after Bosworth, his right to the throne through birth could not be ignored. If the princes were dead, his claim was much stronger than Henry Tudor's and Elizabeth of York's combined.

Richard III's body When the new king's victory parade reached Leicester, Richard's body was buried in an unmarked grave in a local monastery. No other king had been humiliated in death in quite the same way. At the time of the dissolution of the monasteries under Henry VIII, Richard's remains were dug up and thrown into the River Soar.

KEY THEME

Richard III had killed his nephews The exact fate of the princes in the Tower was not known. What if the princes were not dead? Of course, everyone had assumed the worst in the days of King Richard but no one had ever seen the bodies. They had just disappeared. Perhaps they had escaped and fled abroad under false names. If so, they might return to claim their inheritance. Edward V could be a once and future king. If he were actually dead, there was always his brother, Richard, Duke of York. If Prince Richard were alive, then his title to the throne was clear-cut, since he was the brother and the son of a king.

- Even if the princes were really dead and Warwick was still a boy, there were still the sons of Edward IV's and Richard III's sister, Elizabeth. She had married **John de la Pole, Duke of Suffolk** and produced a number of sons. Her eldest, John de la Pole, Earl of Lincoln, had a very strong claim to the throne. He was in his 20s, an able young man, and officially Richard III's heir since the death of the King's young son, Edward of Middleham in 1484.
- Surrounded by so many possible claimants, Henry Tudor – who had no right at all to the royal crown – was right to be nervous.

Henry's suspicions of the nobility

At the same time, Henry was fearful that he could expect no long-term loyalty from any of the great nobles. The Stanleys had only backed him at the last minute when they could guarantee his success; the rest had been neutral or fought for Richard. Admittedly, the apathy of the nobility and their unwillingness to take sides readily in civil conflict might help Henry in the future but it was not the same as positive support and loyalty towards the new regime. Those who did pledge their loyalty might be playing for time and waiting to see how they might be rewarded. Ultimately, there was no one whom Henry could trust. The political instability of recent years had made everyone nervous and suspicious. Immediately after Bosworth, Henry Tudor had less active support than Richard III two years earlier.

Henry's official claim to the throne

When he reached London, Henry's problems became obvious. He called a Parliament, (which met in November), and got them to pass an Act confirming his title to the throne. Parliament declared that Henry's reign had started the day before Bosworth, thus allowing Henry to attaint all those who fought against him on the basis that they were fighting against, not with, the true king. However, the Act also made it clear that Henry was king, not because of his blood claim to the throne, but because God had found in his favour on the battlefield. Furthermore, the Act implied that, as a usurper, Henry owed his throne to the approval of Parliament and the peerage. This was not an idea Henry wished to encourage.

Not until January 1486 did he fulfil his promise, made in Rennes Cathedral, of marrying Elizabeth of York. By delaying the marriage in this way, Henry was hoping to emphasise that he did not owe his crown to her, but the political realities suggested otherwise. In marrying the sister of Edward V, Henry was paying the price for the Yorkist support that had brought him to the throne.

The Roses united. The red rose (Henry VII) was married to the white rose (Elizabeth of York).

Early defections

Unsurprisingly, there were soon signs that Henry's reign would be continuously troubled by insurrection and instability.

- At Easter 1486, Francis, Lord Lovell, together with Humphrey and Thomas Stafford, sons of Sir Humphrey Stafford of Grafton, broke out of **sanctuary** in Colchester and raised the standard of rebellion. This was a rather desperate affair undertaken by followers of Richard III and it gained very little support. The elder Stafford was executed, the younger pardoned and Lord Lovell disappeared. Although very limited in its achievements, it told Henry what he feared most: that there were men out there prepared to plot to overthrow him.

- By 1487, Henry was so worried about the possibility of plots within the royal household that an Act of Parliament of that year set up a special court appointing officials to investigate the possibility that members of the royal household had taken part in 'any confederacy, compassings, conspiracies or imaginings' to destroy or murder the king or any of the great officers of state. Of course, by 1487, Henry had good reason to be worried: he had just survived a very serious uprising led by Lambert Simnel.

HOW SERIOUS WAS THE SIMNEL REBELLION?

It is easy to underestimate the Simnel conspiracy to overthrow Henry VII because it failed. In reality, it was deadly serious and came close to success. Lambert Simnel was a ten-year-old boy, the son of a baker, who was selected by Yorkist sympathisers to play the part of Edward, Earl of Warwick, who was now the surviving male heir of his uncle, Edward IV. The boy was trained by an Oxfordshire priest, Richard Simons. The plot began late in 1486 and rapidly acquired serious backing.

John de la Pole, Margaret of Burgundy and the Irish rebels

An important supporter of the Simnel cause was John de la Pole, Earl of Lincoln. In February 1487, de la Pole suddenly fled from court and turned up in the Low Countries at the court of **Margaret dowager Duchess of Burgundy**. As she was, in reality, Margaret of York, sister of both Edward IV and Richard III, she was determined to see Henry VII overthrown and her family returned to power. Operating outside England, with considerable political skills and a lot of money, she was a formidable foe for Henry Tudor. Joining these two came Francis, Lord Lovell, who had escaped from Henry's clutches the year before and now determined to cause more trouble.

Margaret equipped the rebels with some 2000 experienced troops under an equally experienced captain, Martin Schwarz.

- Resisting the temptation to make a swift, direct attack across the Channel, these forces sailed to Ireland to rendezvous with Lambert Simnel.
- In Ireland, a former Yorkist stronghold – indeed, birthplace of George, Duke of Clarence, the father of the real Earl of Warwick – there was strong support for the conspiracy. Although kings of England claimed to be kings of Ireland as well, their power there was minimal.
- The real – if uncrowned – King of Ireland at this time was Gerald FitzGerald, eigth Earl of Kildare, who had built up a strong power base across Ireland. Henry Tudor had upset the earl by refusing to confirm his official position as deputy-lieutenant of Ireland and now the earl decided to throw his considerable political weight, together with a few thousand Irish troops, behind the Simnel conspiracy.
- On 24 May 1487, just nineteen days after the successful landing of Lincoln, Lovell and Schwarz in Ireland,

Simnel was crowned and proclaimed as King Edward VI. The Archbishop of Dublin performed the ceremony and crowned young Lambert with a golden circlet taken from the statue of the Blessed Virgin Mary in the cathedral.

A contemporary account of Simnel

This extract is from an Irish book called *The Book of Houth*. The Lord of Houth did not support Simnel!

Soon after, it was blown abroad that Edward the young Earl of Warwick was broken out of the Tower and a priest called Richard Simons sailed with a child into Ireland and there he declared to certain of the nobility there that this child was the young Earl of Warwick. And so they called him king and so sent their letters secretly into England and also to Flanders, to Lady Margaret, sister of King Edward, to further his purpose with all his might and power. Sir Nicholas, Lord of Houth, perceiving all this but a mad dance, sent over to the king and advertised to him of all these matters from the beginning to the ending who was the doers and maintainers of these matters in Ireland and Flanders.

Simnel's invasion of England and the Battle of Stoke, 1487

Able to gather forces in Ireland without opposition, the conspirators then landed unopposed in England on 4 June 1487. They were welcomed near Barrow-in-Furness by Sir Thomas Broughton, one of Richard III's northern affinity. The landing place was deliberately chosen to gather more support from the followers of the previous king, who had built up a powerful body of supporters and clients in the north. Moving speedily, they marched across Lancashire and Yorkshire unopposed and it was here that King Henry's weakness became clear. None of the local nobles made any attempt to stop the invasion. The Earl of Northumberland, confirmed by Henry in his control of the north, did nothing to oppose the malcontents. In a situation reminiscent of the successful invasions by Edward IV (1471) and by Henry Tudor himself (1485), an invading army was allowed to march several hundred miles into England without hindrance.

KEY EVENT

Battle of Stoke (1487)
Though the Irish troops proved ineffective, Schwarz's mercenaries were a different matter. Oxford's line buckled under their assault and Henry, who was observing the battle from a safe distance, did nothing to help. During the battle, the rebel leader, the Earl of Lincoln, was killed. All the conflicts of the previous 30 years had shown that the outcome of battles was usually down to random or unpredictable factors; for example, Richard's charge at Bosworth, the snowstorm at Towton and the fog at Barnet.

KEY TERM

Turnspit An unimportant member of the kitchen staff in a great household. His main task was to turn the meat as it cooked over an open fire.

In early June, Henry moved north from Kenilworth near Coventry and met up with Stanley forces from Cheshire and the north-west before intercepting the rebels near the village of Stoke, not far from Newark in Nottinghamshire.

- Both sides at the **Battle of Stoke** were similar in scale to those that appeared at Bosworth. The king had the larger army but the rebels, as at Bosworth, had a core of well-trained foreign mercenaries.
- However, the king did not have the outright support of any of the great nobles. His forces were led by the Earl of Oxford and by Lord Stanley's son, who had escaped death at the hands of Richard III at Bosworth.
- The battle was fought on 16 June and the king's forces won the day. The Irish, who were lightly armed, proved easy meat for Oxford's bowmen and they were shot 'full of arrows like hedgehogs'.

Henry could afford to be merciful to the young and bewildered Lambert Simnel. He was taken into the royal household where he acted as **turnspit** in the kitchens, later rising to the rank of the king's falconer. It was a calculated piece of propaganda by Henry, akin to his sarcastic remark, on hearing of Simnel's coronation in Ireland, that the Irish 'would crown apes at last'. However, this should not blind us to the seriousness of the threat posed by Simnel. The Battle of Stoke was close fought and the losses fairly even – 4000 rebels died but so, too, did some 3000 royal troops.

The serious nature of the Simnel threat

It is easy to think that the Simnel conspiracy was not a serious threat because Lambert Simnel was so obviously an impostor. To emphasise the point that Simnel was a fake, Henry VII had the real Earl of Warwick paraded round the streets of London. However, this did not really help Henry's cause. The rebels merely claimed that Henry's Warwick was the impostor! By parading the real earl around London, Henry reminded even those who believed the king's side of the story that a very good Yorkist claimant was alive and well.

- The rebels, even if they knew that Simnel was bogus, wanted merely to use him as a focus for the Yorkist claim to the throne. In this he was brilliantly successful as he gathered support from Ireland, the Low Countries and England. Once they had defeated and killed Henry VII, the rebels could then free the real Earl of Warwick, or, if rumours of his mental incapacity proved true, they could always substitute the next best Yorkist claimant, John de la Pole, Earl of Lincoln.

- The Simnel conspiracy was stronger than it looked because it did not aim to put the impostor on the throne of England. The Yorkists, after all, had two perfectly legitimate claimants whose right to the throne was much clearer than Henry VII's.
- The Simnel conspiracy was also very dangerous because it mirrored exactly Henry Tudor's successful rebellion just two years before. Both of these invasions relied mainly on foreign support, both marched unopposed for several hundred miles across the kingdom, and both forced the king to fight a battle.
- Hindsight – the knowledge that Henry won the battle and defeated the conspiracy – has also tended to blind us to the dangers it posed at the time. No one was in a better position to appreciate the seriousness of the situation than Henry Tudor.

The Northern rebellion of 1489

While nothing like as serious as the Simnel rebellion of 1487, the Northern rebellion of 1489 indicated again that the king's control of the kingdom was far from secure. It was a rebellion against Henry's heavy tax demands.

- The king wished to raise money to pay for men to defend Brittany from French aggression. This seems to have met with widespread opposition, especially in the north.
- Opposition was associated with some new methods the king used in order to increase the yield of his taxes.
- At the same time, the king seems to have acted insensitively in not allowing the north its usual **tax rebates**.

The rising came to a head when Thomas Percy, Earl of Northumberland was murdered in Topcliffe in Yorkshire. He was attempting to explain the need for the new taxes to a crowd of people when he was set upon by the angry mob and killed. Interestingly, his own retinue of men stood by as their master was lynched, perhaps indicating the depth

KEY TERM

Tax rebates Refers to a situation where the government decreases the amount of tax demanded, usually to win favour with angry taxpayers.

of resentment felt by ordinary people over the high taxes being demanded.

Thereafter the rising became more serious as the rebels feared that the king would punish the whole region for the murder of his chief tax collector. The king probably felt little sympathy for Percy, who had turned up at Bosworth but refused to fight on either side. However, he was **Warden General** of the East and Middle Marches towards Scotland and his death, leaving an heir who was a minor, might mean trouble and conspiracies in the north. In fact, the rising was soon over.

- One leader, John à Chambré, was executed.
- Sir John Egremont escaped royal justice by fleeing to Margaret of Burgundy in Flanders, where he was welcomed and added to the list of those who might overthrow the king.

Although it was soon over, the Northern Rising of 1489 was another reason for Henry to feel insecure in a kingdom which he still did not really know or understand and which saw him as a foreign usurper.

The Warbeck rebellion, 1491–9

Warbeck and the princes

Having overcome a serious uprising from the Yorkists, Henry Tudor might have felt more secure. With Simnel safely in custody and Lincoln dead, the Yorkist cause was seemingly diminished. In fact, it was far from finished. Four years after Simnel, another young impostor, **Perkin Warbeck**, appeared, claiming to be Richard, Duke of York, the younger son of Edward IV. Immediately, the threat to Henry's position was serious. He was still seen as a Welsh usurper by many among the nobility and no one knew for sure what had happened to **the princes** in the Tower. If Warbeck turned out to be genuine, then, of course, his

Perkin Warbeck, enemy of Henry Tudor (French School, 16th century).

KEY TERM

Warden General A special post in the north of England that gave the holder the right to raise troops to oppose any sudden Scottish invasion or raid.

KEY PERSON

Perkin Warbeck (1474?–99) First appeared in the Low Countries and may have been a native of Flanders and the son of a tax collector. Many contemporaries claimed that he was very like the real Duke of York, which has prompted some historians to speculate that he might have been an illegitimate son of Edward IV, conceived when Edward was in exile in the Low Countries in 1470–1.

KEY THEME

The princes In 1483, it was widely assumed that both boys had been cruelly murdered by their uncle, Richard III; eight years later, there were many who wondered whether one or other of the boys might not have escaped from imprisonment in the Tower. The key problem for Henry VII was that he had no bodies (alive or dead) and therefore could not prove that Warbeck was an impostor.

claim was superior to that of Henry Tudor. He was the son of the last undisputed king of England (Edward IV) and his legitimacy was implicit in the fact that Henry VII had married his sister. Henry had promised to marry her on the basis that her two brothers were dead; if one had survived, then the king was in trouble.

Early moves

The first major player to recognise the 'true' identity of Warbeck was one of Henry's greatest of enemies: Margaret of Burgundy, supposed aunt to the young duke. She seems to have taken the boy into her household and coached him in his new role while proclaiming him as her long-lost, disinherited nephew. It is clear that many important figures in England began to wonder if this boy could be the lost prince. If he was who he said he was, the nobility were supporting a usurper and, with the usual caution displayed by the nobility in this period, many, including the king's uncle, Sir William Stanley, thought they ought to make some contact with Warbeck and his supporters just in case he was genuine.

Warbeck in Ireland and France

In 1491, Warbeck, now claiming to be King Richard IV, arrived in Ireland attempting to raise support in the country that had done so much to support Simnel. Finding the Irish unwilling to support another expedition to England, Warbeck moved to the French court in 1492. There he was welcomed by the French king, Charles VIII, and treated as a royal prince. From Henry VII's point of view, this made Warbeck a very serious threat. The French, after all, had funded his own successful expedition to overthrow Richard III less than ten years before. If Charles' government became convinced that Warbeck was genuine, there was a strong possibility of a French invasion.

Furthermore, by 1492, the French were not pleased with Henry VII.

- Not surprisingly, Charles VIII's government was deeply upset when their protégé, the man they had helped to the throne, seemed to turn against them. Henry had been giving help to the Duchess of Brittany in her attempt to stop her duchy being acquired by France. In 1489, he signed the Treaty of Redon with the Bretons, which was designed to help stave off a French takeover of the duchy that had protected Henry during his long exile.

- At the same time, the French were infuriated that in the same year, 1489, Henry had signed a treaty of friendship with Spain (**Treaty of Medina del Campo**).

Therefore, the French were encouraging their ancient ally, Scotland, to invade England from the north. French emissaries found that the ambitious **King James IV** (who may have been involved in the overthrow and murder of his father, James III, in 1488) was very interested in a joint invasion of England, especially as a new king such as James IV needed to assert himself by means of military expedition.

Henry's invasion of France, 1492

The seriousness of the position was immediately apparent to Henry VII. It was so serious that it determined the course of his foreign policy. Desperate to avoid encirclement by an alliance of his enemies, Henry launched an invasion of France in 1492. He laid siege to Boulogne with an army of some 15,000 men, but quickly turned to negotiations with the French rather than fighting them. The result was a compromise.

- The French agreed not to support any more claimants to Henry VII's throne.
- Henry was paid off by means of the restoration of the **French pension** paid to Edward IV and the terms of trade between the two countries were improved.
- However, Henry was forced to allow the French to complete the peaceful acquisition of his ally, Brittany.
- As well as a betrayal of old friends, the loss of an independent Brittany meant that the whole of the Channel coastline west of Calais was now in French hands.

The fact that Henry was prepared to pay such a heavy price to prise Warbeck away from the French shows how worried he was.

Vergil on the French invasion

This is how **Polydore Vergil**, writing probably in 1513, described Henry VII's invasion of France in 1492:

In the meantime, the king crossed to Calais, where he prepared all things necessary for the campaign. Then, moving out of Calais, he led his army in four columns to Boulogne ... There were besides many who believed him to have come to an understanding with Charles before he crossed the sea, partly through fear and partly through a desire to acquire money. Nevertheless (as some argue), it was neither fear nor greed. Henry, a man in general of the most prudent disposition, did not fear the enemy, to whose forces his own were not unequal; nor did he aim to secure cash, but was rather driven by a desire for honour and for his own safety. For it was at that time learned that Margaret, widow of Charles, Duke of Burgundy, had raised from the dead one of the sons of King Edward her brother, a youth by the name of Richard. This youth was with Charles to persuade the French king to supply him with arms against Henry. Not without reason, Henry feared that if he should continue the war (which he could avoid doing at that precise time because of the honourable conditions of the proposed peace), Richard would stir up many treasonable activities in his kingdom.

The chief terms of the treaty that were agreed upon were, first, that Charles should pay Henry an enormous sum of money to cover his expenditure on his expedition; second, that he should pay annually 50,000 francs to Henry.

English 'support' for Warbeck

During 1492–3, Warbeck reappeared in the Low Countries with Margaret of Burgundy and even seems to have made a trip to Vienna where the **Holy Roman Emperor, Maximilian von Habsburg** recognised him as King Richard IV of England. By 1494, it was clear that Warbeck was gaining support from some of the English nobility. Henry VII's abrasive character was making him many enemies and, not surprisingly, some were prepared to open negotiations with Warbeck's agents. The problem for Henry was that the plot to overthrow him in favour of Perkin Warbeck seems to have gained support even in the royal household among people who were in close proximity to his own person. Sir Robert Clifford was an active plotter who turned double agent when he discovered that Warbeck was not the real Duke of York. He saved himself by claiming that John Radcliffe (the king's steward) and Sir William Stanley (the king's uncle and Chamberlain) were plotting to overthrow their sovereign. This was a sensational claim that led to the execution of both men in 1495.

Sir William Stanley's treason

Vergil, writing in 1513, claimed that Stanley was by no means fully committed to Warbeck's cause:

> When William [Stanley] was talking with Robert Clifford about the man Perkin, who claimed to be [King] Edward's son, he asserted that if he were sure that the man was Edward's son, he would never take up arms against him. Such feelings would indicate lukewarmness towards King Henry rather than treason. Yet he openly admitted his offence, hoping that by ready confession he would obtain his life from the king. Indeed, the king might have granted this, partly through mercy and partly to avoid upsetting Thomas, Earl of Derby, William's brother. But Henry feared such leniency to be dangerous to himself – others would be encouraged by William's avoidance of punishment and would undertake similar acts of folly. The upshot was that William Stanley was condemned and a few days later beheaded.

Henry's decisive strike was vitally important to his security, but Stanley's treachery was very disturbing indeed. Sir William's words, if accurate, underline the precariousness of Henry's position. Stanley had placed the crown on Henry's head at Bosworth, yet now he was showing just how lukewarm his support for Henry Tudor was. If Warbeck was Richard, Duke of York, he would do nothing to defend Henry against him.

The impact of this betrayal on Henry was to reinforce his suspicion of everyone. If Warbeck's agents could subvert his steward and his Chamberlain, the king was far from safe. Faced with this imminent and continuing danger, Henry reorganised his household, withdrawing increasingly to his own private chamber surrounded by guards and seeing only his trusted officials - lesser men who owed everything to the king. Warbeck may not have overthrown Henry but he further eroded the normal working relationship between the Crown and the nobility. Warbeck's rebellion changed the nature of Henry's rule.

Attempted invasions of England

Yet still this was not the end of Warbeck. In the summer of 1495, he sailed from the Low Countries with an army of mercenaries and attempted to make a landing in Norfolk. Failing there, his expedition sailed south to Kent and some of his troops got ashore in Deal, not far from London. While Warbeck wisely stayed in the boat, those of his men who did manage to land were quickly arrested. Despite this failure, the danger to Henry was clear. If Warbeck could land unopposed, as Henry himself had at Milford Haven in 1485, his chances of success would become real, since the king still did not have a standing army and might have difficulty in raising a large fighting force.

The Spanish ambassador, de Puebla, wrote the following in a letter to Ferdinand and Isabella, King and Queen of Spain, just days after the attempted landing in Kent of Warbeck's forces:

> Friday the 3rd July, the so-called Duke of York came to England with all the ships and troops he had been able to obtain from the Duchess Margaret, the Archduke and Flanders. A portion of the troops disembarked, but the people rose up in arms against them without the intervention of a single soldier of the king. The peasants of the neighbouring villages made great havoc on the troops who had been disembarked, and if the vessels had not been at hand, not a single man of them would have escaped alive. A hundred and fifty were slain and eighty made prisoners.

From Kent, Warbeck headed back to Ireland where the Earl of Desmond was in revolt against the king. However, with his forces failing to take Waterford, he eventually found safe haven in Scotland.

Support in Scotland and another invasion

Warbeck arrived in Scotland late in 1495 to a warm welcome from James IV. There was immediately talk of an expedition into England and James underlined his confidence in Warbeck by allowing him to marry his kinswoman, Lady Catherine Gordon, daughter of the Earl of Huntley. Despite the diplomatic pressure on him from France and Spain, James was determined to back Warbeck. By 1496, James IV had made preparations for the invasion of England, which was duly launched in September of that year. Warbeck's proclamation, issued as the Scots forces crossed the River Tweed, sounded ominously confident and showed a good grasp of propaganda techniques:

> *Richard by Grace of God, King of England, Lord of Ireland, Prince of Wales: to all those who will see or read our present letters, greeting.*
>
> *It hath pleased God, who putteth down the mighty from their seat and exalteth the humble and suffreth not the hopes of the just to perish in the end, to give us means to show ourselves armed unto our lieges and people of England ... Our mortal enemy, Henry Tudor, a false usurper of the crown of England, knows in his heart our undoubted right [to the throne], we being the very Richard, Duke of York, younger and now surviving heir male of the noble and victorious Edward the fourth, late King of England. This Tudor, our mortal enemy, agreeable to the meanness of his birth, hath trodden under foot the honour of this nation, selling our best confederates for money, and making merchandise of the blood, estates and fortunes of our peers and subjects by feigned wars and dishonourable peace, only to enrich his coffers.*

Despite the confident tone, the actual invasion was something of a damp squib. It lasted all of four days and the Scots decided to retreat in the face of an English force led by Lord Latimer.

Warbeck and the Cornish Rising, 1497

Despite this apparently easy success, Henry remained unconvinced. He took the threat from Scotland and from Warbeck very seriously indeed and, as with France, decided to retaliate by raising his own invasion forces. He raised great sums of money from Parliament and spent the early months of 1497 raising troops for the largest invasion of Scotland ever seen. Despite the continued presence of the Earl of Surrey on the Scottish border, Henry now planned a great two-pronged attack on the Scots. Lord Willoughby de Broke was given command of a naval force to assault the

Scots by sea, while **Giles, Lord Daubeney** was to take charge of an army of 10,000 to invade across the border. However, just as these forces were being marched north, Henry faced the most serious rebellion of his reign.

In the West Country, in Cornwall, Devon and Somerset, there was a great rising in protest at the huge taxes that Henry was attempting to raise to fund a seemingly unnecessary war at the other end of the kingdom. The rebellion was also about Henry's methods of government as well as the level of taxation. Men like John Oby, Provost of Glasney (who was murdered by the rebels) and **William Hody** were among a growing number of Henry's agents in the south-west. For many years there had been complaints about misgovernment at the hands of the King's men and the demand for high taxes, which some of these men now attempted to collect, was the spark for widespread rebellion.

The scale and geographical extent of the rebellion against misgovernment was spectacular. In the summer of 1497, the rebels raised some 10,000 armed men, across much of the south-west, who marched all the way from Cornwall to London. To make matters worse, Henry had been caught out by the timing of the rebellion, since his army was marching north to deal with the Scots. However, the rebellion makes it clear that the great landowners in the south were not loyal to the new Tudor regime. Like Sir William Stanley, they might not join in rebellion but at the same time they did **nothing to stop it**. The rebellion was also serious for Henry because it had support from the gentry and landowners as well as the masses. Indeed, it was led by **Lord Audley**, who objected to what he saw as Henry's harsh regime and general misgovernment. The rebels reached Blackheath on the outskirts of the capital but were routed by royal forces under the Earl of Oxford and Lord Daubeney. About 200 rebels were killed and Lord Audley and several other leaders of the rebellion were executed.

A second Cornish Rising, 1497

The Cornish Rising, however, did not end there. Though the rebels were pursued to the West Country, royal forces decided it would be unwise to enter Cornwall. Perkin

Warbeck decided to seize his chance. He landed in Cornwall in September 1497, where his forces rallied many of the rebels. Together, they assaulted and nearly took the city of Exeter in a two-day battle, after which they moved to Taunton in Somerset. Here the second rebellion ended when the rebel forces fled at the approach of the royal army under Daubeney. Warbeck was caught and sent to the king. He made a confession of his imposture and seems to have been kept under house arrest at court until he apparently attempted to escape in June 1498. After that, he was sent to the Tower, where he joined the unfortunate Earl of Warwick, who had been there since the reign began. The next year, probably under pressure from the Spanish monarchs, who were unwilling to send **Catherine of Aragon** to England while there were still pretenders to the throne alive and well, Henry decided to put both men on trial for treason. Warbeck was hanged on 23 November 1499 and the pitiful Earl of Warwick beheaded five days later.

The Spanish ambassador on Warbeck

Writing to Ferdinand and Isabella, the King and Queen of Spain, their ambassador wrote in optimistic mood in the aftermath of Warbeck and Warwick's executions:

> *The English have not always remained in peaceful obedience to their king. This is because there were too many heirs to the kingdom. The claims of these heirs were so strong that there were disputes between the two sides. Now it has pleased God that all should be thoroughly and duly purged and cleansed. Not a doubtful drop of blood remains in this kingdom except the true blood of the king and queen and above all of the Lord Prince Arthur. And all this has come about since the execution of Perkin and the son of the Duke of Clarence.*

How serious was Warbeck's threat to the regime?

There is no doubt that Warbeck, despite being an impostor, posed a most serious threat to Henry's person and to his continuance as King of England.

- Warbeck gathered support from every country in close proximity to England. He showed that the nobility of England had little enthusiasm for their new king and that many might welcome 'regime change'.

- Warbeck was able to invade England three times and, while these all failed rather miserably, there were probably also plots to have King Henry assassinated.
- Warbeck also dictated Henry's foreign policy. He forced Henry to invade France and attempt the same against Scotland. He threatened to jeopardise the new Spanish alliance and showed that Henry's initial truce with Scotland was worthless.
- Warbeck unwittingly sparked off a very serious popular rebellion; the same kind of rebellion that had prefigured the overthrow of Edward IV by Warwick and Clarence in 1469. The rebellion showed that Henry's methods of government and high taxes were highly unpopular and might bring him down.
- Warbeck was serious because he lasted so long. From 1491–9, some nine years, he was a constant threat to Henry, who, without the help of hindsight, could not know what the outcome would be.

Polydore Vergil, writing about the events of 1492, did not underestimate the threat from Perkin Warbeck. He claims that as soon as Warbeck appeared, many were keen to join him:

> *Conspiracies immediately began to multiply. On the one hand, there were criminals who were tempted by poverty or bribes to break forth and flock to Perkin in Flanders. On the other hand, many among the nobility turned to conspiracy. Some were motivated by mere foolishness. Others, believing Perkin truly to be Edward's son, Richard, supported the claim of the Yorkist party. There were others who considered themselves badly rewarded by King Henry for the services they had eagerly given him. Lastly, there were others whose desire for revolution flung them headlong into this conspiracy.*

Vergil's surprisingly frank assessment of the dangers posed by Perkin Warbeck and of the lack of support for King Henry among the nobility certainly ring true.

The continuing Yorkist threat, 1499–1509

Edmund de la Pole
Yet still the Yorkist threat to Henry's throne was not over. Henry continued to be denied the security of tenure that Edward IV had known in his second reign because there

were still worthwhile Yorkist princes in the offing whose claim to the throne by blood outranked Henry's feeble title. John de la Pole had been killed at the Battle of Stoke in 1487 but he had at least two younger brothers.

- The elder brother, Edmund, had apparently made his peace with the regime but was needlessly upset by the king when his father died in 1492.
- Henry restricted the lands that Edmund could inherit, reduced his title from Duke of Suffolk to Earl, and charged Edmund a hefty fine of £5000 for the privilege of inheritance.
- In 1498, Edmund fled the kingdom but was persuaded to return only to flee again, this time to the court of the Emperor Maximilian in 1501.
- For the next five years, Edmund and his brother, Richard, were a serious threat to the regime. Henry's fear and annoyance can be seen in his cutting off of English trade with the Low Countries (where Edmund was being sheltered) in a desperate attempt to force the ruler there, **Philip of Burgundy**, to hand the earl over.
- This was not achieved until a storm in the Channel drove Philip and his wife, Joanna, onto the rocks on the Dorset coast in 1506. Taking advantage of Philip's weak position, while treating him with all the trappings of an honoured guest, Henry was finally able to persuade Philip to change his mind about harbouring Edmund.

However, even when Maximilian's son eventually handed Edmund over to Henry in 1506, the king seems to have been too fearful of aristocratic reaction to execute him. Edmund's double flight and even his mere existence – he was Richard III's and Edward IV's nephew, after all, and brother of Richard III's heir – posed a serious threat during Henry VII's last years.

Tudor deaths

At the same time, the renewed threat from real Yorkists was strengthened by deaths among Henry's close family and Henry's bouts of serious illness before his ultimate demise in 1509.

- In 1500, the king's youngest son, Edmund, died.
- In 1502, just weeks after his marriage to Catherine of Aragon, Arthur Tudor, Prince of Wales and heir to the

KEY PERSON

Philip of Burgundy (1478–1506) Known as Philip the Fair, he was the son of the Emperor Maximilian and Mary of Burgundy. He was married to Joanna, who became Queen of Castile in 1504, and was set to be a major player in Europe but died suddenly in 1506. He was the father of the future emperor and King of Spain, Charles V.

throne also died. It was a shattering blow to both Henry and his wife, Elizabeth. In an age of piety, it seemed to portend God's anger towards the regime.

- Then, in 1503, Queen Elizabeth herself died in childbirth, trying but failing to add to the king's declining stock of children. Her death, too, could have serious consequences. Perhaps those less radical Yorkists, who supported the regime because the queen was Edward IV's daughter, might now reconsider their allegiance. Despite a flurry of intense diplomatic activity, Henry failed to marry again, so this left all Tudor hopes resting on the young shoulders of Henry, Duke of York (the future Henry VIII).

- At the time of Arthur's death, Henry was only ten years old, the same age as that other Duke of York, younger son of Edward IV, who was murdered in the Tower. So, in his declining years, King Henry realised that his son's **succession** was always in doubt.

At the same time, the king suffered from bouts of serious illness in 1504, 1507 and 1508. Each time his life was feared for and his heir was still a minor. Henry VII's increasing paranoia about the succession may be further illustrated by another incident that occurred in 1501. In that year, Sir James Tyrell, an important supporter of Richard III, who was believed to be plotting with Suffolk, was executed for treason. After his death, Henry VII reported that just before his death Tyrell had confessed to being the man who had murdered the princes in the Tower in 1483. Even with Warbeck dead and a self-confessed impostor, it seems that there were still rumours that one or other of the boys was still alive!

CONCLUSION

While there was only one battle during Henry's reign, it is clear that there were unprecedented levels of political instability. From first to last, there was a serious Yorkist threat to overthrow him, which helped to shape the regime and its attitude to those it governed. Insecurity and fear were the hallmarks of the regime and we should not swallow Henry's propaganda attempts to minimise the threat from other claimants to the throne. Far from his government being strong and just, Henry's regime was harsh and repressive. Becoming more, not less, secure as the

Elizabeth of York, queen of Henry VII, painted c.1500.

KEY THEME

Succession Memories of the events of 1483 were not far away in 1499. In 1499, it was reported by one government agent that he had overheard several conversations among great men of the realm who were speculating, even before Arthur's death in 1502, that Henry VII would be the only Tudor ruler of England. Some, the agent claimed, spoke of the Duke of Buckingham as future king, while others thought Edmund de la Pole would get it, and no one, apparently, spoke up for Arthur.

reign went on, it descended into tyranny and injustice. This happened not because the regime was powerful but because it was frightened. This permanent state of fear, a legacy of the earlier conflicts in England, arose squarely from Henry's minimal claim to the throne and was cemented and confirmed by the desperate insecurity of Henry's early years. This insecurity does not fit well with the old view that Henry VII's greatest success was that he ended the Wars of the Roses. In retrospect, it is clear that Henry VII faced so many problems because, far from ending the Wars of the Roses, he restarted them! One Florentine merchant who visited England in 1496 summarised King Henry's insecurity in this way:

> *The king is very powerful in money, but if some lord of the blood royal rose against him and he had to take to the battlefield, he would fare badly. His people would abandon him because of his greed. They would treat him as they did King Richard, whom they abandoned.*

SUMMARY QUESTIONS

1 To what extent did Lambert Simnel pose a greater threat to Henry VII's regime than Perkin Warbeck?

2 How effectively did Henry VII deal with the threats to his throne?

3 'The political instability of Henry VII's reign shows that the monarchy was weak, not strong.' To what extent do you agree with this judgement?

4 To what extent was Henry VII's regime more secure after 1495 than before?

5 'Far from ending the Wars of the Roses, Henry VII was actually responsible for restarting them.' To what extent do you agree with this verdict on Henry VII's reign?

SECTION 6

HENRY VII AND THE PERSONNEL OF GOVERNMENT: NOBILITY AND THE 'NEW MEN'

Did Henry VII govern in a new way?

KEY POINTS

- It used to be thought that Henry VII governed in a way that was very different from that of his predecessors – that he was a 'new monarch'.
- All medieval kings, in fact, governed in their own way because medieval monarchy was a personal monarchy and was shaped by the ambition and abilities (or lack of them!) of each ruler.
- In many ways, Henry VII governed in a way which other medieval kings would have recognised. There were no important changes in the institutions of government during his reign.
- Henry VII, unlike Edward IV, worked very hard at the business of government. He seems to have revelled in paperwork and used it to exert a greater degree of control over the country than his predecessors had enjoyed.
- Henry VII made less use of the nobility in central and local government than his predecessors. He made more use of his own servants in government. As a result, his governing style was different from that adopted by the previous three monarchs.
- The nature of his government changed, becoming more oppressive as his reign went on. He paid less attention to the law, extracted more and more by way of taxes and became a tyrant.

OVERVIEW

The nature of English government and administration has been much debated by historians and there is still no clear consensus about the extent to which Henry VII was a new monarch who governed in a new way. Those who put forward the idea of novelty in government did so because:

- they thought that the Wars of the Roses were a long succession of bloody wars, lasting 30 years, so it followed that Henry VII must have governed in a different way so that the wars were ended.
- they saw 1485 as a natural turning point in the history of English government because a new family (the Tudors) took the throne. Many believed that the Battle of Bosworth marked the end of the medieval period and the start of the early modern period. Thus it followed that the nature of government not only changed but it also became more efficient and lawful.
- the Tudor period saw big changes in English government: Henry VIII became Head of the Church and broke from Rome; Parliament became more powerful and a more regular element in government; Thomas Cromwell introduced (according to Professor Elton) a revolution in government during the 1530s. It was natural to look at the reign of Henry VII and to see the origins of these changes for the better in his reign.

On the other hand, many historians play down the extent of change in government and administration during Henry VII's reign.

- Led by S.B. Chrimes, they have analysed the institutions or organs of government and found that they changed very little between 1485 and 1509.
- They have played down the significance and impact of the Wars of the Roses and thus do not need to find changes in government to explain Henry's continuing hold on power.
- They have stressed the evolutionary nature of change and the way in which change was a reaction to events rather than a blueprint imposed from above.
- They have pointed to the difference between what the government says in official documents and what actually happens.
- They claim that Henry VII's reign, far from being stable and a model of good government, was, in fact, chronically unstable and the regime was characterised by increasing suspicion, paranoia and oppression.

The view taken here will be in line with the second series of points. As has been seen in the last section, Henry VII's government was seriously and persistently troubled by opposition and treachery. To counter this, Henry VII's government became increasingly tyrannical. This tyranny was unleashed not through new institutions of government but through Henry's personal way of governing, which relied more and more on a small group of trusted advisers. Henry VII thus increasingly departed from the medieval system of governing through the nobility and set up a regime that was harsh and greedy. In this way, his regime was different from that of Edward IV and Henry VI but it was not inherently stable. When he died in 1509, his son, Henry VIII, was quick to restore what he and the nobility saw as the proper system of medieval government.

Henry VII's relationship with the nobility

The scale of the problem in 1485

Much credit has been given to Henry VII for taming the English nobility: an aristocracy that had unleashed and sustained the terrible Wars of the Roses. Henry VII did indeed control the nobility more closely as the reign went on, but this was not really a useful achievement. By increasing pressure on the peers, Henry invited rebellion and an aristocratic backlash. His reign was tense and brutal and a long way from the model of good government. In addition, it is clear that the nobility did not, as a class, pose a threat to the new king. Individuals like John de la Pole did rebel but most of the great men remained aloof or decided to acquiesce in the new regime.

It is also clear that the impact and scale of the Wars of the Roses have been much exaggerated. They were largely over by 1461 or certainly 1471. While a few overmighty nobles, such as Richard, Duke of York and Richard, Earl of Warwick, sustained the conflict, most sought ways of avoiding violent confrontation.

Thus the nobility, which Henry VII inherited, did not pose a great threat to the new regime. With the death of Richard III in 1485, there were no overmighty subjects left for the new king to worry about. While Edward IV was brought down by Warwick, and Richard III faced rebellion from the Duke of Buckingham, Henry VII had no kingmaker to pay off. Like his predecessors, he was a usurper, who had claimed the throne by violent means, but none of the great nobles in 1485 was likely to rebel against him. With the death of the young Richard, Duke of York, there was no one to inherit his title and thus no threat from that quarter. The point was underlined by the new king when he gave the title to his own second son. The Duke of Norfolk, a loyal supporter of Richard III, had been killed at Bosworth and his son, the Earl of Surrey, was keen to regain his lands and titles by supporting the new regime. The Earl of Northumberland had been no friend of Richard III, had taken no part in the Battle of Bosworth, refused to support Lambert Simnel and was then killed in a brawl over taxes in Thirsk in 1489. His son, like the son of the Duke of Buckingham (executed by Richard III in 1483), was a minor and thus the king's ward and no threat to the regime.

The king's family

At the same time, the scale of the 'noble problem' was much diminished in Henry's reign because of the small size of his own immediate family. Most of the trouble in the 1450s and 1460s was caused by the king's immediate family. Edward IV's problems stemmed from one of his brothers (George, Duke of Clarence), while Edward V's arose from another of those brothers (Richard, Duke of Gloucester). Richard, Duke of York – the cause of much instability in Henry VI's reign – was the king's cousin, and Warwick the Kingmaker, so destructive in the 1460s, was also a cousin to Edward IV. Close relatives, then, were the main cause of the political instability of the period 1459–85.

After 1485, however, the situation was transformed and made much easier for the new king because he had so few close relatives. His one uncle, Jasper, was loyal and had no children, so Henry had no cousins. Henry VII also had no brothers or brothers-in-law, so there were no dukes who were heirs to the throne as George of Clarence had been and as Richard of Gloucester thought he was. At the same time, Henry never had an adult male son during his lifetime, itching to get his hands on power and build up a powerful court 'in waiting' as the future Henry V had done during his father's lifetime. Henry VII's eldest son, Prince Arthur, died at the age of fifteen and his second son, Prince Henry, was just seventeen when his father died. So Henry VII was fortunate in not having to worry about noblemen in his immediate family.

In addition, the number of titled and powerful noblemen (dukes, marquises, earls and viscounts) in England shrank by almost 50 per cent during Henry's reign. While there were 23 in 1487, there were only twelve by 1509.

Date	Dukes	Marquises	Earls	Viscounts	Barons	Total
1487	3	1	16	3	34	57
1509	1	1	10	0	31	43

Loyal nobles

More positively, there were, of course, nobles who were prepared to support the regime from its inception. Thomas, Lord Stanley, who was related to Henry through marriage (he was the new king's stepfather), was one of the few nobles to be rewarded by Henry. He was created Earl of Derby. Jasper Tudor, the king's uncle, was elevated to the dukedom of Bedford and acted as loyal viceroy for Henry in Wales. John de Vere, Earl of Oxford was a loyalist from Henry's days in exile. He fought with him at Bosworth and remained steadfast thereafter. In addition, Henry VII was in a stronger position than he seemed in 1485 because he had support from Yorkist elements such as Thomas Grey, Marquis of Dorset, who was bitterly opposed to the supposed regicide Richard III. So, although a Welsh pretender who had lived most of his life in exile, Henry Tudor's position in relation to the nobility was much stronger than it seemed in 1485. At the same time, he inherited the goodwill of much of the political nation, who wanted to see peace return to the kingdom.

Why did Henry distrust the nobility?

Despite the apparent security of his position, Henry VII was chronically suspicious of all the nobility of the kingdom. With hindsight, this seems like an over-reaction, but to Henry, it was immediately clear that the nobility could not be trusted.

- It should be remembered that, unlike Edward IV, Henry VII was not a great nobleman. While Edward IV and indeed Richard III were brought up in great aristocratic households, at the centre of aristocratic affinities and aristocratic politics, Henry was brought up in exile.

KEY THEME

Trust The idea that it was foolish to trust anyone was one Henry VII passed on to his son, Henry VIII, in the training manual *Speculum Principis* ('A Mirror for Princes'), written for the young prince by John Skelton.

- As a pawn in the politics of the day, Henry had no friends or family he could **trust** (apart from his mother, Margaret Beaufort). He had been brought up in the household of the Yorkist Earl of Pembroke and had then been forced to flee for his life. He only just escaped the clutches of Richard III's agents in 1484 and in 1485. He knew that many of his supporters were at Bosworth because he had promised to marry Elizabeth of York, not because they thought that he was the rightful king.
- Henry Tudor would never be able to throw off the fact that he was a usurper. His reign would be dogged throughout by rebellion and opposition headed by Yorkists, who seemed to have a better claim to the throne than he did. The Earl of Lincoln's support for Simnel was disturbing enough, but Sir William Stanley's apparent betrayal of Henry ten years after his accession was more alarming.

An uncertain succession

The succession to the throne would never be fully settled during Henry VII's reign. Other kings had come to the throne with sons already born to them but not so Henry VII.

- Henry married Elizabeth of York in 1486, after Bosworth, and then had to wait many years for his children to grow to maturity. Then, just as the matter of the succession seemed to be secure, disaster struck.
- Prince Arthur, Henry VII's eldest son, died at the age of fifteen in 1502, when his second and only surviving son, Henry, was just ten.
- Prince Henry was only seventeen when his father died in 1509. As the regime became more unpopular, so more men might have dreamt of a non-Tudor succession. The men of the Calais garrison, discussing the succession in 1499, failed to consider the claims of the young Arthur Tudor.

Early cooperation between king and nobility

At first, Henry VII, despite the Simnel rebellion of 1487, tried to work with his nobility.

KEY TERM

Great Councils Called occasionally by the king as a means of discussing plans and policy with the titled aristocracy.

- He held **Great Councils** on several occasions early on in the reign in order to consult with (and be seen to consult with) the nobility.

- Furthermore (as we have seen), he led his nobility in an invasion of France in 1492. Just as Edward IV had done in 1475, Henry used this method to unite the barons behind him in an expedition against the common enemy.
- In addition, King Henry, in his early years, was keen to promote the idea of a king governing with his nobility. He called his first son Arthur and may have been responsible for the **Arthurian Round Table**, which still hangs in Winchester Cathedral where the heir to the throne (Arthur, of course!) was both born and christened. In this way, Henry sought to legitimise his dynasty by linking it to the mythical figure of King Arthur, who, as everyone knew, was meant to return to rule England once again. At the same time, the promotion of the Arthurian myth put forward a model of government where the king rules as chief among equals with his knights of the Round Table.

However, right from the start of his reign, Henry's relationship with the leading magnates was less cordial than that enjoyed by Edward IV in his second reign. Polydore Vergil, who was there for the last eight years of Henry's reign, claimed that: 'The king wished, as he said, to keep all Englishmen obedient through fear, and he considered that whenever they gave him offence they were motivated by their great wealth.' This clearly outlines Henry's policy towards the nobility. He distrusted them; he thought they could be neutralised by financial means and decided that the best way to keep them obedient was through fear. Though relations between king and nobility were rarely easy, no other king was so distrustful of or so harsh towards his nobility.

How did Henry use attainders?

As with Edward IV and Richard III, King Henry was able to pass attainders against all those landowners and aristocrats who had fought against him at the Battles of Bosworth and Stoke, and those involved in the Warbeck conspiracy. What was different about Henry was his unwillingness to reverse attainders on men who subsequently proved their loyalty. Reversals were rarer than under Edward IV and when they did occur were often partial – only some of the land and/or titles were granted back.

- Robert Fitzwater, for example, was attainted in 1495 and later executed. Ten years later, his son paid the king £2000 to reverse the attainder and to receive some (but by no means all) of his father's lands.
- Edmund de la Pole, brother of John, who was killed fighting against King Henry at Stoke, had to pay £5000 to receive some of his brother's lands. He was granted only the earldom of Suffolk even though his father had been the duke.
- It was the same story for Thomas Howard, Earl of Surrey. He was given back his earldom in 1489 and was granted lands other than those held by his father, the late Duke of Norfolk. Only after further payments to the king in 1492 was he allowed some of his father's estates, and it was not until he had defeated the Scots in 1513 that he was given back his father's dukedom by a grateful Henry VIII.

There are more examples but these show that Henry VII was rather less generous than Edward IV in reversing attainders and that he used partial reversals as a means of political control and financial gain.

At the same time, it is clear that Henry VII continued to use attainders as a means of exerting his control. While Edward IV issued only 27 attainders after 1463, Henry VII issued 51 in the **Parliament of 1504** alone, which was the biggest haul of the entire reign and at a time when Perkin Warbeck, the last serious pretender to the throne, had been dead for five years! This was a further measure of Henry's continuing fearfulness and harshness.

How did Henry use bonds and recognisances?

Like attainders, bonds and recognisances were not new. They were part of the normal method of estate management where there was a danger of an official or subordinate being corrupt. Essentially, the king (and other landowners for that matter) could force a landowner to sign a bond or recognisance in which they would agree to pay a fine in case of future misbehaviour. All medieval kings had used them but under Henry VII they were used much more widely and systematically as a way of enmeshing most great men in a system that involved serious fines if the king decided they had acted illegally. In Henry VI's reign, between 1437 and 1458, 22 peers were under bonds and recognisances at one time or another (i.e. one peer per year); under Edward IV and Richard III, the figure was 20 (i.e. fewer than one peer per year); but under Henry VII, it reached 46 (i.e. two peers per year!). This was a particularly high average as the peerage had shrunk significantly during Henry's reign. Forty-six peers represented some 75 per cent of all peerage families!

In addition, Henry imposed bonds on 23 families more than once during his reign, while under the Yorkists only one family received such treatment. The sums of money Henry collected under this system were also impressive. In 1507, Lord Burgavenny was fined a staggering £70,000 by the king, a sum he could never hope to pay. Generously, the king agreed to take £500 a year for the next ten years. The beauty of bonds and recognisances was that they operated outside the law because:

- Henry imposed them as and when he saw fit and the victim had no right of appeal
- as Henry was the law, he not only decided on the guilt of those put under bonds but also decided on the level of fine or suspended fine.

As the reign progressed, Henry and his agents became more proficient in using the system of bonds and recognisances. Only twelve peers were on the receiving end in the first seventeen years of the reign, but after 1502 the number prosecuted shot up, reaching 36 in the last seven years of the reign. The exact figures have been questioned recently but there is no doubt that more bonds were imposed in the later years of the reign. Once again, this confirms the view that Henry's regime became harsher and more lawless after 1500.

At the same time, bonds could be used against the less wealthy by getting one of their wealthy relatives to sign the bond and thus risk their own fortune on the behaviour of their relative. **Edmund Dudley**, a lawyer who was one of Henry's main agents in imposing bonds and recognisances, confessed later that Henry's policy was 'to have many persons in his danger at his pleasure'. Polydore

Vergil later claimed, with some truth, that Henry's policy was to fine men especially harshly so that not only were the guilty men unable to raise rebellion but that their descendants would be equally impoverished. The more systematic use of bonds and recognisances (even used against loyal supporters like the Earl of Oxford) were deeply unpopular with the victims. In this way, Henry's policy in the area of attainders, bonds and recognisances was in danger of becoming political overkill.

While bonds and recognisances were used extensively against the nobility, they were used even more against the gentry and other landowners. It may be that in the later years of the reign hundreds of gentlemen, who had been involved in law suits of one kind or another, found that they were bound to the king in some sort of recognisance and under financial penalty in case of misbehaviour. Sir Thomas Brandon, for example, signed a recognisance to the king for £500, which would be forfeit if his household servants failed to keep the peace with the servants of Lord Broke. Such constraints may have made Henry feel easier but they were bound to increase tension between the king and the natural rulers in the shires.

Other measures of control

As king, Henry VII had many special or **prerogative rights**, which had traditionally been held by medieval monarchs. Not surprisingly, Henry exploited and over-exploited these rights with ruthlessness in order to increase his control of his greater subjects.

He set up a number of commissions whose job it was to seek out where royal rights to land or income had been concealed.

- After 1500, there appeared the so-called Council Learned in the Law, led by the lawyers **Empson and Dudley**, who were commanded to discover where royal rights were being infringed and to maintain the Crown's legal causes in the courts.
- With the uncertainties of the English legal system, and the hard-nosed and often unscrupulous methods employed by its servants, this Council reaped large rewards for the Crown (and for Empson and Dudley). Meeting almost daily after 1500, the Council Learned

KEY TERM

Prerogative rights Special rights or powers enjoyed by the king by virtue of the fact that he was king. As they were not written down, the existence of these special rights allowed a king like Henry VII to increase his power.

KEY PEOPLE

Empson and Dudley Sir Richard Empson (1450–1510) and Edmund Dudley (see page 124). Both were lawyers and both were used as scapegoats for the crimes of Henry's later years. Henry VIII had them arrested and executed soon after his accession to the throne in 1509.

used spies and informers to build up evidence and took over the enforcement of bonds and recognisances. Dudley later admitted that many of the charges they brought against individuals were false but, backed by the king's authority, they could usually persuade the victim to pay a large fine in order to 'compound' for his alleged crime.

- In 1508, the potential for financially terrorising landed families (including the nobility) received a further boost as Henry appointed Sir Edward Belknap to the new office of Surveyor of the King's Prerogative.

Meanwhile, Henry also concentrated on exploiting his traditional rights with maximum efficiency. As king, he had the right to the wardship of the children of major landowners. When a landowner died leaving an heir who was legally still a child, that child became the king's ward. Wardship was always a lucrative business for the king; he could control his ward's income, taking a large slice for himself; he could charge a large **entry fine** when the heir came of age and wished to take control of his own lands, and he could sell the marriage of the young heir to the highest bidder. In 1503, Henry created the post of Surveyor of the King's Wards and the income from wardships increased dramatically during the reign. In 1487, wardship had brought in about £350; this increased to £1600 by 1494 and reached a very respectable £6000 by 1507.

Aristocracy at arm's length?

The measures taken by Henry indicate that he remained deeply distrustful of the nobility and that this distrust got worse, not better, as the reign went on. In terms of court ceremonial as well, one can see that the aristocracy were largely kept at arm's length. As an outsider, Henry's court ceremonial, certainly in the second half of the reign, had more in common with France and Burgundy than with England. Where Edward IV was at the centre of a court where many of the great men resided for long periods, and where the king mixed freely with these men at council and at table, Henry VII's ceremonial stressed the king's remoteness from those around him. The notion of a monarch who was aloof and different from other men was stressed and this fitted well with Henry's dislike of many of the aristocracy. This remoteness and royal isolation was dramatically reflected in a serious change to the layout of the king's court after the arrest and execution of Sir William Stanley in 1495. He had been the king's Chamberlain and had daily access to the king as the man who organised court life.

After Stanley's disgrace, the authority of the Chamberlain was restricted and the king increasingly withdrew to his private or **privy chamber**. So, in the second half of the reign, the king partially withdrew from his court. He spent his days working on his papers in the privy chamber, attended by a relatively small number of household servants. From the chamber came streams of orders and papers from the king and to the chamber came money and men, servants and suspects.

- This system meant that the privy chamber became one of the most important centres of government.
- It also meant that the king was not pestered by courtiers and great men for favours, patronage or changes in Crown policy.
- Instead, Henry re-emphasised his control of affairs and kept people guessing as to what his intentions were.
- Without access to the king, the nobility were forced to react to events rather than shaping them. It certainly meant an end to the aristocratic faction fighting that had helped to destabilise previous regimes. In Henry's reign, no nobleman exercised power and influence at the expense of the others.

Limits to the loss of aristocratic power

Nobles in central/regional government

However, it would be wrong to think that the king invented a new system of government that did not depend on the great landowners. Henry did employ great men (and one great woman) in the day-to-day running of government.

- His mother, Lady Margaret Beaufort, was granted special powers. She had been the main cause of his success (he was her only son) and, in 1485, an Act of Parliament granted her the right to control her own property and act independently of her husband, the Earl of Derby. By 1499, she had her own household, had effectively dissolved her fourth marriage by taking a vow of chastity, and had taken charge of a great regional household, centred on her palace at Collyweston, which oversaw local government throughout much of the Midlands.

- Henry's uncle, Jasper Tudor – elevated to the dukedom of Bedford – ruled much of Wales, while Thomas Butler, Earl of Ormond did much the same for Ireland.
- John de Vere remained in favour throughout the reign, while the Earls of Derby and Shrewsbury were generally supportive.
- John Morton – Chancellor and Archbishop of Canterbury from 1486–1500 – was another key man in the regime.
- These great personages dominated the government. Most were long lived and all were indisputably and unswervingly loyal to Henry's regime. This was partly because none of them had any legitimate children and thus no heir beyond the king himself.
- The nobles in Henry's government were joined by the Earl of Surrey when he was made Lord Treasurer in 1501.

At the same time, we know that King Henry did make use of 43 peers during his reign as councillors who gave advice, at one time or another, at meetings of the **King's Council**. Nearly 70 per cent of the peerage attended more than one meeting during the reign. While such figures may show that the peers were not widely used as councillors, that may be because many of them did not suit that role. Most were courtiers who could advise the king in more informal circumstances rather than at one of the 130 or so official council meetings during the reign. Certainly the balance between peers, clergy and lawyers who were appointed as councillors during Henry's reign is very similar to that of previous reigns. All kings in this period needed political support from the nobility, but they also needed and relied on technical advice from the clergy and lawyers in their household.

The composition of Henry VII's council

Polydore Vergil, in his *Anglia Historia*, gave the following list of those in the King's Council in the early years of the reign. Notice that noblemen dominate the list.

He established a Council in his household by whose opinion all things should be justly and rightly governed and causes brought to it to be decided without the bitterness of lawsuits. And for this Council, he chose men renowned for their singular shrewdness, loyalty and reliability, John, Earl of Oxford; Jasper, Duke of Bedford; Thomas Stanley, Earl of Derby ... John Morton, Bishop of Ely; Richard Fox, Edward Poynings ... and he chose other wise men to council for specific business among whom were Richard Thomas, a Welshman ... Thomas Grey, the Marquis of Dorset, a good and prudent man; George Talbot, Earl of Shrewsbury, wise and moderate in all things; Thomas, Earl of Ormond, an Irishman; William Say, a prominent knight ... Thomas Howard, Earl of Surrey, a man of great wisdom, reliability and loyalty ... William Blount, Lord Mountjoy, very well spoken and cultured ... and many other good councillors and the chief bishops.

Great men in the localities

Meanwhile, in the localities, the king still relied on the aristocracy and great landowners to oversee local government, especially since local officials such as sheriffs and JPs were unpaid. Their traditional powers as local landowners could not be seriously eroded and there is no sign that Henry wished to do this. In a country as disturbed by rebellion and plot as England was under Henry VII, the nobility had to play their normal role in the government of the shires. Henry's tough and shrewd political methods ensured that most of the aristocracy remained loyal, though, as **Sir Francis Bacon** noted, it was the obedience of acquiescence rather than the obedience of enthusiastic support:

For his nobles, although they were loyal and obedient, yet they did not cooperate with him, but every man went his own way.

The need for retaining

Henry continued to depend on the nobility in the matter of the retaining of armed men. It used to be claimed that Henry VII abolished **livery** and **maintenance**. In fact, he did no such thing. Nor did he do much to control the retaining of men by noblemen. The practice was extremely common throughout the Middle Ages, as all great men needed armed retinues to enforce justice and to protect their servants and tenants. At the same time, the king, who

KEY PERSON

Sir Francis Bacon (1561–1626) A Privy Councillor to James I (1603–25), he wrote *A History of the Reign of Henry VII* and in 1622 presented a copy of it to the future Charles I (1625–49). His purpose in writing this book was to contrast the hard-working nature of Henry VII with the corruption in government that Bacon thought had taken hold in his own day. As a propaganda piece, its judgements on Henry VII need to be treated with caution.

KEY TERMS

Livery When a lord gave a retainer or a retained man a uniform or badge.

Maintenance When a lord interfered illegally in a court case to get his retainer declared innocent.

had no standing army, relied on his own household men and the retinues of his great men to form the basis of the national army sent to France in 1475 and 1492.

Statutes on retaining

While retaining might mean the existence of small private armies, the system was usually self-regulating depending on the qualities of the king.

- Under the feeble Henry VI, the system helped make civil war between noble families and the Crown a reality.
- During Edward IV's second reign, it was rather more under control as the causes of unrest had largely been removed.
- Henry VII passed laws about retaining in 1485 and 1487, largely repeating the **statute on retaining passed by Edward IV** in 1468.
- So Henry VII's early actions did little to inhibit the practice of retaining but, of course, after 1487, the realm was in greater quiet and so armed men were not so much in demand. Retaining men was an expensive business as these men had to be maintained by their lord so that they could fight, intimidate or at least appear at their lord's request at a moment's notice. Naturally, therefore, noblemen did not retain excessively.
- Henry VII's next statute on retaining had to wait until 1504 and the last Parliament of the reign. This Act did include a new feature. Lords were now supposed to receive Henry's written permission to retain men and to give the king a list of their retainers for his approval. We do not know whether this attempt to regulate the number of men retained worked in practice, but we do know of three cases where huge fines were imposed by the king for illegal retaining, which then became recognisances.
- Only one of these fines was levied on a peer – the unfortunate Lord Burgavenny in 1506. In reality, this looks more like a continuance of Henry's terror tactics against individuals whose loyalty he suspected was not 100 per cent. Interestingly, Lord Burgavenny's **indictment** was reversed by Henry VIII in 1510.

Overall, much of Henry's work against illicit retaining was carried on informally and we simply do not have the records to make a clear judgement on the issue. As the statute of 1504 was so late in the reign, at a time when the realm was enjoying relative peace and prosperity, its appearance may have more to do with the harsh regime of Henry's last years than with a genuine attempt to emasculate the military power of the nobility. The nobility were already in a weakened state and Henry merely took advantage of their plight.

Henry VII and retaining

Francis Bacon gives us this famous story about Henry VII fining one of his loyalist subjects, the Earl of Oxford, for illegal retaining. However, there is no independent or contemporary corroboration of or date for the story, so we cannot be sure that it is true. It is just the kind of story that could be made up about Henry VII – that he was so greedy that he even fined his most loyal earl who was, on this occasion, also the king's host. It seems inherently unlikely that one of the king's closest advisers for so many years could be so ignorant of the king's policy on retaining as this story suggests.

> *There remaineth to this day a report that the king was once entertained by the Earl of Oxford, that was his principal servant both for war and peace, nobly and sumptuously at his castle at Hedingham. And at the king's going away, the earl's servants stood in a seemly manner, in their livery coats with badges, ranged on both sides, and made the king a lane. The king called the earl to him and said, 'My lord, I have heard much of your hospitality, but I see that it is greater than the speech. These handsome gentlemen and yeomen which I see on both sides of me are surely not just your household servants?' The earl smiled and said, 'It may please your Grace that these are not my household servants. Most of them are my retainers, that are come to do me service at such a time as this, and chiefly to see your Grace.' The king started a little and said, 'By my faith, my lord, I thank you for your good cheer, but I cannot endure having the law broken before my eyes. My attorney must speak with you.' And it is part of the report that the earl was fined no less than 15,000 marks.*

The definition of nobility

One important clue about Henry's rather uneasy relationship with the nobility comes from a play written in the household of Cardinal Morton, one of Henry's closest advisers. The play was called *Fulgens and Lucres* ('Splendour and Wealth') and was in the form of a dialogue between two suitors who wished to marry a beautiful heiress.

- One of the suitors was of an ancient noble family and based his claim to win the lady on his birth and name.
- The other candidate was a man who had risen to prominence through royal service and he based his claim on his public service to the country.
- Needless to say, it was the second candidate who won the lady in question.
- Nonetheless, the moral of the tale was not that noble birth in itself was a bad thing, but that true nobility came through service to the state and was defined by what a man did rather than through birth alone.
- Thus loyal nobles like the earls of Oxford, Surrey and Shrewsbury, who served the king conscientiously, were truly noble and deserved their high status.
- Equally, **'new men'** who dedicated themselves wholeheartedly to Henry's view of government could become noble through their actions. They might not be elevated to the peerage but they were worthy servants of the nation. This was the outlook of the 'new men'.

Conclusion

Henry's relationship with his nobility was, ultimately, a failure. As an outsider to the English political system and as a usurper with little claim to the throne, he over-reacted to uncertainties of the time. In reality, his position in 1485 was relatively strong and this strength was enhanced by his overcoming of the Simnel threat and by his successful expedition to France in 1492. At this stage, one might have expected the relationship between Crown and nobility to revert to the normal medieval model, which Edward IV had largely revived during his second reign. Instead, Henry Tudor grew increasingly distrustful of his peers, driven on by the continuing conspiracy around Perkin Warbeck and the demise of members of his close family and of loyal and long-serving servants after 1500. As a result, Henry's regime became increasingly tyrannical, not because the nobility were too strong but because they were too weak.

The 'new men'

In contrast to the difficult relationship between the king and the nobility, Henry's reign saw the rise of a group of men who the king did trust to keep him safe and secure on the English throne.

- They were the ones who enforced royal policy and executed the royal will in the capital and in the localities.
- Most of them were lawyers and many of them were ambitious to gain land and power for themselves and their families; all of them were **loyal to the king** who had given them power.
- What was different about Henry VII was the extent to which he employed such men and his willingness to let them bend the law to bolster royal security.

Who were they?

Many were lawyers and/or trusted administrators. **Sir Reginald Bray** began as steward to Lady Margaret Beaufort. Edmund Dudley was a brilliant lawyer who gave lectures at the Inns of Court explaining how the king's rights overrode the rights of the nobility. Sir Edward Belknap, made Surveyor of the King's Prerogative in 1508, was the man who helped to put down the Cornish rebels in 1497. These trusted men wore their chains of office with great honour, were entrusted with important tasks for the regime and were rewarded with a wide range of offices and perks. When that erstwhile Yorkist pretender, Edmund de la Pole, was finally handed over to Henry VII in 1506, the delicate matter of transporting him safely to the Tower of London was given to two of the 'new men'.

Transept window in Great Malvern Priory, showing Sir Reginald Bray.

Henry Wyatt was despatched to Calais to pick him up and Thomas Lovell went down to Dover to deliver the prisoner to the king.

Many of these 'new men' had earned Henry's gratitude by sharing his exile. Sir Edward Poynings was involved in the 1483 uprisings against Richard III before joining Henry in Brittany. Thomas Lovell, Reginald Bray, John Risely, Richard Guildford and Giles Daubeney were all from that happy band who had actually seen their patron and their political fortunes crowned on Bosworth Field.

Bronze relief of Sir Thomas Lovell

The ambitions of the 'new men'

All these men aimed to re-establish royal authority in order to put an end to the political instability of the period. Although many were lawyers, they all had an inflated idea about the importance and extent of royal powers.

- The troubles of the previous 30 years and the problems of Henry's own reign meant that they were prepared to abuse the law in order to maintain and enhance royal authority.
- They also came to enjoy the fruits of their power and hard work. They had their portraits done, often dressed in dark, sober clothes and with serious faces.
- They built up landed estates for themselves and their families and many put up buildings, religious and secular, often decorated with Tudor badges. There is a splendid instance of this in the magnificent transept window of Great Malvern priory church. Lovell and Bray probably promoted the project and the window depicts not only them but also the king, the queen and Prince Arthur. Here we can still see the 'new men' and their devotion to the royal family they served with unswerving devotion. While the nobility might be aloof and unreliable, these 'new men' were quite the opposite.

Henry Wyatt (1460–1537) He was opposed to Richard III's seizure of the throne for which he was imprisoned. The story goes that he was saved from starvation by a cat that brought him a pigeon every day! Henry VII made him a Privy Councillor and he was also guardian to the young Henry VIII. In 1492, he was allowed to buy the castle and estate of Allington near Maidstone in Kent.

Thomas Lovell (d.1525) The son of Sir Ralph Lovell, who held estates in Norfolk. Thomas Lovell joined Henry in exile in Brittany and fought for him at Bosworth. He also fought at Stoke in 1487, and it is said that Simnel attended Lovell's funeral in 1525 as the last survivor of the battle. He was an MP and Speaker of the House of Commons. In 1485, he was made Chancellor of the Exchequer; in 1487, he was knighted; in 1502, he was appointed President of the Council and, in 1509, became Constable of the Tower.

Sir Edward Poynings (1459–1521) The second son of a baron and involved in a rising against Richard III in Kent, after which he joined Henry Tudor in exile. He was employed mainly as a military commander by Henry VII, most notably in Ireland where he snuffed out the opposition around Perkin Warbeck and brought the Irish lords back to nominal allegiance to the English Crown.

What did they do?

The men were engaged in many tasks and proved
extremely flexible in approach.

- *Commissions of the peace.* These were lists of men
  appointed as Justices of the Peace by the king. In order
  to ensure that the JPs acted as the king would wish, he
  often added some of his royal servants to act as overseers.
  Sir James Hobart turned up on commissions of the
  peace in Norfolk and Suffolk. Sir Thomas Lovell
  appeared in places as far apart as Yorkshire and Sussex,
  especially when important cases were to be tried. At the
  same time, these loyal servants could articulate royal
  policy and report back to the king on the attitudes of
  the other JPs.
- *Financial administrators.* The 'new men' ran the royal
  finances. Sir Thomas Lovell and then Sir John Heron
  were Treasurers of the King's Chamber, which not only
  oversaw the receipt and expenditure of an increasing
  percentage of royal income but also coordinated the
  other financial institutions. The duchy of Lancaster
  managed most of the older Crown lands and was run by
  Reginald Bray. He also oversaw the education and
  training of other men such as Richard Empson. The
  latter, together with Edmund Dudley, essentially ran the
  so-called Council Learned in the Law with its far-
  reaching financial tentacles. Dudley was especially
  responsible for the collection and sometimes the
  invention of royal debts. A lot of money from the
  collection of debts found its way to the royal Jewel
  House, which was run by Henry Wyatt. A number of
  these men also worked for the Exchequer, the older
  institution for the collection of royal revenue. The
  Chancellor of the Exchequer for much of the reign was
  Thomas Lovell.
- *Inquisitions post mortem.* Using their legal expertise,
  several of this group of men were able to use their local
  influence to question the ownership of land where the
  landowner had recently died. Often the heir might
  'compound' (pay a fine) to receive his inheritance or it
  would be 'proved' (rightly or wrongly) that some of the
  land actually belonged to the Crown.
- *Tax collection.* These men not only administered the royal
  finances, they also collected taxes and debts themselves.

Often they were subsidy commissioners, collectors of benevolences and customs duties on the importing or exporting of goods.

- *Military leaders.* The aristocracy still played an important part but many of the 'new men' were also able to raise considerable forces of **bowmen** and **billmen** to fight for the king. In 1492, for the expedition to France, Bray raised 156 men, while Lovell brought some 143 – this at a time when earls or dukes might bring 300 or so. In the same expedition, Sir Edward Poynings, a major military commander, who was not from the aristocracy, captured the town of Sluys and was later to lead a military expedition to Ireland. At the time of the Scottish expedition, Sir Thomas Lovell actually amassed 493 men for the king, an indication of the way in which the powers of these 'new men' increased as the reign went on.
- *Retaining.* At the same time, these men were often given licenses by the king to retain men. This allowed them to retain men among the local élites, who realised that attachment to one of the king's favourites would enhance their own political and financial standing.
- *Men of business.* These men also made lots of money from fees, pensions and other perks obtained when they sold the king's favour to the highest bidders. They were masters of patronage and charged high fees for their favours. As King Henry increasingly sold offices, favours, town charters and the like, these men acted as go-betweens and could hope to make money, even from applicants who eventually failed to be appointed. Edmund Dudley did a nice line in appointments to major offices in the Church. By the end of the reign, the enterprising Dudley made twice as much from the Church in England as the Pope did! Sir Thomas Lovell made money on the sale of town charters such as the one granted to Wallingford.

Results

The 'new men' favoured by the king became very rich for the most part and translated much of their wealth into land for the future endowment of their families.

- Bray, whose father earned about £10 a year, had an income in excess of £1000 a year.

Bowmen Archers who used the traditional and highly effective longbow.

Billmen Infantry (foot soldiers) who carried a bill, which was a long pole (often 2–2.5 metres long) topped with a range of hooks, spikes and blades. These were carried vertically before battle but lowered to the horizontal position when battle was joined.

- Lovell 'earned' perhaps twice as much as Bray, which put him in the same income bracket as an earl or marquis!

As men with considerable amounts of cash, they were also able to act as moneylenders and collected land when their clients were unable to pay them back. Sir Henry Wyatt got hold of lots of land in his home area of Kent in this way. Others bought wardships from the king and the right to marry wealthy heiresses. In a society where hard cash was in short supply, these men made a killing.

As the king's eyes and ears in the shires, they helped to establish increasing royal control and to stamp out feuding among the gentry. However, the regime which they were part of was essentially lawless and tyrannical. They were the agents of a king who, increasingly after 1500, had more the image of a mafia Godfather than an upright law-giving sovereign. In this way, the king's paranoia fed the ambitions of the 'new men'.

At the same time, the way in which these men were allowed to increase their regional and local influence, often at the expense of the local magnates, meant that direct royal control in the shires was rather greater than in the reign of Edward IV. Edward had delegated power in the regions to powerful men, such as Richard of Gloucester, who acted as mini-viceroys. This worked well enough provided the aristocracy remained loyal. Henry VII's increasing reliance on 'new men' in the localities was better at safeguarding royal control but it did not mean that the country was better governed. In many ways, **aristocratic paternalism** had been replaced by the greed and ambition of the 'new men' and their insecure royal master.

KEY TERM

Aristocratic paternalism
The idea that the aristocracy should govern in a reasonable and sympathetic way in offering the people their protection and the protection of the law. As great men, they should govern for the good of all rather than attempting to govern in their own interests.

The king's household officials

Although Henry VII became more and more reliant on men from below the rank of the nobility, the employment of such men in the business of government was not in itself new. In terms of the workings and the administration of government, kings had always needed educated and reliable men at the heart of government. In addition, the nobility, as a class, were not interested in the machinery and bureaucracy of government but in the patronage and power that came from royal favour. At the heart of government for all the kings in this period there were the king's household officials, men who had daily access to the king, many of whom were also major office holders and nearly all of whom came from the ranks of gentry or even yeomen families. Richard III's secretary was John Kendall, his chamber treasurer Edmund Chadderton, his solicitor Thomas Lynam, and none of these men were of aristocratic birth. Chief power-brokers in his reign were Catesby and Ratcliffe, both gentlemen from his affinity (group of followers), who were natural key advisers when he usurped the throne. These men were just the same class as Bray, Daubeney, Guildford and Lovell in Henry VII's reign. All were ambitious men (quite often younger sons) with some land and/or legal training, who used royal service to advance their own and their families' fortunes. At best, their reward might be elevation to the peerage and the acquisition of landed estates.

Leading churchmen

At the same time, as we have seen, the English Church, like the royal administration, was also staffed by men from the lower orders and not from the nobility. In France, many of the bishops were younger sons of the nobility, but this was rarely the case in England. Apart from Lionel Woodville, who was made Bishop of Salisbury on the back of his sister's advancement to the throne as Edward IV's queen, the English bishops were not political appointments. Instead, the Crown had always used the Church to reward loyal royal servants.

- In the reigns of Edward IV and Henry VII, John Morton was very influential. The son of a minor landowner, Morton won favour with both Lancastrians and Yorkists. Edward IV made him Master of the Rolls and then Bishop of Ely and tutor to Edward V, while Henry VII advanced him to the post of Archbishop of Canterbury as well as Chancellor of England, with a **cardinal's hat**.
- Richard Fox, who moved from the bishopric of Exeter to the richest see in England (Winchester) via Bath and Wells and Durham, was certainly of yeoman stock and one of Henry VII's most trusted officials.

The last ten years

Henry's increasing paranoia

In the last ten years of the reign, Henry's government became more oppressive.

KEY TERM

Immediate warrants In general, these were written instructions and commands issued from the privy chamber. More specifically, they were instructions by which the king used his prerogative power to interfere with a legal case currently being heard in one of the common law courts.

KEY EVENT

Prince Arthur died in 1502 A contemporary account tells us, 'When the king understood those sorrowful heavy tidings [the news of Arthur's demise], he sent for the queen, saying that he and his queen would take the painful sorrows together.' In the same source, we are told that Queen Elizabeth comforted her husband and told him that they were young enough to have more children. How ironic then that the queen died only months later while giving birth to a daughter, who also died.

- He tended to spend his days in his privy chamber issuing orders and **immediate warrants** and scouring official papers of all sorts.
- He personally intervened in all aspects of government and in all sorts of legal cases.
- He read every page of the royal financial accounts (both receipts and expenditure), signing each entry to show that he had read and approved it.

His increasing paranoia was fuelled by the deaths of many of those who were closest to him. Though his mother would outlive him by a few months, others did not.

- Cardinal Morton, Archbishop of Canterbury and the Chancellor of England died in 1500.
- **Prince Arthur died in** 1502, his beloved wife Queen Elizabeth of York and Reginald Bray in 1503.

Increasingly, Henry VII was isolated and alone, feeling embattled, ill and bad tempered. The fear of insurrection and revolt was never fully quelled. The king failed to marry again and the future of the dynasty hung on the life of his young son, Henry. The two Henries, so different in character, did not get along well. As his family fell apart (his daughter, Margaret, went to Scotland in 1503), the king became embittered, increasingly short-sighted and even more determined to maintain his control.

The lack of immediate family, which had done so much to secure his position in the early days, now came back to haunt him. The death of his wife he took particularly hard. They seem to have been a devoted couple and there is no hint that King Henry was ever unfaithful to her. In all, Henry's wife presented him with eight children (three sons and five daughters) but only three of them survived her. At the queen's death, we are told that Henry 'privily departed to a solitary place, and would no man should resort unto him'. The last years of Henry's reign were thus overshadowed by domestic tragedies, increasing illness and the disintegration of his family. Henry had aged prematurely, his eyesight was failing and his life was feared for on at least three occasions before his death in the spring of 1509. No wonder that in these last years his government became increasingly harsh and lawless.

SUMMARY QUESTIONS

1 To what extent did the nobility represent a serious threat to Henry VII's regime?

2 'Docile, quiescent and largely cooperative.' How accurate is this assessment of the nobility during the reign of Henry VII?

3 To what extent, if at all, can Henry VII's regime be seen as 'a model of good government'?

4 Why did Henry VII's government become more oppressive in the last decade of the reign?

5 To what extent was the nobility's power eclipsed by the power of Henry VII's 'new men'?

SECTION 7

HENRY VII AND THE WORKINGS OF GOVERNMENT: COUNCIL, FINANCE, PARLIAMENT AND THE CHURCH

> ### To what extent did Henry VII strengthen the monarchy?

KEY POINTS
- The structure of government changed very little during Henry VII's reign and remained similar to that already analysed under Edward IV (see Section 3, pages 46–54).
- Henry VII did work harder at the business of government than Edward IV and his regime became more oppressive as the reign went on.
- The Crown became more powerful during Henry's reign but this was more to do with his changing style of government than with changing institutions of government.
- The increase in the power of the Crown during Henry's reign has often been exaggerated.

Aspects of central government

The King's Council
The King's Council under Henry VII remained very similar in make-up and function to that of Edward IV. The Council was not a fixed body but groups of councillors called upon by the king as the fancy took him. The Council had two main functions.

- As an administrative body, it could advise the king about policy in all areas of government as and when he asked for that advice.
- In addition, the Council, with or without the king, could operate as a law court and dispense justice.

The key to the King's Council under Henry VII, as under his predecessors, was its flexibility and, in a sense, its informality. The king never called all of his councillors together: instead, he called different councillors at different times according to the nature of the business to be discussed and the availability of his advisers. At any one time there might be about 20 or so councillors and often the king might call together six or seven of them to advise him.

Council meetings were not only not attended by fixed groups of men: they also happened sporadically rather than at fixed times. There were 135 known meetings of the Council under Henry VII spaced over the 24 years of the reign. This informality was just the same under Edward IV and we know that 29 of Henry VII's councillors had served under the Yorkist king as well. In addition, the social origins and functions of Henry VII's councillors were very similar to their counterparts under Edward IV. Of the 225 councillors who we know something about, 43 were peers, 45 courtiers, 61 churchmen, 27 lawyers and 49 'officials'. This analytical profile is very much in line with the practice under Edward IV and earlier kings.

The Star Chamber

For many years, historians argued that Henry VII had set up a new law court called the Star Chamber, which showed up his desire to crack down on the nobility and his willingness to innovate in the structure of government. This idea derived from an Act of Parliament passed in 1487, which was given the title *Pro Camera Stellata* ('in the Star Chamber'). It was thus thought that Henry VII was inventing new councils and courts to underpin a new strong government after the carnage of the so-called Wars of the Roses. The Council Learned in the Law was later given much the same treatment by historians.

In fact, as Stanley Chrimes noted in his 1972 biography of Henry, the Act of 1487 did not establish a whole new law court at all, it merely established a temporary tribunal at a time when there was serious unrest because of the Simnel conspiracy. Far from being used by the king to curb the nobility, he pointed out that the few cases we know about (only a dozen) originated with the supposed victims of crime rather than with the king or his Council. Furthermore, the defendants were rarely of noble stock. So, in fact, an Act of Parliament, which was once used to show that England was being better governed under Henry VII, actually reveals the continuing lawlessness of the land in the early years of the reign.

Justices of the Peace

In the same way, historians have often over-interpreted Acts of Parliament that urged Justices of the Peace to carry out their judicial functions with vigour and zeal. There were 21 such statutes during the reign.

- Most rehearsed the traditional duties of the JPs and reveal royal anxiety about whether these men were enforcing law and order or whether they were, on the contrary, corrupt officials who added to rather than curbed the lawlessness of the times.
- One Act of 1488 paints a pretty bleak picture of the state of the realm with many references to all the crimes and misdemeanours being perpetrated. Five of the statutes give JPs advice how to cope with riots.
- The crucial thing to bear in mind is that the JPs, who were judges in local courts and also policemen, who quelled disturbances, were unpaid officials. They were appointed to the Commissions of the Peace for each county by the king and they assumed the office because of the prestige it would give them among their neighbours and political rivals. Therefore it also gave them a chance to swear in corrupt juries and to allow their followers to escape from justice. The level of corruption among these officials is unknown but there is no reason to think that they became less corrupt during Henry's reign.
- Indeed, we have seen already in the analysis of the 'new men' on pages 133–138 that Henry's regime was always more concerned with its own power than with the strict legality of its actions.

Law and order in the reign of Henry VII

The more optimistic accounts of Henry VII's reign tend to claim that the first Tudor re-established law and order after the anarchy and lawlessness of the Wars of the Roses. The following sources seem to paint a rather different picture.

First there is an Act of 1489, which acknowledges the corruption amongst Justices of the Peace.

> *The king has noticed that every day within this realm, the coin is traitorously counterfeited and murders, robberies and felonies are grievously committed. At the same time, the king is grieved*

by the number of unlawful pleas, extortions and the wrongdoing of sheriffs and others in authority ...

And now it has come to his attention that his subjects are little eased of these said mischiefs by the said Justices but by many of them, they are rather hurt than helped. And if the said subjects complain to these Justices of the Peace of any wrongs done to them, they have no remedy and these mischiefs do increase and are not subdued.

Portrait of Henry VII, painted in 1505.

Any person having a grievance about anything that a Justice of the Peace may decide must take his complaint to a different Justice of the Peace. If he still receives no satisfaction, he must take his complaint to the Justices of the Assize when they come into his shire. If he still has no remedy, he must come to the King's Highness or to his Chancellor and show his complaint. And his Highness shall send for the said Justice of the Peace to find out why his subjects are not helped and his laws carried out.

(From the introduction to the *Statute Against the Negligence of the Justice of the Peace*, 1489.)

This next Act from 1495 paints a similar picture of the lawlessness of government officials.

*The king our Sovereign Lord, well understands the heinous and detestable perjuries daily committed in this realm in inquests and juries to the high displeasure of Almighty God. He is likewise aware that such perjuries are increasing through the unlawful retaining, maintenance and **embraceries** committed by sheriffs and other officers of the law.*

Now we have complaints made in the 1490s. Harry Uvedale, against whom the complaints were directed, was a member of the king's household, an MP in 1491–2 and 1504, who lived in Corfe Castle.

> ### KEY TERM
>
> **Embraceries** Corrupting juries to give unlawful verdicts in court.

John Hill, a labourer, was arrested on suspicion of theft. He was sent to the gaol in Dorchester. There he fell ill and died. Harry Uvedale took from John Hill's wife two cows with calves, a mare and 20 sheep.

A French ship was wrecked and seven sailors came to land alive. They asked for help. Harry Uvedale and his servants saved the sailors' goods but kept them for Uvedale's own use. And so the poor men departed with little or nothing but the clothes hanging on their backs.

William Wolfe was robbed. The thief was captured and taken to Harry Uvedale, who found he was carrying stolen belts of silver and gilt. This thief was sent to Dorchester gaol and was later hanged at Shaftesbury. William Wolfe came many times to Harry Uvedale and asked for his stolen goods back. Harry Uvedale would not give them up because he was keeping Wolfe's possessions for his own use. This was against the king's law
(From official complaints from people living in Dorset.)

Commentary

The first two sources are entirely typical of fifteenth-century statutes. When Parliaments met, the king would be harangued with lots of complaints about lawless behaviour and these two statutes (Acts of Parliament) tell us that the laws were often being broken by officials, such as JPs and sheriffs, who should be enforcing the law, not abusing it. Lawlessness of this kind was a normal part of life in the fifteenth, and every other, century and the sources quoted above make it hard to claim that there was any improvement in the overall level of law and order in Henry VII's reign, compared to earlier and later regimes. Judging by the increasing harshness of Henry's regime, the use of 'new men' and the king's increasing isolation from his people, we are at liberty to suppose that law and order were perhaps less in evidence in Henry Tudor's reign than before or afterwards.

In the third source, it is impossible to tell how typical Harry Uvedale was. We do not even know for sure whether the complaints against him were well founded. However, it seems more than likely that this local power broker was dishonest and that he used his status in local government, buttressed by his membership of the king's household, to escape conviction. People were able to make these official complaints about Harry Uvedale's behaviour but it seems pretty clear that Uvedale did not suffer loss of royal favour or local power since he is still recorded as an MP and member of the king's household after 1500.

Royal finances

Henry's reputation

Francis Bacon claimed of the first Tudor that 'of nature assuredly, he coveted to accumulate treasure'. Contemporaries and historians alike have agreed that the former penniless refugee was most concerned about the accumulation of treasure and wealth once he reached the throne. Giovanni de Bebulcho, an Italian merchant, claimed that Henry was 'more feared than loved, and this was because of his greed,' and that the only man who really had any influence over the king was Reginald Bray, 'who controls the king's treasure.' The Milanese ambassador was more optimistic about the political benefits of Henry's greed for money. He claimed in 1496 that 'Everything goes well with the king, especially as he has an immense fortune in his treasury.' It is clear, however, that Henry's sustained interest in the accumulation of treasure made him unpopular and brought him little by way of political advantage.

Sources of income

Henry VII did not discover or set up any new sources of revenue for the Crown, but he exploited existing revenues in a more determined and systematic way than his predecessors had.

- *Royal lands.* Like all landowners, and as the greatest landowner in the land, the king enjoyed the rents from his lands. Because of the circumstances in which he took the Crown and despite the fact that he was a usurper with no real claim, Henry VII enjoyed the greatest landed estate of any king since William the Conqueror. Annual income from royal lands increased during his reign from £12,000 in 1485 to perhaps £40,000 by 1509. This healthy increase arose from a more systematic exploitation of rents but more significantly from the increase in the amount of land in royal hands. The attainder of Richard III and his supporters at Bosworth meant that more lands now reverted to the king. As the family of York was the second largest landowner after the Crown, this was a very important addition to the stock of land held by the king. At the same time, these Yorkist lands had themselves been bolstered by marriage, particularly by the marriages of George, Duke of Clarence and Richard, Duke of Gloucester to the daughters and heirs of Warwick the Kingmaker. As a result, many of Warwick the Kingmaker's lands also found their way into the king's hands. At the same time, there were a total of 138 attainders during the reign of the first Tudor and these confiscations increased royal lands still further. Furthermore, the miserly Henry gained even more land from the deaths of his near relatives! His uncle, Jasper, died in 1495, leaving the king as sole heir to his extensive estates. When Prince Arthur died in 1502, most of his lands reverted to the Crown, bringing in an extra £6000 a year. Although some of these lands were then granted out to Prince Henry when he became Prince of Wales, Henry rewarded himself with his son's duchy of York lands!

Furthermore, Henry VII was reluctant to alienate Crown lands in the way that the previous King Henry had done and he exploited his lands in a much more systematic way than Edward IV had done. All of this meant that, by means of good fortune allied to the hard-headed approach of a shrewd businessman, royal income from land increased significantly during the reign.

- *Feudal dues*. Henry and his agents exploited his feudal rights as king with increasing zeal and efficiency. For example, the king benefited greatly on the death of the great landowners and nobles, who were technically the king's tenants-in-chief. Henry appreciated this system so much that, in 1501, he declared that all 'large' landowners were now also tenants-in-chief. This greatly widened the number of those whose deaths could be exploited. In 1503, he created a new post called Master of Wards to ensure that wardship was being properly exploited. In the same way, the king was concerned to make more money from his other feudal dues. In 1508, as already noted, there appeared a new official called the Surveyor of the King's Prerogative whose job was to discover where the king's special rights had been infringed. This post merely formalised what Henry and his legal team (the likes of Empson and Dudley) had been doing for years.

- *Bonds and recognisances.* Combining prerogative rights and the profits of justice, it is clear that Henry made large sums of money from the imposition of bonds and recognisances.

- *Trade.* Like his predecessors, Henry was allowed to tax trade, both imports and exports. He was granted **tunnage and poundage for life** in the first Parliament of the reign in 1485. For the first ten years of the reign, this brought in, on average, £33,000 a year but this increased to nearer £40,000 for the remainder of the reign.

- *Parliamentary grants.* The traditional parliamentary grant was the Fifteenth and Tenth. This tax was assessed as a fixed sum on each community and would normally bring in £30,000 for each Fifteenth and Tenth granted. These extraordinary grants were for the purpose of security at home and war abroad. Eight were granted to Henry during his reign, three in 1491 for the invasion of France, and two in 1497 to take on the Scots. One unusual (but not unheard of) demand by the king was for a parliamentary subsidy in 1489. The unusual nature of this tax, based on individual income, not the wealth of the community, helped to spark off the Northern Rising of that year when one of the king's tax collectors, the Earl of Northumberland, was lynched by an angry mob. However, the tax failed. The king hoped to raise £100,000 to pay for archers to defend Brittany but only a meagre £25,000 was actually raised.

- *Knighting of the king's eldest son and marriage of his eldest daughter.* There was more trouble in the Parliament of 1504, when the king demanded money for the knighting of his eldest son and the marriage of his eldest daughter. As Arthur had been knighted back in

1489 and had been dead for two years, and since Margaret had been married to the King of Scotland the year before, Parliament was not impressed by these retrospective demands. Henry may have hoped to use these two specific claims to set in train a wide-ranging investigation of the true extent and value of his prerogative rights. If so, then his ambitions were thwarted by Parliament's decision to offer him an 'aid' worth £30,000 instead!

- *Loans.* Like all his royal predecessors, Henry could and did ask for loans to boost his income. Some were from merchants and other moneylenders. At the same time, Henry could ask for benevolences or free loans and these were not usually repaid. Chancellor Morton is especially associated with the demand for a benevolence from the great and the good in 1491. He personally visited many of those who were asked for money to encourage prompt payment!

- *French pension.* Like Edward IV, Henry was the beneficiary of a French pension, which brought in a total of £160,000 during the reign. This was negotiated in the Treaty of Etaples in 1492 after Henry's invasion of France. In order to avoid any fighting, the French king, Charles VIII, bribed Henry to go away.

- *Sale of offices.* It was normal for a king to expect some financial reward for awarding a powerful and financially rewarding office to one of his courtiers. However, Henry seems to have exploited this source of revenue more systematically than his predecessors. It may be one of the things he learnt from his time in France where the open sale of offices to the highest bidder was becoming more common. Henry twice sold the office of Chief Justice of the Common Pleas for £330. John Yonge paid £1000 to the king to become Master of the Rolls, while £100 was enough to secure the Attorney-Generalship for John Erneley. At one stage, there seems to have been an auction for the office of Speaker of the House of Commons. Daubeney's bid of £100 on behalf of his associate, Robert Sheffield, was trumped by Reginald Bray who secured the post for his man, Thomas Englefield. The disputed election was handled by

Thomas Lovell who no doubt also profited from the deal, probably from both bidders!

Henry VII's search for concealed lands, 1486

This source indicates how Henry VII, as a new king who had never lived in England, had to work hard to find out exactly what land he owned. Instructions such as these would have been commonplace and, in a world where land ownership was so important and where it could be so often disputed, the king may well have got his agents and lawyers to bend the law in his favour. When a landowner died without an heir, the Crown could claim all the lands. If there was an heir, he had to pay the king a serious 'entry fine' in order to take possession of his lands. If the heir was a child and thus the king's ward, the king controlled the heir's lands and marriage. In all circumstances, then, the king stood to gain from death! Notice at the end of the source the reference to commissions post mortem. The deaths of landowners then were usually occasions for serious disputes about landownership.

> *Commission to John Fisher, serjeant at law, John Mordaunte, Richard Godfrey, Richard Sheldon, John Stanford and William Collet, to enquire in the county of Bedford of all concealed lands, goods and chattels, and on lands transferred to religious houses or corporations without royal permit; and of all lands acquired by Edward IV and Richard III and which belonged to those kings. They are also to enquire into all the lands which the persons named in the attached schedule held at their death in the said county.*

Chamber finance

One novelty about the administration of royal finances under Henry VII was the degree to which income was paid directly into the King's Chamber. Most medieval kings had some money paid into the Chamber when it was needed for quick expenditure, especially when the king was making preparations for war. For the first ten years of the reign, the king, who was a complete novice in terms of understanding and operating the machinery of financial administration, allowed most of the royal finances to be received by the Exchequer in the usual way. After that, however, a rapidly increasing percentage of revenues was received by the

Treasurer of the Household (who was also the Chancellor of the Exchequer), Sir Thomas Lovell.

Period	Money received by the King's Chamber
1487–9	£17,000 pa
1489–95	£27,000 pa
1502–9	£105,000 pa

This table indicates the gradual way in which the King's Chamber came to oversee most of the king's income. Ten years after his accession, the Chamber was still only handling around 25 per cent of the king's total income. Only in the later years did the Chamber receive the vast majority of that income. This was the time when Henry personally checked all the items of income received in the Chamber and signed each one.

Expenditure
Henry VII has often been seen as a miser – a man who accumulated money for its own sake and who spent as little as possible. This view is clearly wide of the mark. Though contemporaries thought of him as a miser because of his merciless (and sometimes illegal) exploitation of all possible sources of revenue, it is important to realise that Henry VII also spent a lot of money.

- The king kept a fairly lavish court where he enjoyed gambling.
- Henry was also a builder of note. He began rebuilding the palace of Sheen in 1495. He spent some £20,000 on it and, on its completion in 1501, renamed it Richmond after his father's (and his) earldom. He also built Greenwich Palace.
- After 1491, he spent perhaps £300,000 on plate and jewels.
- The political instability of his reign also cost him dear. On the one hand, he had to spend a lot to defeat his enemies. He had to pay to defeat Simnel in 1487 and Warbeck, with his eight-year campaign to unseat the Tudor, cost him even more. In 1492, Henry had to launch a major invasion of France to persuade Charles VIII to desist from his support for young Warbeck.

- At the same time, Henry also spent vast sums on diplomacy during his reign. To woo the Spanish and Philip the Fair of Burgundy (ruler of the Low Countries), Henry spent lavishly indeed. A special meeting with Philip in 1500 was **an expensive event** and the surprise next meeting in 1506, after Philip was forced to seek shelter in England, was similarly costly. Given his origins as a penniless refugee, it is entirely predictable that Henry would want to use his new-found wealth to persuade foreign leaders and diplomats (as well as himself) that he was here to stay.

With such high levels of perhaps unnecessary expenditure, it is legitimate to query Henry's financial achievement. More secure by 1500, he could have cut back his expenditure and saved the realm from his high taxes and dubious financial penalties. The truth is that throughout his reign Henry raised money and spent money on a scale not seen before in peacetime.

Assessment

Although Henry undoubtedly increased royal income during his reign, the scale of his financial achievement, compared to that of Edward IV, should not be exaggerated. It is impossible to provide accurate figures for royal income at any one time and even contemporary officials would have had only a general idea.

- The best estimates suggest that Edward IV had restored royal finances after the disastrous reign of Henry VI.
- In the last eight years of his reign, Edward had achieved solvency (he earned more than he spent), had paid off debts, and had maintained an impressive royal household and government without recourse to Parliament.
- By the end of his reign, Edward had a regular annual income in the region of £70,000.
- By comparison, Henry VII reached an income nearer £100,000 per annum by the end of his reign and left behind plate and treasure possibly to the value of two years' income.

However, this was not in itself a great achievement. The king's grasping nature in his last years made him seriously unpopular. Polydore Vergil claimed that the king was

KEY THEME

An expensive event One historian, Ben Thompson, has calculated that £342,000 (or the equivalent of three years' income!) was spent on diplomacy with Philip and his father, the Emperor Maximilian, in the period 1505–9 alone!

rather feared than loved because of his greed, high taxes and oppressive government.

Giovanni de Bebulcho wrote in 1496 that the king's greed was well known and hated. 'The king,' he wrote, 'is very powerful in money, but if some lord of the blood royal rose against him and he had to take to the battlefield, he would fare badly. His people would abandon him because of his greed.' So more money and treasure, far from bolstering Henry's position, may have helped to undermine it.

Furthermore, money and plunder did not, of itself, make the king more powerful than his predecessors.

- Apart from the setting up of the colourful Yeomen of the Guard to act as his private bodyguard, Henry, like his predecessors, still lacked a standing army.
- At the same time, Henry's officials largely remained unpaid and, as we have seen, exploited their offices to make money rather than to administer government and justice in a fair and impartial way.
- If Henry had used his increasing income to fund a paid bureaucracy, we could perhaps speak of a real increase in his royal authority.
- In the same way, Henry did not find any new sources of income for the English Crown, so it remained underfunded. The increased exploitation of royal revenues was personal to Henry himself and it did not outlive him.
- He failed to introduce new institutions of financial administration, which might have made his financial advances more permanent.
- The limited nature of Henry's achievement is highlighted by the rather greater income enjoyed by his rivals, the kings of Spain and France. For sixteen years of his reign, he remained a pensioner of the French.

Parliaments and Great Councils

Parliaments under Henry VII fulfilled exactly the same functions as they did under Edward IV and there was little or nothing of significance in the development of Parliament during the reign of the first Tudor.

Sessions

Parliament was called and dismissed at the king's instigation. Apart from the initial Parliament, which confirmed his claim to the throne, the king was not obliged to call Parliament. As the table below shows, Henry called seven Parliaments in all during his reign, with growing infrequency.

	Date of session	Approximate length of session
1485 Parliament	07/11/85–10/12/85	1 month
1487 Parliament	09/11/87–??/12/87	1 month
1489 Parliament	13/01/89–23/02/90	1.5 months
1491 Parliament	17/10/91–04/11/91	0.5 month
1495 Parliament	14/10/95–21/12/95	2 months
1497 Parliament	16/01/97–13/03/97	2 months
1504 Parliament	25/01/04–??/04/04	2.5 months

Parliamentary sessions lasted for about one year in a reign of more than 23 years, giving some idea of the limited importance of Parliament at this time. The first Parliament was undoubtedly the most significance of the reign.

- This Parliament crucially recognised the fact that Henry was indeed king and allowed him to date his reign from the day before Bosworth so that all who fought against him could legally be called traitors. This prevented the king's opponents from claiming that they were merely obeying the orders of their sovereign when they fought for Richard III.
- In addition, this Parliament secured the king a grant of tunnage and poundage for life. Henry ensured that relations remained favourable by not asking for a grant of taxes in this Parliament.

Thereafter, all other Parliaments were called together largely to grant the king money, which all six did.

Finance

As we have seen, Parliament did grant the king extraordinary taxes on several occasions during the reign, the only trouble occurring when the king asked for a subsidy in 1489. Most of these grants were associated with measures to secure the realm from foreign invasion and, as such, they seem to have generated little opposition. The size of parliamentary grants tended to fall as the reign progressed.

Legislation

Laws could not be made without the assent of the Houses of Lords and Commons and the laws passed in this reign should not be overrated in importance. **Henry's laws** (and most of them did originate with the Crown rather than with either of the two Houses of Parliament) were mainly to do with attainders (20 per cent) and law enforcement (20 per cent). As we have seen on page 142, one of these laws *Pro Camera Stellata* in 1487 set up a new tribunal to punish rioting and illegal retaining. Another such tribunal, this time looking into perjury, was created in 1495, but neither of these bodies actually heard many cases and cannot have added significantly to the level of justice in the land.

Great Councils

Just to underline the limited role of Parliament in advising the king or, indeed, in approving of his policies, it must be remembered that the king used Great Councils when he wished to announce new plans or to formally take advice from the English political élite.

- Great Councils were formal assemblies of nobles, leading churchmen and councillors to discuss pressing matters and to get the assent of the political nation to Henry's policies. Five were summoned during the reign between 1487 and 1502, and they were an important point of contact between the king and his barons and a way of binding these men to the aims and the letter of royal policy.
- One of these assemblies was called when Henry had decided on the invasion of France and another, **ad hoc** Great Council was assembled in the fields of France to underwrite Henry's decision to end that campaign without fighting but with a large French pension. Although the king had decided to go home, the assembled great men were made to sign documents pleading with the king to return to England!

KEY TERM

Henry's laws Francis Bacon, writing during the reign of James I (1603–25), claimed that in King Henry's times, 'good commonwealth's laws did excel' and that the legislation of this period was 'the pre-eminent virtue and merit of this king'. However, Bacon's judgement is not to be trusted as he was concerned mainly to impress on his own king the merits of good laws.

KEY TERM

Ad hoc Short for the Latin phrase *ad hoc tempus,* meaning 'at that time' or unplanned.

Local government

Local government and the nobility

Local government changed little during Henry's reign. Although the king may have made little use of his nobility in the workings of central government, their predominant power in the localities remained assured. Any attack on their powers might have led to a full-scale aristocratic revolt. Therefore Henry apparently used the nobility in local and regional government in the usual way.

- The Earl of Oxford was used in the government of East Anglia and especially in Essex, where most of his estates (centred on Hedingham) were located.
- From the 1490s, Henry Bourchier, Earl of Essex, served regularly on Commissions of the Peace in Hertfordshire and Essex.
- The Earls of Shrewsbury and Northumberland had power in the north of England, and the Earl of Surrey, even though on the wrong side at Bosworth, served Henry loyally in the same area.
- The Duke of Bedford and the Stanleys exercised enormous regional power (in Wales and the north-west, respectively) during Henry's reign.
- One newcomer to regional government was Henry's mother, Margaret Beaufort, Countess of Richmond, who was given extensive powers over the Midlands, which she ruled from her palace at Collyweston.

It is clear, therefore, that Henry used the nobility in just the same way in local government as his predecessors had done. Most of the time he was rewarded with loyal service from the nobility, which was obedient after 1487.

Local government and the gentry

Below the great power brokers in the social order came the gentry and lords of the manor, many of them JPs, who were responsible with the sheriff for government in the many communities up and down the country. The function of JPs may have shifted a little during Henry's reign. While retaining their function as local judges, they acquired wider administrative powers, but we do not know how effectively they carried out royal commands. They remained unpaid officials who were likely to see and

KEY TERM

Choosing JPs The historian John Guy has suggested that Henry attempted to split up aristocratic affinities or power networks (made up largely of gentry) by bringing in some JPs who were outsiders but who had royal backing. Clear evidence for this view is hard to come by, but perhaps we can say that the intrusion of many of Henry's 'new men' in the government of the shires, and Henry's increased use of immediate warrants (written commands/instructions often designed to allow the king to interfere in legal cases) in the later years of the reign, probably did increase royal power in the localities.

interpret royal commands and new Acts of Parliament in the light of local circumstances. Henry VII may have taken care in **choosing JPs** who would be loyal and reliable, and we know that some of his special agents or 'new men' ended up as JPs. However, all kings took care in the choice of JPs and sheriffs, often balancing out the competing claims of different powerful families for whom the government of the shire was a vitally important power base.

Local government and social mobility

Some historians argue that Henry may have managed to strengthen relations between the central government and the local gentry as a counterweight to the nobility whose influence he wished to diminish. However, there is only limited evidence for this and, once again, we can find examples of gentlemen being advanced to the ranks of the aristocracy and to increased local power in the reigns of Edward IV and Richard III.

- It is easy to think that late-medieval England was a static world, socially and politically, in which everyone knew and stayed in their social position. In fact, there was a lot of social mobility throughout the period. Noble families died out on average after four generations; new families rose from the ranks of gentlemen, or even yeomen, to the ranks of the aristocracy.
- The increasing power and fortune of Lord Hastings in Edward IV's reign and the power given to Richard III's northern associates (e.g. Ratcliffe and Brackenbury) in the south of England are good examples of this process.
- At the same time, it should be borne in mind that Edward IV and Richard III were powerful titled aristocrats before they came to the throne. They were brought up in a world of close-knit affinities based on family and service. Henry VII did not have this advantage, which may explain why he made more use than his predecessors of 'new men' in local government.
- However, as with so many of Henry's supposed achievements in government, the success of the 'new men' depended on the close personal supervision of the king and this level of supervision died with him.
- Even if Henry spent long hours working on his papers, he did not have the ability personally to supervise events

in a thousand different communities and he did not have the paid agents who could do this for him. Beyond the confines of the royal palaces and the court, Henry VII's writ may not have been as effective as we sometimes think.

The Church

In the reign of Henry VII, relations between the king and the Church remained very similar to those in the previous two reigns.

Relations with the papacy

England, of course, remained a Roman Catholic country and relations between Henry and the papacy were cordial at all times. The Pope realised that the king was the *de facto* head of the Church in England and did nothing to upset this long-standing arrangement.

- Pope Innocent VIII recognised Henry as the rightful King of England and granted a dispensation (special permission) for him to marry Elizabeth of York since the two were cousins.
- Pope Julius II granted a more significant dispensation for Catherine of Aragon to marry her brother-in-law (Prince Henry) after the death of her first husband, Prince Arthur, in 1502.
- At the same time, Pope Innocent proclaimed that rebels against Henry were excommunicated by definition and Henry even received special gifts from the papacy in the shape of a papal sword and a **Golden Rose**.
- Financially, the papacy was rewarded for its benevolence by being allowed to preach its special Jubilee Indulgence throughout England in 1501, which raised some £4000 for the papal coffers.
- Henry improved relations with the papacy still further by sending **Christopher Bainbridge**, the new Archbishop of York, to Rome to act as a kind of resident ambassador to the Pope.

The Pope's good relations with the king were also underpinned by the fact that Henry was a faithful and pious son of the Church. He founded three religious houses during his reign and built the splendid new chapel at the eastern end of Westminster Abbey, where he and his wife

were buried and where he paid for 10,000 masses to be said
for his soul. His mother, too, was pious and put her money
into religious foundations. She and Bishop Fisher
re-founded God's House in Cambridge as Christ's College
and gave much support to St John's College in the same
city.

Henry and the bishops

Not surprisingly, then, successive popes made no objection
to Henry's choice of new bishops. John Morton was moved
to Canterbury in 1486, and **Henry Deane** and **William
Warham** went there afterwards. In Henry's reign, rather
fewer of the bishops were theologians than in previous
reigns. It seems that Henry preferred civil lawyers to
theologians, perhaps to ensure that theology did not get in
the way of loyalty to a grasping and hard-headed regime.
At the same time, the papacy was apparently unconcerned
that Henry deliberately moved several bishops, when there
was only one vacancy, in order to **make more money for
the Crown**. So when Morton died in 1500, Deane was
moved from Salisbury to Canterbury, Audley went from
Hereford to Salisbury, and Castello to Hereford. This round
of musical chairs (or rather musical bishoprics) helped to
maximise Henry's profit
from the Church.

Henry's financial grip
on the Church did not
end there. He fined
churchmen with the
same enthusiasm as he
did laymen and via the
same agents.

- James Hobart, the
  Attorney General
  and member of the
  Council Learned in
  the Law, pursued
  churchmen for their
  money.
- Even **Bishop Fox**,
  the most loyal of
  churchmen, was

**Bishop Fox (oil on panel by
Hans Corvus, painted
between 1512 and 1544).**

fined £2000 in order to obtain a royal pardon. Edmund Dudley, when cooling his heels in the Tower of London early in Henry VII's reign, listed seventeen cases of churchmen being mistreated by Henry VII.

For the most part, the king was able to exploit the **Statutes of Provisor and Praemunire**, which meant that the **church judges and church courts** could not encroach on common law. Once again, the Henrician regime exploited the law to enrich the king.

Benefit of Clergy and sanctuary laws

In two areas of legislation, Henry confirmed and increased his power over the Church in England. Benefit of Clergy was a special privilege whereby churchmen who were accused of crimes could have their case heard in an ecclesiastical, rather than in a civil court. This, in practice, meant that the penalties, if the individual were found guilty, were rather more lenient. The problem with this system was that a lot of men could claim to be clergy when they were not actually in holy orders. A statute in Henry's reign tightened up the definition of a clergyman to restrict the numbers of people who could claim this special privilege.

At the same time, Henry ruled that in treason cases no one could claim the right of sanctuary. This right meant that those accused of a crime (usually fugitives from justice) could avoid arrest temporarily as long as they remained inside a church. In 1486, when the Stafford brothers attempted to raise rebellion, Henry's officers apprehended the rebels in a church and the king's judges ruled that the king had acted legally.

Assessment

The close and amicable relationship between the king and the Church was to the benefit of both.

- The Church was an important department of state. The bishops and many of the lesser clergy were, in fact, government officials at both local and central levels. Men could hope to advance far up the clerical (and therefore political) ladder, where the only qualifications needed were education and a patron, rather than birth.

- At the same time, the churchmen appreciated the powers of the king. After the conflict between York and Lancaster, and with the persistent instability of Henry's reign, the Church's message about obedience to God and obedience to the king being one and the same thing was particularly useful. At the same time, the clergy tended to feel that a strong monarchy (even if operating at the borders of legality) was preferable to a weak monarchy and a confused polity.

KEY THEME

Religious convulsions In the 1530s, Henry VII's son would repudiate the Pope's power over the Church in England and make himself the Church of England's Supreme Head.

During the reign of Henry VII, then, the Church remained a vital part of the governing process in terms of practical administration and in terms of ideology. At the same time, there was no hint in Henry VII's reign of the great **religious convulsions** to come in the next reign. Indeed, there was very little religious violence at this time. Seventy-three people were put on trial for heresy during the reign, but only three were burnt. Most of those accused were from the lower orders and belonged to a small-scale heretical sect called the Lollards (see page 54). Thus the Church in England was united and cohesive and Church and State were apparently indivisible. All this was nothing new. Henry VII exploited the Church more systematically but in the same ways as his predecessors had done.

CONCLUSION

What was true of the Church was true of government and administration as a whole.

- Henry's government was not new in the sense that it was based on new institutions or new methods of government. It was only new in the sense that it was, like the government of every other medieval king, *sui generis* – of its own type. In other words, it was different in style but not in substance.
- Henry's regime became increasingly harsh and unpopular as the reign went on and he alienated many of his natural allies in the governance of the country, amongst the nobility and gentry.
- Henry's reign was unstable because he had no real claim to the throne, and he over-reacted to the threats. After 1495 (the betrayal by Stanley) and 1497 (the Cornish Revolt), Henry became increasingly harsh and paranoid and there was a real danger of an aristocratic backlash at

any time against the 'new men'. In fact, that backlash did not occur until Henry died. The fact that it happened then and not before was a tribute to the essentially quiescent nature of the English aristocracy.

* After 1487, none of the great men gave overt support for regime change and Henry should have been able to establish a sound and more even-handed government on the model of his predecessors and along the lines of Edward IV's successful second reign. Instead, Henry became increasingly harsh and repressive because his government was that of a usurper who, unlike the usurpers Edward IV and Richard III, was not a member of the aristocracy and who, in the final analysis, was always undermined by his lack of title. He claimed the throne through battle not inheritance, which allowed others to do the same.

* Henry's inherent weakness in 1485 and during the long years of exile dictated the nature of his government of the realm. The Crown was in some ways stronger in 1509 than in 1485, but the real comparison needs to be made between Edward IV's second reign (1471–83) and Henry's reign. From this perspective, it seems that, in many ways, Henry's government was stronger (i.e. harsher) than Edward IV's, but in another way it was weaker because the government presided over a realm in tension, where unresolved conflicts between ruler and ruled always threatened to spill over into civil unrest.

* At the same time, the government was weak because it was so often threatened by political instability (pretenders and rebellion), which was not a feature of the earlier period. Ultimately, Henry's government became stronger than earlier regimes but also rather more brittle!

SUMMARY QUESTIONS

1 'Different in style but not in substance.' How accurate is this comparison between the governments of Henry VII and Edward IV?

2 How important a role did Parliament play in government, 1485–1509?

3 How 'new' was the monarchy of Henry VII?

4 To what extent did Henry VII revolutionise Crown finances?

5 To what extent did Henry VII increase the power of the monarchy during his reign?

ENGLAND'S RELATIONS WITH FOREIGN POWERS DURING THE REIGN OF HENRY VII: UNHELPFUL ALLIANCES?

How successful was Henry VII's foreign policy?

KEY POINTS

- Henry's foreign policy was very similar to that of Edward IV.
- The main aim of English foreign policy was to strengthen the political and dynastic security of the king.
- As Henry VII was the first of a new dynasty and a usurper, his foreign policy negotiations were undertaken very seriously, since he needed to establish his position in Europe.
- England was not a great European power. As an island cut off from the Continent and as a monarchy, which was not wealthy by European standards, England was a small-time player in the entanglements of European diplomacy and a power that became less important in European politics as the reign of Henry VII unfolded.
- It is easy to see Henry's foreign policy as a success, since it helped to keep Henry on the throne and quashed the threats from pretenders.
- In reality, the judgement on his foreign policy needs to be rather more mixed.

TIMELINE

1486   Henry's marriage to Elizabeth of York.

       Birth of Prince Arthur.

1488   Expedition to Brittany (unsuccessful).

1489   Treaty of Redon (aid for Brittany).

       Treaty of Medina del Campo with Spain.

1489	Birth of Princess Margaret.
1491	France takes control of Brittany.
	Birth of Prince Henry.
1492	English invasion of France and Treaty of Etaples.
1493–6	Trade embargo with Low Countries.
1494	Charles VIII of France invades Italy.
1496	Intercursus Magnus with Low Countries. Scottish invasion of England, supporting Warbeck. New marriage treaty with Spain.
1497	Truce of Ayton with Scotland.
1501	Marriage of Prince Arthur and Catherine of Aragon.
1502	Treaty of Ayton with Scotland.
	Death of Prince Arthur.
1503	Princess Margaret marries James IV of Scotland.
1504	Death of Queen Isabella – internal troubles in Spain.
1506	Philip of Netherlands agrees to hand over Suffolk. Intercursus Malus.
1508	League of Cambrai v Venice – Henry VII left out.

OVERVIEW

The foreign situation in 1485

At first glance, it would be easy to think that Henry VII's position in relation to the other powers of Europe was rather weak. After all, he was a pretender who owed his throne to French aid. If he could be so successful, so could another foreign-backed pretender. As the first of a new dynasty, his family had no dynastic links (via marriage) with the other ruling families of Europe. Furthermore, as a bachelor in 1485, it would take many years before his prospective children could make advantageous diplomatic marriages.

However, the diplomatic position for the new king was much stronger than it seemed.

- Only France had the power to launch a serious invasion of the country and, having just helped Henry to the throne, they were unlikely to immediately start backing new pretenders. The government of France was, in 1485 still a weak minority government for the young Charles VIII.
- Scotland had recently been invaded successfully by Richard of Gloucester and was no real threat to English security.
- A greater threat might emerge from Ireland where there was serious Yorkist support, but the Irish were not notable fighters.
- In the immediate aftermath of Henry's crushing victory at Bosworth in 1485, there seemed little chance that the Yorkists might launch attacks on Henry's throne. Furthermore, Henry was committed to marrying Elizabeth of York and ruling jointly with her, so he actually had support from many leading Yorkists.
- The defeat at Bosworth had also left the Yorkist heirs in a weak position. The princes in the Tower were dead, Lincoln swore loyalty to the new regime and Warwick was soon under lock and key.
- The prospects for serious intervention by foreign powers in English politics in 1485 or 1486 seemed remote.

1485 was not like 1470-1

Henry Tudor was also in a stronger position in 1485 than Edward IV's regime in 1470 or Henry VI's regime in 1471. In some ways, the French-backed Tudor triumph of 1485 seemed to mirror the twin triumphs of **foreign-backed invasions both in 1470 and 1471**, when first Henry VI and then Edward IV regained the throne. In fact, the circumstances were far different after 1485. The multiple crises of 1470–1 were brought about by the existence of two men who had been crowned king of England. The readeption of Henry VI came about because that monarch was still alive, his wife was French (which brought about French support) and two great magnates (Clarence and Warwick) had turned against Edward IV and forced him to flee. Edward IV was able to invade successfully in 1471 because he had backing from Burgundy, Clarence changed sides, Warwick was discredited and Margaret of Anjou was late in arriving.

> ### KEY THEME
>
> **Foreign-backed invasions in 1470–1** The coalition of forces put together by Louis XI of France, which caused Edward IV to flee in 1470 and brought about the Lancastrian invasion of 1471 led by Henry VI's wife, Margaret of Anjou, and his son, Edward, Prince of Wales. In a sense, Edward IV's successful invasion of 1471 was also a foreign-backed invasion since it was backed by his brother-in-law, Charles the Bold, Duke of Burgundy, and foreign mercenary troops.

In 1485, Henry VII was in a rather stronger position because none of these factors obtained and the situation was far less tangled. In 1485, the previous king, Richard III, was safely dead and his reputation as a murdering usurper meant that few men were prepared to fight for his cause. Richard also had no son to fight for the throne since his only child, Edward of Middleham, the Prince of Wales, had died in 1484. Furthermore, by 1485 there were no overmighty subjects left who might ally with France in the way that Warwick had done in 1470. Warwick had died without male heirs in 1471 and the Duke of Buckingham (who may have had ambitions of becoming king) was executed by Richard III in 1483, leaving an heir who was a small child. In all these ways, Henry Tudor, in 1485, appeared to be in the same strong position as Edward IV at the start of his second reign (see Section 3, pages 43–46). On both occasions there was no obvious alternative king to the present incumbent!

Of course, this is all clear with hindsight. At the time, Henry naturally felt insecure and did all he could to establish friendly relations with most powers in close proximity to his new kingdom. Nonetheless, his position was stronger than it looked and so the apparent strength of his position at his death does not mean that his foreign policy was especially brilliant and successful. It meant that Henry, largely through good fortune, had survived.

Relations with France

England, France and Brittany

In the first few months of the reign, Henry made a one-year truce with France, which was later extended from 1486 to 1489. Immediately, Henry had neutralised the main (but at this time not very serious) threat to his regime. Fortunately for him, the regency government of France wanted to be assured of English neutrality while it sought to take over the duchy of Brittany. The independence of Brittany was an affront to the French government and, with its duke, Francis II, getting old and having only an unmarried daughter, **Anne of Brittany** (aged nine in 1485), to succeed him, the French thought it would be an excellent idea for the young Charles VIII to

KEY PERSON

Anne of Brittany (1477–1514) Francis II's only child and thus his heiress. She was forced to marry Charles VIII in 1491 and his successor, Louis XII, in 1499 to ensure that Brittany remained part of France. She had one daughter, Claude, by Louis XII, who then married the future Francis I of France.

England and her Continental neighbours

marry her, thus bringing the duchy peacefully under French control. Over the years, Brittany had been a thorn in France's side as it tended to ally with England and France's other main enemy, Burgundy.

For Henry, the situation was rather difficult because he had spent so much of his exile in Brittany and he did not wish to see the whole of the French coast across the Channel from England fall into French hands.

However, the powerlessness of Henry's position soon became clear.

- He made a commercial treaty with Brittany in 1486 and, when Francis II died in 1488, he signed the Treaty of Redon (February 1489) with the Breton government, promising military aid to defend the duchy from French incursions.
- In April 1489, he despatched 6000 men (mainly archers) to aid the Bretons. Although these troops, led

by Daubeney, helped to defeat the French at Dixmude in June 1489, the French were not seriously molested and soon bought off Maximilian von Habsburg, the ruler of the Low Countries, who had also joined forces in support of Brittany.

- With Maximilian gone, Henry knew he had to concede. In December 1491, Charles VIII of France married Anne of Brittany and the duchy was actually (but not formally) **annexed** by France.
- To talk of Henry's betrayal of his ally is perhaps a little harsh because the episode underlined England's military weakness. In the light of this, it would clearly be too dangerous to antagonise France too much by giving continued aid to the lost cause of Brittany.

The invasion of France, 1492

Despite caving in over Brittany, Henry VII was soon at war with France. In October 1492, he led a large army of 26,000 men, which landed in Calais (England's last possession on the Continent), and proceeded to advance on the port of Boulogne and then laid siege to it. The **cause of this war** was the appearance of Perkin Warbeck in 1491 and the welcome he received at the French court (see Section 5, pages 104–106). Unable to resist this opportunity, the French government welcomed young Warbeck as though he were Richard IV and allowed him to live honourably at court. Polydore Vergil later recalled in 1513 that some people thought that the real motive for the English invasion was financial. Henry's greed for money, they claimed, had led him to emulate Edward IV's invasion of France in 1475 to re-secure the French pension granted to Edward but which had lapsed since his death.

Luckily for Henry, the French were quick to offer terms. As it was late in the campaigning season, it is doubtful whether the English would have been able to take Boulogne and, if they did, Henry might well have become concerned at the spiralling costs involved in maintaining it. Exactly the same problem with Boulogne occurred late in the reign of Henry VIII and the outcome was the humiliating sale of the port back to France by the Duke of Northumberland, since the maintenance of the English garrison and fortifications had proved ruinous to royal finances.

The Treaty of Etaples, 1492

In the peace treaty drawn up by both sides at Etaples in 1492, Henry was paid off by the French.

- The French paid his expenses in launching the invasion and restored the pension paid to Edward IV, which amounted to some £12,500 each year for the next fifteen years.
- The French also promised to abandon Perkin Warbeck and not to support pretenders to the English throne in the future.
- Henry acknowledged that Brittany was now part of France and that England must now face a potentially hostile coastline from Calais westward.

Although peace with France was secured, Henry could not be sure of French good faith. He was a French pensioner again but the future might bring about a serious worsening of Anglo–French relations.

Peace with France, 1492–1509

The fact that there was no further outbreak of war between the two countries was largely down to Henry's good fortune. At a time when the French were emerging from a long period of conflict with Burgundy and could perhaps be a greater threat to England, their interests were channelled to the south, not the north. On attaining his majority in 1492, Charles VIII, brought up on chivalrous and crusading tales, determined to lay claim to the Italian kingdom of Naples. If the best came to the best, he would use Naples as a 'springboard' for a **crusade** to recapture Jerusalem for the Christians. So, luckily for Henry VII, the French were keen to buy off the English late in 1492 because they wanted to invade Italy. Even more fortunate for Henry was the fact that the French conquest of Naples in 1494 set off a whole series of battles known as the **Italian Wars,** which would guarantee hostility between France and Spain for most of the period up to the **Treaty of Cambrai** in 1529. This long-term hostility between France and Spain, in turn, meant that France (and Spain for that matter) wanted England as a friend or at least a neutral power. For the rest of the reign, the threat from France was lifted and Henry should have breathed a big sigh of relief.

Why did Henry continue to fear France?

However, Henry continued to engage in furious diplomacy with the likes of Spain and the Low Countries, which showed up his insecurity. By negotiating alliances with these powers, he risked bringing about the main thing he feared, namely a French invasion of England. In particular, Henry was keen on an alliance with Spain and, when **Philip the Fair of Burgundy married Joanna of Castile**, the heir to the throne of Castile, in 1496, there was the possibility of building up a three-way alliance with them against France.

- In 1496, Henry VII became an associate member of the **League of Venice** against France.
- Also in the late 1490s, Henry finally allied himself with Spain (1499) and married his eldest son, Prince Arthur, to Catherine of Aragon (1501).

However, these moves against France need to be looked at critically. It is not clear that playing a part in an alliance system against France was necessarily in England's best interests. Spain and the Low Countries were unlikely to help England if the French should invade. With French attention elsewhere, Henry might have done better to remain on friendly terms with France by marrying his heir (and even himself after Elizabeth of York's death in 1503) to a French princess.

Catherine of Aragon (oil on panel by Michiel Sittow, 1503/4).

- Alliance with France was the best way to guarantee security at home. As a number of important deaths shipwrecked Henry's anti-French diplomacy by 1506, (Prince Arthur in 1502, Isabella of Castile in 1504 and Philip the Fair of Burgundy in 1506), Henry did indeed contemplate a marriage with **Margaret of Angoulême**, who was the sister of the heir to the French throne. However, this marriage never went beyond the early planning stage and one must conclude that Henry, prematurely ageing and often unwell, missed the chance to secure his dynasty with a French match.

- Certainly, when the Pope, Louis XII of France, the Emperor Maximilian, Ferdinand (now effectively ruling Castile as well as Aragon) and the Archduke Charles (nominal ruler of the Low Countries at the age of eight!) all signed up to the **League of Cambrai** in 1508, Henry Tudor was notable by his absence. Perhaps Henry would have done better to abandon the diplomacy with Spain and the Habsburgs and to concentrate his energies more exclusively on an alliance with his next-door neighbour, Scotland.

Relations with Scotland

Friendship at first

The possibility of war with France, which continued to overshadow the reign, meant that Henry needed to take decisive action to neutralise France's normal ally against England: Scotland. Luckily for Henry, the Scottish threat was not that great. The Scots had suffered defeat at the hands of Richard of Gloucester in 1482 and had lost Berwick-upon-Tweed to the English. At the same time, the Scots king, James III, was a rather ineffectual ruler and had to face serious internal unrest and opposition from his brother, the Duke of Albany. In 1486, Scotland signed a three-year truce with England. Luckily for Henry VII, the internal unrest and political instability in Scotland resulted in the Battle of Sauchieburn, which, in turn, led to James III's murder in 1488 and the succession of his young son, James IV (aged fifteen), to the Scottish throne.

Worsening relations, 1488–97

James IV and his advisers were more hostile to England than James III. Indeed, one of the reasons for their hostility to James III's regime had been his desire for good relations with both Edward IV and Henry VII.

- As early as November 1488, the new King of Scotland had received a number of English Yorkist visitors and was apparently on good terms with that arch-Yorkist conspirator, Margaret of Burgundy.

King James IV of Scotland.

- In the summer of 1491, James made a treaty with France, thus renewing the 'auld alliance' between the two countries and Scotland's traditional alliance with the enemy of England. The treaty committed James to invade England if Henry VII should invade France and likewise offered Scotland French help if the English should strike north.
- Although Henry VII then expended much energy in negotiating a truce with Scotland in 1492 (the same year as he made peace with France at Etaples), this truce was torn up in 1495. In that year, Perkin Warbeck appeared on the scene, and the Scots regime welcomed him with open arms. He was married to Lady Catherine Gordon (James IV's cousin) and was given Scottish troops for his ill-fated invasion of England in September 1496. Although the invasion was a complete failure, the Scots danger was so real to Henry that he caused a massive tax strike in the West Country (the Cornish Rising of 1497) when he tried to raise unprecedented taxes for war against the Scots.

Peace and alliance, Ayton, 1502

Luckily for Henry, James IV became tired of supporting Warbeck and began to give serious consideration to Henry VII's offer of an alliance backed by a marriage between James, who was still only 24, and Henry's eldest daughter, **Princess Margaret** (aged only eight in 1497).

- Because of her youth, of course, such a marriage had to be delayed, but the lure of an alliance, together with Bishop Foxe's excellent negotiating skills, meant that

James signed a seven-year truce in 1497 at Ayton.
- This was renewed in 1499 and became a formal Peace Treaty of Ayton in 1502. By this treaty, both sides agreed not to support claimants to each other's throne and James IV promised to marry Princess Margaret.
- The next year, Margaret, still only thirteen, was accompanied to the Scots border amid much pomp and circumstance. Her progress northwards was a royal progress. She called in on the grandmother after whom she was named, Lady Margaret Beaufort, at Collyweston, before spending several days in York as the guest of the Earl of Northumberland. She was then escorted all the way to Edinburgh by the Earl and Countess of Surrey and handed over to her future husband, James IV.
- James and Margaret were married in August 1503 and, as often happened in diplomatic marriages of this kind, there was some disparity in their ages: James was 30, while his bride was not yet fourteen! As it happened, the marriage was successful in terms of the good relations between the two and in terms of the production of an heir (James V).
- The marriage guaranteed that Scotland would not be a threat to England for the rest of the reign. Only when Henry VIII invaded France in 1513 would the 'auld alliance' flourish once more, though it would result in James IV's death and an English regency under Queen Margaret.

Assessment

Henry VII has often been praised for his success in neutralising the Scottish threat but this tends to ignore three key points.

- First, the threat from Scotland was not very grave but there was a Scottish invasion of England and hostile relations between the two kingdoms lasted for a whole decade. A more successful monarch might have established better relations sooner than Henry VII did.
- Second, Henry's offer of a marriage alliance with the Scots was entirely traditional: Edward IV had offered his infant daughter, Cecily, to the future James IV.
- Third, Henry overestimated the threat from Scotland and caused massive unrest in his own kingdom, in the shape of the Cornish Rising of 1497, which underscored

his precarious hold on power and the lukewarm loyalty of his leading subjects to the regime.

So, though his policy towards Scotland was eventually successful, this was no great achievement on Henry's part. French interest in Italy once again diminished its interest in Scotland, so the threat from Scotland was actually limited. As always, Scotland was just too far from London to be a real threat to the English government.

Relations with Spain

The prospect of a Spanish alliance

Six years before Henry's triumph at Bosworth, Ferdinand of Aragon succeeded his father, John II, as King of Aragon. Since he was married to Isabella, who had been Queen of Castile since 1474, this meant that Ferdinand and Isabella now ruled the vast majority of what is now modern-day Spain.

- For Henry VII, this newly united kingdom represented an excellent counterweight to France, and the keystone of his diplomacy, for much of his reign, was to be an Anglo–Spanish alliance.
- For the Spanish, too, an alliance with England would be a useful means of blocking the pretensions of France. The Spanish resident ambassador, de Puebla, was also very keen on the alliance and his influence over Henry grew as the negotiations proceeded.

Negotiations with Spain began in 1488 and led to the Treaty of Medina del Campo in 1489. This treaty outlined the friendship between the two countries, made the usual promises about not supporting pretenders and described a projected marriage alliance between Prince Arthur, who was aged three at the time, and Princess Catherine of Aragon, who was the same age.

The problem, as with the proposed Scottish alliance, was that the children were so young that no worthwhile treaty could be made for many years until the actual marriage took place. Nonetheless, this imposed delay also meant that Henry could throw himself into bouts of further negotiations with the Spanish, especially after the French triumphs in Italy.

- A new Anglo–Spanish treaty was drawn up in 1496 confirming that the marriage was still 'on' and this treaty was itself then officially ratified by Henry in 1497.
- Two years later, Catherine was married by proxy to Prince Arthur: that is, Catherine was not present at the ceremony but her place was taken by the Spanish ambassador.
- A full treaty of alliance was also drawn up in 1499 and this agreement may have spelt doom for Edward, Earl of Warwick and Perkin Warbeck. When it came to it, the Spanish did not wish to send their princess to marry a man whose father might be overthrown.
- So it was that in late 1501, **Princess Catherine** (not yet sixteen) was finally **married to her equally young bridegroom, Prince Arthur**.

How did the alliance end?

Yet by April 1502, the alliance was in disarray when Arthur died at Ludlow. After waiting a few weeks to ensure that Catherine was not pregnant (a son would have been heir to the English throne), it became clear that the alliance was in ruins. Henry agreed that his next son, Henry, might marry Catherine and the betrothal took place in June 1503 even though Prince Henry was still only a boy of twelve.

- In 1504, the undermining of the Anglo–Spanish alliance was compounded by the death of Catherine's mother, Queen Isabella. Her death meant that Spain itself was once more disunited.
- The new Queen of Castile was Catherine's elder sister, Joanna, who was married to Philip the Fair of Burgundy. However, in their absence, Ferdinand of Aragon (Isabella's husband) had claimed the regency of Castile for himself. So now Philip and Joanna were at odds with Ferdinand, who wished to continue ruling the whole of Spain.
- The divisions in Spain saw Ferdinand allying with his old enemy, France, in the **Treaty of Blois** of 1504, which bolstered his position in Spain.
- Meanwhile, Henry VII was moving away from his alliance with Spain and towards an alliance with the Habsburgs, who were now in a position to rule the Low Countries, Germany and Castile.

KEY EVENT

The marriage of Arthur and Catherine (1501) The marriage was a magnificent affair celebrated in St Paul's Cathedral with the Archbishop of Canterbury performing the ceremony. Catherine was escorted up the aisle by Arthur's younger brother, Henry, little guessing that she would marry him eight years later. Afterwards, there were feasts, sports and various entertainments as Henry VII sought to impress everyone with his wealth and power.

KEY TERM

Treaty of Blois (1504) Spain and France were fighting in Naples by 1502, in arguments over the partition (division) of the kingdom between their two countries. By 1504, Louis XII was forced to concede Spanish control over the whole of Naples.

- Philip the Fair's death late in 1506 added a further twist to a complicated tale, as this event left his son, Charles, as heir to Castile and his wife, Joanna, as a mad woman (apparently thrown into insanity by the sudden and unexpected demise of her husband).
- Under these circumstances, Ferdinand regained control of Spain, but the deaths of Isabella and Philip and the madness of Joanna showed up the limited value of Henry's much coveted and long worked-for alliance with Spain.

Failure of a new Spanish match

When Arthur died, the Spanish were apparently keen to renew the alliance by projecting a new marriage between Catherine and the new heir to the English throne, Henry, Duke of York.

- Ferdinand and Isabella agreed to this in 1503 because they, King Henry and Prince Henry were assured that the marriage between Arthur and Catherine had not been consummated, which made it easier to obtain a **papal dispensation** to allow Catherine to marry her brother-in-law.
- The day before his fourteenth birthday in 1505, however, Prince Henry, egged on by his father, publicly protested against the proposed marriage. This was because Henry VII's desire for a Habsburg alliance meant that Catherine of Aragon was of little value to him.
- In addition, there were long-standing arguments about the payment of **Catherine's dowry** for the marriage with Arthur, let alone dowry payments for the new marriage! It had been agreed by the original marriage treaty that Spain would pay Henry VII 200,000 crowns. Now the Spanish demanded the return of the money already paid on the basis that the marriage had not been consummated and was therefore not a true marriage.
- Henry VII, on the other hand, demanded that the dowry be paid in full and that a new dowry would be payable if Catherine wished to marry Prince Henry. For several years these arguments also meant that Ferdinand and Henry argued about who should pay for the princess' upkeep in London. It is much to Henry VII's shame that his miserly attitude allowed his one-time daughter-in-law to be treated in such a shabby way.

KEY TERMS

Papal dispensation
Special permission granted by the Pope to allow people to marry within what was called 'the prohibited degree'. Normally, a man could not marry his brother's widow because the bride and groom were related by blood. However, since the marriage between Arthur and Catherine had not been consummated (they had not had sex), the Pope could more easily allow Catherine's second marriage to Prince Henry. The Pope's dispensation was to be at the heart of Henry VIII's break with Rome in the 1530s.

Catherine's dowry It was traditional at this time for a prospective bride to bring money and goods with her when she married her husband and this was called her dowry. At the level of prince and princess, the sums involved could be considerable and would be an important part of the marriage treaty.

Catherine's debts grew and, amid the continuing recriminations and accusations, there seemed no chance of her marrying Prince Henry.

- The Spanish alliance, so central to Henry's plans after 1488, was in ruins.

Relations with the Low Countries

Background

The Low Countries were a collection of seventeen semi-autonomous provinces ruled over by the Duke of Burgundy. With the death of Charles the Bold in 1477, his daughter and heir, Mary, was married to Maximilian von Habsburg, the ruler of Austria, who would become Holy Roman Emperor in 1493. With the rising power of the Habsburgs on his doorstep and anxious to curb the support given to pretenders by the Yorkist Margaret of Burgundy (widow of Charles the Bold), Henry VII began to explore the possibility of an alliance in that direction.

Trade wars

Henry, at first, allied himself with Maximilian in 1489, when the two of them tried unsuccessfully to stop the French takeover of Brittany. After that, relations became strained when Maximilian recognised Perkin Warbeck as Richard IV and backed Margaret of Burgundy's plans to support the pretender against Henry. The king's response was to impose a **trade embargo** on the Low Countries. A proclamation in late 1493 forbade English merchants from trading with the Low Countries and especially the growing **entrepôt** of Antwerp. Maximilian responded with a counter-embargo of May 1494, which meant a full-blown trade war with England's main trading outlet on the Continent.

Normal trade relations were finally restored by the treaty known as the Intercursus Magnus in 1496.

- This allowed English merchants to trade with the Low Countries (except Flanders), paying the normal customs dues operative over the last 50 years.
- In addition, it included the usual clauses about not harbouring the other's rebels.

However, Maximilian's son, Philip the Fair, who ruled the Low Countries after his father's elevation to the post of Holy Roman Emperor in 1493, then imposed a new import duty on cloth, which saw trade with England again dry up until the autumn of 1498. This, in turn, meant that the treaty was not finally confirmed until May 1499, by which time Perkin Warbeck was in the Tower and soon to be executed. The serious disruption to England's trade with the Low Countries cost the country and the merchants dear and gives the lie to the old view that Henry VII encouraged trade. In terms of diplomatic arguments, the king was quite prepared to sacrifice England's trading interests in pursuit of his own political and diplomatic agenda.

A Habsburg alliance?

While trade disagreements kept England and the Low Countries apart, Henry was keen to pursue closer political ties with the Habsburgs.

- Philip the Fair had married Joanna of Castile in 1496, which opened up the prospect of a three-way (Habsburgs/England/Spain) alliance against the aggressive power of France.
- In 1500, Henry VII met Philip in person in Calais amid much feastings. By 1505, Henry was so keen on a Burgundian alliance that he lent Philip £138,000 to help him in his bid to claim Castile now that Isabella had died leaving his wife, Joanna, as heir.
- The next year fate took a hand in sealing the Anglo–Burgundian alliance. While en route for Castile to take charge of their new kingdom, Philip and Joanna were shipwrecked off the Dorset coast and became Henry's unexpected guests for the next three months. Henry put on the style and the pageantry in order to get Philip to agree to a new alliance in the Treaty of Windsor of 1506.
- This treaty included a new trade treaty, the so-called **Intercursus Malus** (which was never ratified because of Philip's death the same year) together with Philip's agreement to hand over Edmund de la Pole, the Yorkist pretender, currently in exile in the Low Countries. In addition, the Treaty of Windsor outlined two more marriages to seal the Tudor–Habsburg alliance, neither of which came to fruition. Henry himself was to marry

KEY TERM

Intercursus Malus (1506)
'The bad trade treaty' was so called by the Flemish merchants because its provisions seemed to them to favour English merchants at their expense.

Philip's sister, Margaret, who was regent in the Low Countries, and Henry's younger daughter, Mary, might marry the Archduke Charles, Philip's elder son. Once again, this serves to remind us how many diplomatic plans and initiatives came to nothing.

Dissolution of the alliance

However, no sooner was Henry hitched to the Habsburgs than Philip himself died suddenly a few months later, unravelling all of Henry's intensive diplomacy. His anti-Ferdinand policy had failed miserably as Ferdinand (with his daughter, Joanna, declared mad) became regent of Castile, while his agreements with the Low Countries lapsed with Philip's death. Once again, Henry's foreign policy had been less than successful.

Relations with Ireland

Background

As far as Henry VII was concerned, Ireland was not really a foreign country at all. Henry II (ruled 1154–89) had conferred the title of Lord of Ireland on his son, John, in 1177 and, when he became King John in 1199, his sovereignty over Ireland was confirmed. In reality, however, Ireland was a foreign land. The king's authority actually stretched no further than a small area around Dublin known as the Pale and the borders of the Pale itself were far from fixed.

Henry VII's immediate problems with Ireland stretched back to the reign of Henry VI.

- Henry VI had appointed Richard, Duke of York as lord lieutenant in Ireland in 1447. His son, Clarence, was born in Dublin and the duke had extensive estates in the country. This all meant that the Yorkist pretenders received staunch support from the Irish.
- The most powerful Irish lord throughout Henry's reign was Gerald FitzGerald, Earl of Kildare, who held extensive lands in the **kingdom of Leinster** just outside the Pale. In 1486, he refused to come to England to advise Henry on the Irish situation and in the next year he masterminded the Simnel rebellion in Ireland, which saw the boy crowned as Edward VI in Dublin Cathedral. Simnel made Kildare lord lieutenant of Ireland but this

KEY TERM

Kingdom of Leinster At this time, Ireland was divided into four kingdoms called Leinster (south-east), Connaught (west), Ulster (north) and Munster (south-west).

theoretical elevation proved short-lived, as Simnel was defeated at the Battle of Stoke in 1487.

English intervention in Ireland

In the aftermath of Stoke, Henry sent Sir Richard Edgecombe to Ireland with a small force of 500 men. He landed at Kinsale in June 1488 but was not in a strong position. Kildare and the other lords refused to sign bonds for future good behaviour but were prepared to acknowledge Henry VII as their king and overlord. When Edgecombe left after less than a month, Kildare was confirmed in his office as the king's deputy in Ireland, apparently unscathed after his attempt to overthrow the first Tudor.

However, Kildare's attitude to Yorkist pretenders was now more circumspect. He gave no overt support to Perkin Warbeck when he arrived in Ireland in 1491, but Henry remained suspicious and, allying himself with other Irish lords, dismissed Kildare from office in December 1491, when the king raised Irish troops to arrest and imprison delinquents. However, the Irishmen Henry appointed in Kildare's place – notably Walter FitzSimons, Archbishop of Dublin – were unable to stand up to the king's former deputy. By 1488, however, Kildare decided to give bonds for future good behaviour and went to England to consult with the king.

Poynings' Law

Kildare remained in England until 1494, when he returned to Ireland, accompanied by Sir Edward Poynings and an English force of 700 men. Poynings, an experienced soldier and statesman, was the king's new deputy.

His first task was to conquer Ulster where rebellion was commonplace. In this task he failed. Slightly more successful was **Poynings' Law**. This was one of 49 Acts passed in the Irish Parliament, which met at Drogheda between December 1494 and April 1495. This Act merely stated that no Irish Parliament could be called without the king's approval and it was aimed at undermining Irish support for Warbeck. In reality, however, the Irish lords saw little value in supporting this pretender, since this was likely to antagonise the king. What they wanted was a king who left them alone to get on with their feuding, not one who sent soldiers to Ireland. And when Poynings departed in 1495, they got what they wanted. They gave up supporting the Yorkists and Henry responded by appointing Kildare as lord deputy once again in August 1496 and passing a general pardon for all those who had supported Warbeck. Kildare remained in office until Henry VIII's reign and was allowed to summon an Irish Parliament in 1498.

Henry's limited achievement in Ireland

Overall, Henry had achieved a limited success in Ireland. Eventually, he had persuaded the Irish lords to give up their support for the Yorkists. However, he had done nothing to increase the effectiveness of English rule in the Pale, let alone the rest of Ireland. Much of the land was in the thrall of anarchic contending tribal groups and much of the rest was under the sway of two or three great families, who owed no more than nominal allegiance to the English Crown. Given Henry's insecurity at home and the very limited military forces he could dispatch to Ireland, he could not really hope to achieve much more.

Assessment of foreign policy

Was it a policy?

One might argue that all the twists and turns in England's relations with foreign powers during Henry's reign meant that there was no policy at all. Henry certainly had some fixed aims, but the word 'policy' implies a clarity of purpose, which Henry did not and could not have. No monarchs of the period could command events; all reacted to the ever-changing kaleidoscope of international relations. No one could be sure that diplomatic negotiations were being carried on in good faith, since all the countries sought their own advantage. In this way, diplomatic relations and negotiations were certainly intense but it is not clear that they were ever very successful.

Aims of foreign policy

Henry's aims in his dealings with foreign powers were clear enough and were entirely traditional. Ever since the English expulsion from France in 1453, the aims of foreign policy had been fairly consistent. These were:

- to protect the realm from invasion – particularly important since Henry was a usurper and there were many Yorkist plots to overthrow him
- to build up relations with foreign powers to the point where alliances could be made, which would give the new Tudor dynasty recognition in Europe
- to play a part in European affairs
- to protect and possibly improve trade with the Continent.

Apparent success?

Given these aims, how successful was Henry VII? At first glance, he seems to have been very successful, provided one looks at events from the point of view of 1509. Foreign policy had helped to crush the threat from the pretenders, Henry had made a marriage alliance with Scotland and had quelled the threat from Ireland. Most other royal houses wished to negotiate with Henry and wanted his friendship or neutrality; trade with France and the Low Countries had increased in volume and value.

Limitations of Henry's success

However, on closer inspection, this analysis seems too rosy and too much coloured by hindsight.

- Foreign affairs were not so much the relations between countries as the relations between a small group of families. Alliances depended on marriages between these families and relations between them were always at the mercy of births, marriages and deaths. The deaths of Arthur of England, Isabella of Castile and Philip of Burgundy profoundly altered Henry's policy and left it in ruins.
- Foreign powers did back Lambert Simnel in 1487 (Ireland, Burgundy) and Perkin Warbeck (France, Burgundy, Scotland) and, despite Henry's best endeavours, there was no guarantee that they would not do so again. Philip of Burgundy was still sheltering Edmund de la Pole in 1506. Only Philip's shipwreck near Weymouth in that year meant that he agreed to hand over the senior Yorkist claimant to King Henry.
- This event and several others indicate that Henry's apparent success depended on good fortune. Luckily for him, the French were unwilling to fight England in 1492. Any serious campaign by the English in France was likely to prove disastrous, since England's military strength was based on *ad hoc* rather than standing armies. Even more

fortunate was France's preoccupation with Italy after 1493. This meant that there was no real danger of a full-blown French invasion of England, despite Henry's anti-French stance in foreign affairs.

It is also clear that, in many ways, Henry's foreign policy, far from strengthening England in Europe, merely served to highlight residual weaknesses.

- Henry was forced to abandon Brittany and became a French pensioner.
- His much-vaunted Spanish alliance was no sooner cemented than it was broken apart by the deaths of Arthur and Isabella.
- His alliance with Scotland was too long in coming and was probably unnecessary given the limited strength of the Scots without French backing.
- The Intercursus Malus and alliance with Burgundy fell through when Philip of Burgundy died. Henry also failed to take advantage of his widower status after 1503 to contract a new marriage with a foreign power.
- England's military weakness also meant that it was not seen as a major player in Europe. The Spanish raised great armies to conquer Granada between 1482 and 1492. Spain and France, and even the Italian city-states, raised great armies to fight in the Italian Wars. England invaded France once and did no fighting at all. The fact that England did not join the League of Cambrai in 1508 underlined the possibility that England was something of an irrelevance in European diplomacy.
- Henry's foreign policy was also too expensive. He spent vast sums in pursuing the quest for a Burgundian alliance, and he spent vast sums trying to protect England from a very small-scale Scottish threat.
- The reality is that Henry's foreign policy was the foreign policy of a usurper. His desperate search for the recognition of his family led to diplomacy of a peculiar intensity and the king's continuing insecurity, even after 1500, cost the country dear. He over-reacted to perceived threats and overspent accordingly.
- By comparison, Edward IV's diplomacy in his second reign seems rather lazy. After his successful invasion of France in 1475, foreign affairs seemed to take up little time. The kingdom and the king were secure. This was not the case with Henry VII. Partly because of deaths in his own family and because he was a pretender, Henry

continued to worry and those worries mounted as the years went by.

- At the same time, it is not clear that foreign marriages, which Henry promoted for his children, were necessarily beneficial.
  - Henry VII, Edward IV and Richard III had all married within the kingdom and were none the worse for that. Henry's marriage to Elizabeth of York indeed was vital to his regime.
  - The previous foreign queen had been Margaret of Anjou, a formidable character, who did much to foment and continue the instability of her husband's and Edward IV's reigns.
  - At the time of Princess Margaret's proposed marriage to James IV of Scotland, many of Henry's advisers were very much against the match. They claimed, somewhat prophetically, that such a match might later make a Scotsman king of England. This was exactly what happened when Queen Elizabeth, Henry VII's granddaughter, died in 1603. King James VI of Scotland succeeded to the English throne, transforming himself into James I of England because he was Margaret Tudor's great-grandson.
- Henry's foreign policy was also too fearful. France, Spain and the Low Countries had good reason to fear each other because they all had difficult and often ill-defined land borders to defend. England, protected by the Channel, could afford to be rather more isolationist and Henry could have spent his money building up his defences at home – military and naval – rather than spending it on uncertain diplomacy and unhelpful alliances.

The wrong alliance?

This begs the question of whether Henry VII actually chose the wrong ally. In general terms, he was pro-Spanish and sought good relations with the Low Countries, while keeping France at a distance. It is clear, in retrospect, that he might have been better advised to making an alliance with France the cornerstone of his foreign policy.

- France was his natural ally, since the French government funded his successful expedition to England in 1485.

- Henry's truce with France in the early years of the reign meant that Simnel got no support from the French.
- Henry's aid to the lost cause of Brittany and his treaty with Spain in 1489 (Medina del Campo) meant that the French supported Perkin Warbeck.
- Henry's pursuit of a Spanish alliance in the 1490s encouraged the French to stir up Scotland against him and the Scots backed Warbeck in 1495–6.
- Only the French were strong enough to back a successful pretender against Henry. His continuing friendship towards Spain and the Habsburg Netherlands meant that he always risked French hostility.
- The Spanish alliance was short-lived and brought Henry no political or diplomatic advantage. The Spanish would not help Henry if there were a French invasion of England.
- Henry's diplomacy failed anyway as the Low Countries continued to shelter Edmund de la Pole.

By contrast, it can be argued that the French would have been keen on an English alliance while they invaded Italy and their support for Henry would keep him much more secure than the Spanish alliance ever would. In addition, friendship with France would mean friendship with Scotland. So did Henry VII choose the wrong ally?

SUMMARY QUESTIONS

1 What were the main characteristics of England's relations with France during the reign of Henry VII?

2 Why was Henry VII more successful in his relations with Scotland than in his relations with France?

3 To what extent, if at all, can England's foreign policy, 1485–1509, be described as a success?

4 'In the reign of Henry VII, England remained a weak power, pursuing policies towards other countries that were expensive and largely unnecessary.' To what extent do you agree with this judgement?

SECTION 9

1509–13: HENRY VII'S REIGN IN CONTEXT: THE LIMITS OF HIS ACHIEVEMENTS

> **To what extent was Henry VII's regime destroyed by 1513?**

KEY POINTS

- With Henry VII's death, the nature of English government changed.
- The nobility regained the political influence denied them under Henry VII.
- Empson and Dudley were executed.
- Henry VIII was far less interested in government and administration than his father. This led to the advent of a chief minister (Thomas Wolsey) after 1513.
- Henry VIII decided to make war on France.

TIMELINE

1509 Death of Henry VII. Accession of Henry VIII. Arrest of Empson and Dudley.

1510 Executions of Empson and Dudley.

1511 Henry VIII becomes part of a Holy League against France.

1512 Pope Julius II proclaims that Louis XII of France is deposed in favour of Henry VIII. English expedition to Aquitaine, south-west France.

1513 Execution of Edmund de la Pole. Henry VIII invades France. Captures Thérouanne and Tournai. English forces under the Earl of Surrey defeat the Scots at the Battle of Flodden. James IV of Scotland killed, leaving Queen Margaret Tudor as regent for infant James V.

OVERVIEW

Henry VII's death

Henry VII died in his bed on 21 April 1509. The

KEY THEME

Henry VII died When William, Lord Mountjoy heard of Henry VII's death, he could barely contain his excitement. 'Heaven and earth rejoice,' he wrote, 'everything is full of milk and honey and nectar. Avarice has fled the country. Our king is not after gold, or gems, or precious metals, but virtue, glory, immortality.'

---

evidence of his death mask (still housed near his tomb in Westminster Abbey) suggests that he was finally carried off by a stroke. He had not been well for several years. His eyesight was failing and his life had been feared for in 1507 and 1508. Overworked and isolated, the king had aged prematurely. He was just 52 years old when he died, having reigned for 23 years and eight months. The fact that he died in his bed is taken as a great achievement, as is the fact that there was then a smooth succession, since his seventeen-year-old son now

Effigy of Henry VII in Westminster Abbey.

became Henry VIII. Death in bed and a smooth succession seemed a long way off for much of the reign, as he and his dynasty were threatened by opposition from pretenders, by foreign alliances, which failed, and by the premature deaths of his wife and eldest son.

The struggle for power

Yet the smooth transfer of power to Henry VIII masked a serious power struggle within the regime. Henry's death was kept secret for two days. The reason for the secrecy was an aristocratic coup, led probably by the Earl of Oxford, against Henry's 'new men'. During those two days, the aristocrats took charge of the young Henry and persuaded him of the need for reform.

- Henry VII's regime had been increasingly unpopular in its last years and his political opponents celebrated his death.
- The dismantling of the old regime proceeded apace. While the new king took up his quarters in the Tower of London, two leading peers – the Earl of Oxford and **Edward Stafford, Duke of Buckingham** – called together a council made up mainly of peers to take charge of affairs.
- These men resolved that the new king (who was only seventeen) should be brought up 'in all pleasure, for

Edward Stafford, Duke of Buckingham (1478–1521)
Son of Henry, Duke of Buckingham, (executed by Richard III in 1483) he succeeded to the title as a minor and the king's ward. Enmeshed in bonds and recognisances by the unscrupulous Henry VII, he looked for better times under Henry VIII. He was made lord high constable and lord high steward as well as a privy councillor. However, his hostility to Cardinal Wolsey brought him down in 1521, when he was executed on bogus charges of treason. His problem was that, by birth, he still had a better claim to the throne than Henry VIII!

otherwise he should grow too hard amongst his subjects
as the king his father did'. In other words, the peers
were resolved that the new king should not be like the
old king. He would not govern the realm in the
oppressive way his father had: instead he would devote
himself to princely pastimes and the pursuit of glory
and fame.

The end of the old order

The group of men who became most intimate with the
new king were all peers. The Earl of Wiltshire was there,
along with his elder brother, the Duke of Buckingham.
Also on the scene for jousting and sports of all kinds were
Sir Edward Howard, second son of the Earl of Surrey; Sir
Thomas Knyvet, who had married Surrey's eldest daughter;
and **Sir Thomas Boleyn**, who had married the earl's
second daughter. Thomas Grey, restored to his original title
of Marquis of Dorset, Henry Bourchier, Earl of Essex, and
Sir Edward Neville were likewise men of noble birth who
now found themselves places in the new king's circle of
friends.

Character of Henry VIII

The change at court after Henry VII's death could not have
been more marked. While Henry VII fretted over his
papers, Henry VIII wrote music, including the famous
song *Pastime With Good Company*. This little number
summed up the new king's philosophy:

> *Hunt, sing and dance,*
> *My heart is set*
> *All goodly sport*
> *To my comfort*
> *Who shall me let?* [Who shall prevent me?]

Henry VIII, like many of the aristocratic young men who
now rushed to court, had been well educated, rather more
so than his father. He was intellectually able and enjoyed
reading books and being a patron of the so-called **New
Learning**. At the same time, he had chaffed under the
strict regime in which he had been brought up: a regime
that got stricter after the death of his brother, Arthur. He
was surrounded by tutors and learned men, but was not
allowed to enjoy sports such as jousting, which might

prove dangerous. It is not difficult to imagine that young Henry rather resented his father and was determined to both enjoy himself and to remodel the government of the kingdom when his father died.

Power of Henry VIII

That the new king was willing to take on this new role is not hard to explain. His father had always been an outsider, a usurper who won the Crown by chance of battle, a ruler who distrusted the nobility and who faced serious challenges to his authority. Henry VIII, by contrast, had been brought up to be king.

Portrait of Henry VIII in early manhood (c.1520).

- Yorkists and Lancastrians supported him, as he represented the joining of those two families.
- By inclination and character, he wanted to impress. He loved court ceremony and pageantry, hunting and hawking, feasting and revelling.
- Henry VII had remained aloof and cut off from his subjects. Henry VIII wanted to be the centre of attention. This was underpinned by the new king's size. Taking after his grandfather, Edward IV, he was well over six feet tall – always an imposing figure compared to his father.

Attacks on the old regime

Immediately, the new king and his noble councillors attacked the old regime.

- Empson and Dudley, hated architects of the Council Learned in the Law, were arrested and later executed for treason even though there was no real evidence against them.
- Many of the bonds by which Henry VII had trapped the nobility and other landowners were cancelled. Henry VIII claimed that these bonds were made 'contrary to law, reason and good conscience, to the manifest charge and peril of the soul of our late father'.
- The new king also summoned a Great Council of peers, which immediately set up special commissions all across the country to hear and determine complaints against the old regime. This was unprecedented.
- At the same time, Henry, probably urged on by the leading noblemen, determined to marry Catherine of Aragon. His father had put off the marriage and treated

his widowed daughter-in-law appallingly. Now the young Henry would set the record straight. He would marry Catherine amid much pomp and ceremony and then he would be at the centre of a splendid coronation for both himself and his new queen.

Changing foreign policy

The Spanish marriage also signalled a major change in foreign policy. The new king was determined to renew England's Hundred Years' War against France in earnest. He wished to put together a coalition of forces – including Catherine's father, Ferdinand of Spain – which would reassert Henry's claim to the French throne. This policy of all-out war with France did not win favour with some of the king's councillors, particularly those, like Bishop Fox, who had been inherited from the old regime. However, the king, backed by the nobility, got his own way. Another Great Council was convened in 1511, which agreed on an English expedition to Aquitaine (south-west France), which had once been English, the next year.

The invasion of France, 1513

Though the expedition of 1512 was a total failure, English honour was at stake and, in the next year, Henry VIII personally led a huge English invasion of France. With an enormous army of 30,000 men, raised and led by his nobles, Henry enjoyed real success. The towns of Tournai and Thérouanne were captured. French armies were fighting in Italy, so they could only send a small force against the English. When they engaged the English forces, they were overwhelmed in what was called the Battle of the Spurs. For Henry, the expedition became something of a royal progress. By fortifying Tournai, he had built a bridgehead for further expeditions to France and he was confident of eventual victory.

Victory over the Scots, 1513

At the same time, Henry's forces, under the Earl of Surrey, triumphed against the Scots. The 'auld enemy' had dared to invade England while Henry was away but were decisively beaten at the Battle of Flodden in 1513. Even better for Henry was the fact that his brother-in-law, James IV, was killed and the Scots' regency, for his son, James V, was in the hands of the boy's mother – one Margaret Tudor!

All this aggressive foreign policy was proving very successful and was a refreshing change from the tortuous diplomacy and feeble foreign policy of his father. Henry VIII, of course, needed little encouragement to embark on this kind of effort and it was the nobility who once again reaped the rewards. With the realm at peace with itself, there was little else for self-respecting noblemen to do than to bash the French and the Scots.

The nobles rewarded

The peers were still a military caste and the advent of young noblemen, who had full access to the king at court, meant that they shared the king's ideas on chivalry and glory in a foreign field. These were the men who shared the king's love of sports and outdoor pursuits and, when victory was won, they received their rewards. The Earl of Surrey and **Charles Brandon** were elevated to duchies (Norfolk and Suffolk, respectively). Sir Charles Somerset was made Earl of Worcester and Sir Edward Stanley became Lord Mounteagle.

The new power of the nobility was also illustrated by the return to power of nobles with Yorkist ancestry. Henry VII's suspicions had kept them weak and robbed them of political power. Now the new king sought to re-invigorate his nobility as a whole by ensuring that none of the old suspicions remained.

- The Greys and Courtenays, who had strong links to Edward IV and the Yorkists, were restored to their lands and titles.
- **Margaret Plantagenet**, daughter of the Duke of Clarence and sister of the unfortunate Edward, Earl of Warwick (executed by Henry VII), was made Countess of Salisbury and her son created Lord Montague. In doing this, Henry VIII was emphasising that he was a Yorkist as well as a Lancastrian and, as such, patron to all the nobility.
- Henry was a king who rejoiced in his own nobility and the virtues that were associated with that concept. It was all very different from the reign of Henry's father, where the nobility were treated with suspicion and fear.

Charles Brandon (1483–1545) Companion to Henry VIII from an early age, since his father had been Henry VII's standard bearer at Bosworth and had been killed by Richard III. Brandon shared Henry VIII's love of sports and military matters and went on to marry Henry's younger sister, Mary, when her first husband, Louis XII of France, died soon after their wedding. Henry elevated him to the rank of Duke of Suffolk.

Margaret Plantagenet (1473–1541) The Countess of Salisbury, she married Richard Pole and her eldest son was created Lord Montague. Later, the family fell under suspicion because of their Yorkist blood. Margaret was executed on Tower Green, aged 68.

Summary

In all these ways – in dramatic changes to the nature of government and the aims of foreign policy – Henry VII's regime was repudiated by his son and by a newly empowered nobility. Henry VIII reverted more closely to the model of medieval government similar to that of his grandfather, Edward IV, a model that his father, as a usurper, had abandoned. One further and final symbol of the end of the bad old days of insecurity also came in 1513. In that year, Henry VIII had Edmund de la Pole, the last of the Yorkist pretenders, executed. It usually ranks as a small footnote in English history but it was a vital step for Henry VIII in putting an end (in his mind once and for all) to the Yorkist attempts to retake the Crown of England. The execution of de la Pole signalled how much more secure and confident the second Tudor was compared to the first.

Henry VII's reign in context

Contemporary views of Henry VII

Historians have given Henry VII credit for establishing a new dynasty, but when he died that prospect was all in the future. In 1509, nearly all contemporaries who we hear from damned the reign with faint praise at best and overt criticism at worst.

- The lawyer and humanist Sir Thomas More, who would go on to be Chancellor of England, was in no doubt that Henry VII's regime had been oppressive. In a Latin poem for the new king's coronation, More wrote that, 'This day is the end of our slavery, the fount of our liberty; the end of sadness, the beginning of joy.' It was a remarkably daring and public condemnation of the old regime but it clearly won approval with the new men in the new regime.
- More was encouraged to give the new Henry a special presentation copy of his poem, decorated with **red and white roses**. More claimed, too, that Henry VII's reign had seen the oppression of the nobility, the overtaxing of the people and the use of informers. His poem represented a general condemnation of the old regime.

Polydore Vergil, writing a few years later, struck something of the same note. He claimed that Henry VII's virtues as a

KEY THEME

Red and white roses
Symbolised that Henry VIII was the embodiment of the union between his father (the red rose of Lancaster) and his mother (the white rose of York).

king 'were obscured latterly only by avarice, from which he suffered. This avarice is surely a bad enough vice in a private individual, whom it forever torments; in a monarch, indeed, it may be considered the worst vice, since it is harmful to everyone, and distorts those qualities of trustfulness, justice and integrity by which the state must be governed.' As a man who knew Henry VII in his later years, and who wrote up his thoughts early in the next reign, Vergil's views should be taken seriously. He claims that Henry's government lacked 'trustfulness, justice and integrity'. Another writer claimed, in relation to Henry, that 'of the three affections that tie the hearts of subject to their sovereign – love, fear and reverence; he had reverence in height, fear in good measure but so little of love ...' Henry's harsh regime meant that he was literally unloved.

The fan vaulting of Henry VII's chapel in Westminster Abbey

In 1498, Pedro de Ayala, the Spanish ambassador, informed Queen Isabella that Henry VII 'likes to be much spoken of, and to be highly appreciated by the whole world. He fails in this because he is not a great man. He spends all the time he is not in public or in his council, in writing the accounts of his expenses with his own hand.'

All this rings true of Henry. He never felt he was appreciated or loved as king because he did not act in a kingly way. He lacked a nobility of outlook, lacked presence on the public stage and devoted himself to more mundane and bureaucratic tasks. Unlike Edward IV and Henry VIII, he just did not look the part.

Henry VII's tomb
On his death, Henry was buried in the magnificent new Lady Chapel at Westminster Abbey. It had been one of the king's great building projects and he and his queen lie there to this day, beneath the magnificent fan vaulting.

Queen Mary (1516–58)
Ruled as Mary I (1553–8) and
was the daughter and only
surviving child of Henry VIII
and his first wife, Catherine of
Aragon. Mary reintroduced
Catholicism after her father
and half-brother, Edward VI
(ruled 1547–53), broke with
Rome.

**Queen Elizabeth
(1533–1603)** Succeeded
Mary I in 1558 and, as Anne
Boleyn's daughter,
reintroduced Protestantism
and the Church of England.

Originally planned as a new resting place for Henry VI, the
chapel, in fact, houses some of Henry's immediate family.
Just to the north in a side chapel lie his granddaughters,
Queen Mary and **Queen Elizabeth**, while to the south of
the king lies his mother, Margaret Beaufort, a staunch
supporter of the regime, who survived her only son by a
few months.

In the centre of the chapel lies Henry himself and his
queen. Unlike other monarchs, however, his tomb is
surrounded by a beautiful grille or fence. In death, as in
life, he remains aloof and withdrawn from his subjects. The
beautiful effigies of Henry and Elizabeth, executed in the
latest Italianate style and at great expense by Torrigiano,
cannot be seen by the passer-by. The king's magnificence in
death is lost to the world, as it was in life. As you pace
round his tomb, you cannot see him. This is perhaps a
metaphor for Henry Tudor's greatest failing. While other
kings might underpin their royal status by appearing aloof
and withdrawn, with Henry VII the trick did not really
work. He was a usurper and a usurper he remained.
Ultimately, as Ayala suspected, he was not a great man.

Conclusions

So how should the first Tudor's reign be judged? Those
who have praised Henry VII have done so on the basis that:

- he ended the Wars of the Roses
- he survived attempts to overthrow him and brought
  political stability to the kingdom
- his foreign policy was innovative and earned England
  greater security than it had known before
- he founded a new type of monarchy, which was strong
  and efficient and offered justice after years of injustice
  and corruption
- he quelled the threat from the nobility
- he founded a new royal family, which would rule for
  over 100 years: he thus laid the foundations for the
  achievements of his son (Henry VIII) and his
  granddaughter (Elizabeth I)
- his son succeeded to the throne peacefully: this was the
  first peaceful transmission of the Crown from father to
  son since 1422, therefore a great achievement.

The more pessimistic view (expressed here) was that:

- the Wars of the Roses were not a long series of civil wars at all. The worst of the fighting was over by 1461, 24 years before Henry came to the throne. Therefore the realm was not in a state of disorder or anarchy before Henry's accession. Edward IV and Richard III were both strong rulers and the power of the crown was greater in 1485 than it had been in the 1450s. The problems of the 1450's had stemmed from the weak character and eventual madness of Henry VI. Edward IV, however, had re-established the power of the Crown by the end of his reign. Opposition to Richard III came not from power-crazed noblemen but from a wide range of landowners who thought, probably correctly, that he had murdered the rightful king (Edward V) in order to grasp the Crown for himself. In other words, those Lancastrians and Yorkists who backed Henry Tudor and Elizabeth of York in 1485 and those great men who refused to fight for Richard III; all wanted to see a return to legitimate monarchical government and the overthrow of a wicked usurper. They did not act to weaken the monarchy but appealed to a vision of a strong monarchy, which was vital if the realm were to be properly governed. Equally, they believed that an illegitimate sovereign, Richard III, was bound to become a tyrant because of his usurpation of the throne.
- although Henry survived attempts to overthrow him (Lambert Simnel, John de la Pole and Perkin Warbeck), these destabilising threats to the regime went on for most of the reign. They were serious threats to Henry because he lacked support and because he had no real claim to the throne. The Yorkist threat continued to haunt Henry's regime.
- the Cornish Rising, which marched unimpeded to London in 1497, showed that Henry's government at the local level was far from effective. The apparent stability of the regime is partly the result of hindsight: because Henry VII died in his bed, we exaggerate the stability of the reign. Compared to the second reign of Edward IV (1471–83), Henry VII's reign was much less stable.
- Henry's foreign policy was very similar to that of Edward IV. The innovative Spanish alliance was

short-lived and brought little security. Much of Henry's tortuous diplomacy ended in failure. Henry was very fortunate that the one country that could undermine English security – France – became embroiled in the Italian Wars. In fact, the chances of the French, or anyone else for that matter, launching a successful invasion of England were highly remote: they lacked the motive and power to achieve this. Military and financial backing for pretenders was a serious worry not because France was strong but because Henry was an unpopular usurper.

- Henry did not develop a 'new monarchy'. He governed in his own way, within the system of government that he had inherited from his Yorkist predecessors. His regime was different from that of Edward IV, since as an insecure outsider, Henry VII took a keener interest in government matters than King Edward. In the same way, as we have seen, Henry VII's regime was also rather different from that of his son Henry VIII. Every monarch of the period governed in his own personal way.

- Henry VII's chronic distrust of a quiescent nobility led to serious problems. The medieval model of government was distorted by Henry's financial grasping and the activities of his 'new men'. Far from bringing in justice and ending corruption, Henry's regime was harsh and tyrannical, employing methods which bypassed common law and which were often illegal. This new style of government was, in fact, unnecessary, as Edward IV's successful second reign had shown. The reasons for the introduction of this oppressive regime stemmed not from Henry's security but from his chronic insecurity. In John Skelton's book *Speculum Principis* ('A Mirror For Princes'), written for the young prince Henry, the main messages were that a king can trust no one and that many previous kings had ended up being murdered. These views were very much in accord with Henry VII's thinking. The Crown, which he won by violent means, always sat uneasily upon his head. An oppressive regime, so decisively rejected by his son on his accession, was the natural result.

- during Henry's reign, he was unnecessarily harsh towards the nobility. The overmighty subjects, who had caused trouble earlier, were all dead by 1485 and their vast estates in royal hands. Henry's increasing use of bonds and recognisances and futile attacks on retaining merely served to deepen the hostility between the Crown and the natural rulers of the country. The unprincipled activities of his 'new men' deepened the gulf, which resulted in the noble backlash of 1509–13.

- the achievements of future monarchs had nothing really to do with the activities of the first Tudor. If royal government became stronger in the reign of Henry VIII, this had more to do with that king's fierce and unpredictable nature and to the extraordinary 'break with Rome', when Henry VIII divorced England from the papacy. The king then made himself the ruler (or Supreme Head) of the Church in England (soon to be the Church of England) and his power was enhanced. None of this was foreseen in the reign of Henry VII.

- the peaceful accession of Henry VIII was not quite as peaceful as it seems. The repudiation of Henry VII's style of government shows up the serious tensions in early Tudor England, tensions that were the creation of Henry VII. In addition, the transition from one Henry to another might not have been so smooth if Henry VII had died a few years earlier, leaving a child as king. If Henry VII had died in 1503, when his wife did, he would have left an heir aged only twelve; the same age as Edward V when his father died 20 years before.

The reign in its true perspective

Overall, then, Henry VII's reign was not a great success. Ronald Hutton has described the reign as 'one long succession crisis' and this seems a far more realistic way of viewing matters than the older 'new monarchy' and stability model. Even if it turned out all right in the end, the view that an historian needs to convey is the contemporary view – what was it like at the time – rather than the hindsight view. Making judgements from the point of view of 1509, we can praise Henry's success in difficult circumstances and his success in handing on the throne peacefully to his heir. On the other hand, the judgement on the reign, as it unfolded, is somewhat different. The reign was far more troubled and the regime far harsher than that of Edward IV or Richard III. Henry VII was never assured of survival but lurched from one crisis to another. His regime was characterised by watchfulness, suspicion and fear. He abandoned the medieval model of government as a consensus between Crown and nobility, in favour of Crown and 'new men'.

Like Edward IV and Richard III, Henry VII was a child of the upheavals of mid-century. Unlike them, he was not a great nobleman in the normal sense but a penniless refugee. He had been catapulted to the throne by the sudden and unexpected series of events.

- First, the sudden and unexpected death of the outrageously hale and hearty Edward IV just before his 41st birthday.
- Second, the sudden and unexpected overthrow of Edward V by his uncle, Richard.
- Third, the sudden and unexpected death of Richard III at the Battle of Bosworth and the Welsh Henry Tudor's accession to the throne of England. The disease that killed King Edward had much to answer for!

Viewed in this way, it is clear that the problems of Henry VII's reign had one important characteristic, which is often overlooked by historians – they were largely self-inflicted. Henry had problems not because he inherited an unruly and turbulent nobility: they were, in fact, pretty quiescent. The upheavals of mid-century had taught them caution and the overmighty nobles were all dead and gone; the estates that had sustained them and their military power were divided up, with much of the land absorbed by the Crown. This is why the nobility put up so little resistance. After the death of the Earl of Lincoln, there was no one mighty enough to challenge Henry's rule.

However, although the nobility was cowed and cooperative, Henry did not know this and his background, together with his lack of legitimate claim to the throne, meant that he overestimated the political problems that faced him. This, in turn, explains the way in which his regime became harsher rather than more liberal as the reign went on. Edward IV has been accused of idleness and sexual misconduct during his second reign, but at least he was able to enjoy his power! When other claimants for his throne had been disposed of, and with foreign threats muted, Edward IV reacted by enjoying himself and building up the power of his family. Not so Henry VII. He continued to work at his papers, enmeshing landowners in bonds and recognisances, giving free rein to the illegal actions of his 'new men'. Interestingly, historians have always tended to judge kings in terms of how hard they worked. Henry VII was a harsh bureaucrat, so he has been favourably judged. The truth is that Henry VII's regime was highly unpopular and much more severe than it need have been. It was a personal style of government, which did not outlive its creator. Henry's new style of government ultimately led nowhere. He was a bureaucrat, his son was not. He had taken the throne by force and with no claim; his son took it peacefully and had a very good claim, since he was Edward IV's grandson and other Yorkist claimants were in prison or dead.

At the same time, it is clear that, despite the upheavals of the period, the power of and respect for the monarchy were never in doubt. Despite Henry VI's manifest failings and his madness, most of the nobility wished to see him continue as king. As an anointed sovereign, he was the king, ordained by God; he could not be replaced by the agency of men, even a man as powerful as the Duke of York. Edward IV's seizure of the throne was born out of desperation rather than a matter of principle or anything else. After the death of his father, it was the only way to save the family and the family estates. It would take all the trauma of betrayal and the readeption of Henry VI to bring Edward to the terrible crime of regicide in 1471. Despite this crime, Edward IV then prospered during his second reign. There were no uprisings or rebellions, as the nobility accepted the new order of things.

Richard III, of course, was rather less popular than his brother. He had seized the throne from his nephew, who was the rightful king. Despite this, respect for the monarchy as an institution, as opposed to respect for the monarch as a man, was powerful enough to make it look as though Richard III's regime would be a success. So the monarchy that Henry VII inherited was in good shape; it was only his feeble claim to the throne and his refusal to honour his promise to rule jointly with Elizabeth of York that caused him trouble. Once again, Henry VII's success was not that impressive.

At the same time, it is important to look at the reign not from the point of view of the king but from the point of view of those who were governed. From this perspective, it is clear that Henry's so-called successes were not as great as they first seem. For most of his subjects, it made little difference who was king. Their loyalty lay with the local landlord or lord of the manor. Even for lesser landowners and gentlemen, the centre of their political life was the shire they lived in rather than the government in Westminster. Central government could make all sorts of decrees but whether they became effective and operational depended on the reaction of local landowners and the like.

Henry VII refused to rule within the law. He liked bonds and recognisances and immediate warrants because they operated outside that body of custom and precedent that the English called common law. He allowed his agents to flout the law to increase their power and the power of their master. He extended the royal prerogative rights beyond what was deemed acceptable by medieval society. The nobility, apart from those related to the regime, were largely sidelined and Parliament, that important point of contact between Crown and local rulers, met only once (and then rather briefly) in the last twelve years of the reign. Of course, in any regime, those with power are liable to abuse that power, but, in Henry VII's England, that abuse became institutionalised: it came from the top.

The success of medieval government depended on the characteristics of the king. The most successful regimes were those where the king had:

- a good claim to the throne
- ability as a soldier
- ability to rule with the aid of the nobility and other landowners
- ability as a politician
- a willingness to administer justice upon his subjects
- freedom from the threat of foreign invasion.

In these areas, Edward IV (and even Richard III) had rather more going for them than the first Tudor. His claim to the throne was poor. He had no military ability: he appeared in two battles but took no part in the fighting. He failed to rule with the nobility or to administer justice fairly upon his subjects. He did have considerable ability as a politician and as a man who devoted himself more seriously than most of his predecessors to the business of government and holding on to power. He was largely free from the threat of foreign invasion.

All of this leads to the conclusion that Henry VII was very fortunate to hold on to power and to hand the Crown on to his son. Henry's good fortune can be seen in his winning the Battles of Bosworth and Stoke, which could have gone either way; inheriting a nobility that was smaller and less powerful than it had been for a century or more and inheriting a diplomatic situation where England's main enemy, France, took a serious and sustained interest in Italy. Nonetheless, he did face serious threats at home and abroad that could have unseated his regime at any time in the first fourteen years of the reign. In the end, good fortune was more important than good government in keeping Henry VII on the throne!

SUMMARY QUESTIONS

1 To what extent did Henry VIII change the government and administration of England in the first four years of his reign?

2 'The early part of Henry VIII's reign shows how unpopular his father had become.' To what extent do you agree with this judgement?

3 Why did Henry VIII invade France in 1513?

4 'The execution of Edmund de la Pole in 1513 marked the end of the Wars of the Roses.' How valid is this view?

5 'Henry VII restored strong and effective government to England.' With reference to the period 1485–1513, assess the accuracy of this view.

AS ASSESSMENT

This section offers students the chance to improve their skills in answering exam and coursework questions. Questions come in two types:

1 **Source-based questions**. Candidates are presented with a series of sources (both contemporary and secondary) and are asked a series of questions, each of a specific type. This section aims to help students identify the different types of questions and to show how to structure the different types of answer required.

2 **Essay questions**. It is important that candidates spot the different types of essay question on offer in order to structure their answer in the most effective way.

SOURCE-BASED QUESTIONS IN THE STYLE OF EDEXCEL

Study Sources A–E and answer Questions 1–5 that follow.

Source A

The king called his Council and these men thought it good to give a general pardon to all those who would receive the same without any condition or exemption. And after the young Earl of Warwick was brought to Paul's Church through London, where many might see him that thought he was run away and that they might perceive the fondness of the Irish to move war against the king without any just matter. The king, hearing of these men's landing, decided to encounter them straightaway in case that, in long tarrying, he might enlarge their power and increase their numbers. In truth, they were but a few in the beginning. To be short, both armies came within a little to Stoke and the morrow after joined and fought very valiant on both sides, for those Germans were very good and apt soldiers and so was their Captain, Martin Schwarz; his like was not in either army. The Irishmen did as well as any naked men could do and at length they were slain, about 4000 and more. This field was fought the 16 of June 1487.

> From *The Book of Houth*, an Irish history of the sixteenth century, produced by the supporters of Nicholas, Lord Houth. Quoted in I. Arthurson, *Documents of the Reign of Henry VII*, 1984.

Source B

It began to be rumoured that Richard, King Edward's son, was alive and living in Flanders, where he was known as Perkin and held in great esteem. Conspiracies immediately began to multiply, just as in spring the trees always clothe themselves in a multitude of flowers. On the one hand, there were criminals who were tempted by poverty or bribes to break forth and flock to Perkin in Flanders. On the other hand, many of the nobility turned to the conspiracy. There were others who considered themselves badly rewarded by King Henry for the services they had eagerly given him. These people were driven partly by resentment and partly by greed to support this Perkin. Lastly, there were others whose desire for revolution flung them headlong into this conspiracy.

> From Polydore Vergil, *History of England*, 1513. Here he is writing about events in 1492.

Source C

The English have not always remained in peaceful obedience to their king. This is because there were too many heirs to the kingdom. The claims of these heirs were so strong that there were disputes between the two sides. Now it has pleased God that all should be thoroughly and duly purged and cleansed. This is so that not a doubtful drop of royal blood remains in the kingdom except the true blood of the king and queen and, above all, of the Lord Prince Arthur. And all of this since the execution of Perkin and the son of the Duke of Clarence.

> From a letter written to the King and Queen of Spain by the
> Spanish ambassador to England in January 1500.

Source D

Sir Richard, the governor of Calais, said that four years ago when the king lay sick, he [Sir Richard] was in the company of many important men. They were talking of what would happen if the king were to die and who would rule England then. Some, he said, spoke of my Lord of Buckingham and said he would be a royal ruler and gave him great praise. Others of them spoke of the traitor, Edmund de la Pole. But none of them spoke of the Prince of Wales.

> From a letter sent to Henry VII by an informer in 1503.

Source E

There was, of course, nothing new about executing magnates in fifteenth-century England; indeed, many more went to the scaffold under Henry VI or Edward IV than under Henry VII. But the executions in the previous reigns were all carried out by the victorious party in the aftermath of rebellions or coups d'état; there seems to be no immediate precedent for such cold-blooded and 'pre-emptive strikes' as the executions of the Earl of Warwick and Sir William Stanley. These can be called precautionary executions intended to deal with trouble before it took place rather than afterwards. Henry's concern for security has been interpreted by some historians as reflecting a basic insecurity in his regime. But it would be more apt to say that he was not prepared to take any chances at all of suffering the experiences of his four predecessors.

> From A. Grant, *Henry VII*, 1985.

QUESTIONS

1 What can you learn from Source A about the nature of the threat to Henry VII's throne in 1487? (6)

2 Use your own knowledge to explain how Lambert Simnel came to challenge Henry VII at the Battle of Stoke. (10)

3 How far do Sources C and D agree about the chances of Henry VII being succeeded as King of England by Prince Arthur? (10)

4 How useful are Sources A and D to an historian studying the security of Henry VII's regime? (10)

5   Study Sources B and E and use your own knowledge. Do you agree with the view that after
    1490 Henry VII's regime remained essentially insecure?   (24)

HOW TO ANSWER SOURCE-BASED QUESTIONS

General points

• Do not read all the sources before looking at the first question. Instead, read the first
  question and then read the source it refers to. In this way, you know what you are looking for
  as you read the source for the first time.

• Another idea is to use a pen or highlighter to pick out words or phrases that will help to
  answer the question.

• Answers to some questions might well be balanced answers. Part of your answer might say:
  'In some ways, the source is useful because ...' The second part of your answer might say: 'In
  other ways, the source's usefulness is limited because ...' Balanced answers of this type are
  often very successful. It does not mean that you are contradicting yourself, provided one part
  of the answer is more substantial than the other. A good answer on a reliability question, for
  example, would be saying overall either that the source is essentially reliable but with one or
  two limitations, or that the source is basically unreliable though not totally so.

• In reliability questions, be careful not to say that a source is reliable because the author is an
  eyewitness. Often eyewitnesses, especially those who take the trouble to write down their
  reactions afterwards, are often doing so because they are biased in favour of or against the
  individual or incident that they are recording.

• Also think carefully before saying that a source lacks value because it is unreliable. Value for
  an historian includes the attitudes of contemporaries to the matter under review.
  Government propaganda to persuade people to agree with a certain viewpoint will be
  unreliable and inaccurate but is still valuable to an historian who wants to know how
  government propaganda operates.

Possible approaches to the questions

While possible approaches to the questions are offered in the following examples, these are not
the only lines of argument; they are merely suggestions. The important thing is that you keep
thinking hard about what the question is asking and that you are prepared to develop a range of
ideas in your answer.

1   What can you learn from Source A about the nature of the threat to Henry VII's throne
    in 1487?   (6)

• This is a question designed to test your ability to extract relevant information from a source
  and make inferences that are supported by direct reference to phrases in the source. As you
  read it, pick out words and phrases to show that the Simnel threat was serious. Then see if
  there is any evidence to suggest that the threat was not that serious. As you start your
  answer, you must put forward an inference (a conclusion) in your own words about the nature
  of the threat to Henry VII. You might start with: 'This source shows that the threat to
  Henry VII from Lambert Simnel was serious.' Then bring in the words/phrases you have

highlighted to back up this idea. In the second part of your answer, you might want to balance your answer by showing that the source also claims that the threat was not that serious. You should start a new paragraph with a sentence such as: 'At the same time, Source A hints that the danger to Henry was not that serious. The author says that the Irish troops were "naked" and that "they were slain, about 4000 and more".' Do not worry that this second part seems to contradict the first part of your answer; it is designed to show that you are thinking carefully about the information and ideas in the source. However, the best balanced answers will have rather more inferences and support for them from the source on one side of the argument than on the other.

- Remember that if you are asked, 'What does the source reveal', 'What can you learn from the source', or 'What does the source tell you about ...' you need to do just that. Outside knowledge is not required. It will not gain you any credit and may mean that your answer loses focus and so loses marks. The examiner will not be impressed because s/he will begin to think that you have not read the question before answering it!

---

2   Use your own knowledge to explain how Lambert Simnel came to challenge Henry VII at the Battle of Stoke. (10)

- This question depends squarely on your own knowledge of the topic and you should not bring in material from any of the sources. The answer is essentially descriptive rather than analytical, and the more you know about the Simnel conspiracy before the Battle of Stoke the better your answer will be.

---

3   How far do Sources C and D agree about the chances of Henry VII being succeeded as King of England by Prince Arthur? (10)

- This is an agreement/disagreement of sources question, involving careful cross-referencing between the sources. Read each source carefully, trying to get a clear sense of what each implies about the chances of a smooth Tudor succession, in the shape of Prince Arthur, when Henry VII dies. In Source C, the Spanish ambassador, writing in 1500, seems confident that Arthur will succeed in due course. In Source D, however, Arthur's succession seems far from secure. The informer says that in discussing the succession 'none of them spoke of the Prince of Wales.' (Note that it is still Prince Arthur because, although the author is writing in the year 1503, the year after Arthur's death, he is discussing an incident four years previously, i.e. 1499.) You must then start your answer with a clear statement about this disagreement in your own words: 'Source C disagrees fundamentally with Source D about the chances of a smooth Tudor succession on Henry VII's death. Source C claims ...'
In the next paragraph, when you examine Source D, restate your argument clearly: 'While Source C claims that Arthur is certain to become king, Source D disagrees completely. This disagreement is even stronger because both seem to be written after the executions of

Warwick and Warbeck. Source C states this and Source D has it by implication, since neither is mentioned as possible successors.'

- In most questions of this type, you might follow the section on disagreement (or agreement) with a shorter balancing section on limitations to the agreement or disagreement: 'Although the sources basically disagree about this issue, they do agree that ...' In most cases, sources do not agree or disagree totally, as they seem to do here!
- Notice that this question is not an 'evaluation of the source' question. It does not ask you to evaluate the reliability of the sources. It does not ask you why they disagree but just the *extent* to which they disagree. However, although a paragraph of evaluation of the sources is not reqired, you need to bear in mind the author of each source and bring that in where appropriate. You might, for example, decide to introduce a few meaningful asides. So you might say that while the Spanish ambassador was naturally keen to play down the threats to the regime (he wanted the marriage between Catherine and Arthur to go ahead), the informer naturally enough (since he is an informer) might want a good story about threats to the regime.

| 4 | How useful are Sources A and D to an historian studying the security of Henry VII's regime? (10) |

- This question is a classic usefulness/reliability/value question, which asks you to evaluate the given sources. Having already answered Questions 1 and 3, you are already familiar with what both sources say; you must now consider their usefulness.
- The first rule is to always use the key word in the question throughout your answer. In this case, the key word is 'usefulness', **not** reliability or value. At the same time, notice that questions on 'value' usually have a qualifying phrase after the key word. You are not being asked to evaluate the usefulness of sources in general but usefulness for an historian studying the security of Henry VII's regime.
- As a general rule, consider each source separately, bearing in mind that a really good answer might also compare the usefulness of the two sources under review. This can easily be done, not at the beginning of your answer but as you start your comments on the second source. So you might start that section with a new paragraph beginning: 'While Source A is very useful for an historian, Source D is rather less so.'
- In thinking about your answer, you need to consider two main things in relation to each of the sources specified in the question. First, you should consider the circumstances in which each source was produced and whether there was a specific purpose in its production. Is the source an example of propaganda designed to persuade people for or against something or someone by giving an exaggerated or biased account of events? All these considerations will affect the source's usefulness. This means that you must look carefully at each source's attribution – usually written above or below the source. For Source A, you need to consider whether an Irish author might have exaggerated aspects of the Simnel threat because of his nationality. If so, is this evident in what he says in the source? Now look through the source for evidence about bias or support for one side or the other. Is the source useful because it

lacks viewpoint and merely records what happened? Is it useful because the Irish author actually seems hostile to the Irish forces involved in the campaign against Henry VII?

- Second, you need to look at usefulness by measuring what the source says against your own knowledge of the events referred to. Did Henry VII parade Warwick through the streets of London? Was Martin Schwarz likely to be a good commander? Were the Irish naked? Even if you do not know the answers to these questions for certain, does what the author say seem likely or unlikely given your knowledge of the topic?

- Once again, you will probably want to put forward a balanced (but not too balanced) answer. If, having considered the question, you think the source is basically useful, start with a paragraph explaining why it is useful, giving your own knowledge and quotations from the source(s) as appropriate. The next paragraph can then look more briefly at limitations to the source's usefulness. After that, you can move on to consideration of the second source and make a judgement about whether it is more or less useful than the source you have just written about.

---

5   Study Sources B and E and use your own knowledge. Do you agree with the view that after 1490 Henry VII's regime remained essentially insecure?   (24)

- This question is the classic question asking you to integrate sources and own knowledge in order to agree or disagree with a particular contention.

- As the question is worth the most marks (40 per cent of the total) it is important that you plan your answer carefully to ensure that you produce a consistent line of argument. Only in this way can you put forward the sustained judgement that merits the top marks.

- Always start planning by using your own knowledge. What episodes seem to back up the idea that Henry's regime was essentially insecure after 1490? After considering those ideas and facts, think about ideas and evidence to back up the idea that the regime was, in fact, pretty secure. Hopefully, one side of the argument will appear more convincing and you should now make a conscious decision to adopt that line of argument in your answer. If you think that the regime was insecure, you need to be able to play down those ideas that make it seem secure. On the other hand, if you take the line that the regime was actually secure after 1490, then you will play down the significance of those factors that make it seem insecure.

- After this, you might consider whether you wish to introduce a more sophisticated argument to answer the question. You might argue that, while the regime was still insecure by 1509, it had become more secure after 1499 and the executions of Warwick and Warbeck. Or you might want to argue that the regime was more secure than it seemed after 1490 but actually became less secure after 1501 with the deaths of Arthur and Queen Elizabeth and the failure of the Spanish alliance. At the same time, you might consider the question from two different perspectives. Would an historian with his built-in hindsight take a different view from contemporaries like Henry VII, who did not know that the regime would survive? Is it possible that contemporaries would have seen the regime as less stable than it actually was?

At this planning stage, then, you should consider such possibilities and be able to develop your own line of argument.

- Now and only now, are you ready to integrate the specified sources, B and E, into your plan. Source B reminds you about Perkin Warbeck, who is probably already in your plan. It tells of all the men and nobles who were apparently prepared to flock to Perkin. Pick out a couple of quotations and add them to the section of your plan dealing with Perkin Warbeck and your view of how serious a threat he was. Then do the same for Source E. Alexander Grant thinks that Henry's regime was, in fact, pretty secure because of his 'precautionary executions'. You may agree and add in a couple of quotations to back up this view in your plan. However, you may disagree with the source. You might, for example, wonder whether delaying the execution of Warwick for fourteen years (after all, he was put in the Tower soon after Henry VII won at Bosworth) can really be seen as a pre-emptive.

- The important point to notice is that, since the two sources take different views about the security of the regime, you will need to be critical of one of them and explain why you think its ideas about the security/insecurity of the regime are exaggerated. This ability to use sources critically is a key feature of top-level answers.

- Finally, remember that you must use *both* the sources *and* your own knowledge in your answer, as half the marks are awarded for each skill. A brilliant answer that only uses the sources or only uses own knowledge can only receive half the marks, and quite a good answer will be marked out of twelve rather than twenty-four.

ESSAY QUESTIONS IN THE STYLE OF AQA AND OCR

While source-based questions are an important way of assessing your understanding of the period, essay questions are also a natural way of working out your ideas about a topic.

Reading the instructions

Make sure you understand the demands of the question. Look at the instruction words, usually at the beginning of the question. There are basically three types of question:

1) **Reasons questions**, which are asking you to explain a series of inter-related reasons for something. Such questions may start with the words:

   - Why ...
   - Assess the reasons for ...
   - Account for ...

   For example:

   - Why was the English monarchy so much stronger in 1509 than it had been in 1483?
   - Account for the deep-seated political instability in England between 1459 and 1471.

2) **Judgement questions**. Nearly all other questions ask you to make a judgement of some sort. These questions start with such phrases as:

- To what extent ...
- Assess the importance of ...
- How valid is the view that ...

For example:

- To what extent was Henry VII's foreign policy motivated by financial considerations?
- 'Far from being in decline, the English monarchy was stronger at the death of Edward IV than at his accession.' How valid is this viewpoint?

Here, rather than explaining reasons, you are being asked to construct a line of argument running throughout the essay in which you give a direct and consistent answer to the question. These judgement questions are often more difficult than 'reasons' questions because there is more room for disagreement and argument, i.e. there is no right answer and you have to construct a line of argument that remains consistent throughout the essay.

3) **Reasons and judgement questions**. Just occasionally, you may be asked a question that combines the first two types outlined above – asking for reasons and a judgement. These questions start with the following words:

- To what extent and for what reasons ...

For example:

- To what extent and for what reasons did the English nobility become less powerful in the period 1470–1509?

Here you need to combine the approaches of the first two types and it is best to deal with each part separately. Explain the reasons first and then answer the 'to what extent' part.

Notice that exam questions rarely ask you to describe or narrate the events of the period specified in the question, so if you find yourself doing this in your essay, you are unlikely to gain much credit. Your essay will always be rewarded in terms of how well you answer the question set, not in terms of how much you know about the topic.

Planning your essay

You cannot answer a question effectively unless you plan carefully and systematically beforehand. A good plan will ensure that every part of your answer is directly relevant to the question set and is structured in the first place around a series of relevant ideas and not around facts and events. Outside exams, the proper and detailed planning part of the essay-writing process may take longer than the actual writing up of the essay, since planning involves reviewing your ideas and information and thinking hard about how the ideas and information you have can be applied to the question set. Remember, however, that you will be able to write your essay more quickly, more fluently and more directly if you have planned properly!

Write the question at the top of a blank piece of paper. Read through your notes, relevant chapter(s) in the book and any other relevant material you possess. As you read, think about the question and try to write down some relevant ideas. These should be fairly broad and you should then be able to use your notes to add in relevant information or examples to back up or substantiate your ideas. When you have worked carefully through all your material, review your plan and think how you might organise the ideas you have.

If you are answering a 'reasons' question, you should end up with a series of reasons, clearly stated with details and examples, which back up each one. To add weight to your argument, you might think about putting your reasons in order of their importance so that in the finished essay you will evaluate the relative importance of each reason as you come to it. In most cases, it is best to start with the most important reason and deal with the others in descending order of importance. One other refinement is to divide your reasons into long term and short term and then to decide which group is more significant.

If you are answering a 'judgement' question, you will need to organise your ideas into two groups: those that support the contention in the question and those that oppose the contention. When this has been done, you need to weigh up the arguments on each side and decide which side looks the stronger. This is the stage where you have to think very carefully in order to evaluate the relative importance of each of your ideas and then the collective importance of each of the two groups of ideas. On this basis, you must then decide which group is the more convincing so that you start the essay with a clear idea of your overall answer. You will either basically agree with the contention or judgement in the question or basically disagree. Avoid the comment that the contention is true 'to a certain extent'.

With 'reasons and judgement' questions, follow the procedures for each of the two parts as outlined above. The most common failing with answers to this type of question is that students often fail to tackle the evaluation/judgement part of the question directly. Having spent a lot of time on the reasons, the crucial second part of the question is forgotten or sidelined into a short final paragraph. Clear planning on your part should ensure that this cannot happen.

In all cases, as you start writing your essay, you must be clear in your own mind about your overall line of argument. You can only do this with confidence if you have spent time planning your answer and thinking through the main ideas.

Writing your answer

- *The first paragraph*. It is vital to get your essay off to a good start, so the first paragraph must start the argument. You should not think of the first paragraph as an introduction to the question or the topic. It should not set the scene for the essay or merely define some of the key words in the question. Nor should it be used to tell the examiner how you are going to set about the answer, e.g. 'First I will look at ... then I will consider ...' Above all, you should not include further questions at this stage; instead, you must start the answer. If you have thought carefully and planned thoroughly, your answer to the question should be uppermost in your mind as you start writing.

In 'reasons' questions, you should start by explaining your first reason and its relative importance. The best approach is to start with the most important reason. So, in your first sentence, you should briefly outline that reason and say that you think it is the most important reason. Then explain and explore that reason more thoroughly and add relevant supporting evidence. You should not use the first paragraph to give a list of all your reasons, as this will lead to unnecessary and time-wasting repetition later on when you explain each of the reasons you have thought of.

In 'judgement' questions, you should outline your overall argument in clear and reasonably bold terms in order to catch the examiner's attention. The overall answer, agreeing or disagreeing with the viewpoint in the question, should be stated in the first sentence. You should be fairly decisive in the first paragraph and avoid too balanced an argument, which will make you look uncertain. You must show that you basically agree or basically disagree with the contention in the question. Do not go down the 'middle of the road' and collect the catseyes! You can add reservations later on when you are arguing in detail. Try to finish the first paragraph with another sentence that clearly answers the question. If this sounds as though your opening paragraph is a concluding paragraph, it is meant to. You are not trying to keep the examiner in suspense until the last moment; you are writing a history essay where the answer must be clear from first to last. Remember, too, that you do not need to explain your argument in detail in the first paragraph – that will come later. You can use the first paragraph to put forward clear, relevant but unsubstantiated ideas that will have the examiner wanting to read on.

One exciting refinement might be to look at a specific detail or episode and/or give a brief contemporary quotation (better than an historian usually!) that helps to illustrate your answer. Then explain how this example/quotation answers the question and clarifies the line of argument you will be pursuing in the body of your essay.

- *The body of the essay.* Every paragraph of your essay should start with a relevant idea, which directly, if partially, answers the question. If possible, you should also try to include a link back to the previous point, as this will add to your control of the argument. Once you have established the basic idea for each paragraph, you should explain and expand it, and then add facts and evidence to back up your idea. Evidence and information, therefore, comes later in the paragraph, *not* at the beginning. Only mention those pieces of information that clearly back up the main idea of the paragraph.

In a 'reasons' question, each paragraph starts with a new reason. In a 'judgement' question, start each paragraph with an idea that either supports or undermines the judgement in the question.

Consider this question: 'To what extent can Richard III be blamed for the crises of 1483 and 1485?' In a 'judgement' question of this type, you need to consider both sides of the argument. At the planning stage, you will have thought about ideas that support the contention and ideas that seem to contradict it. In some ways, Richard III can be blamed; in other ways, he cannot be blamed. To avoid writing two parts of an essay that just contradict each other, you can adopt the following strategy.

If you basically disagree with the contention, start the body of the essay by discussing those factors that support the contention, but, as you consider them, play down their importance. A favourite device is to start this section with the phrase: 'At first glance, it is easy to see why Richard III might be blamed for the crises of 1483 and 1485.' After briefly putting forward ideas and evidence to support this view, you then put forward the arguments that disagree with the assertion in the question. This section of the essay, where you come on to the most important points, might start with a sentence such as this: 'Although it is easy to blame Richard III for the crises of 1483 and 1485, the reality is that England's political difficulties at that time were the result of deep-rooted problems rather than just Richard III's desire for the Crown.' You then write most of the essay in support of this idea and therefore end up with a clear line of argument running throughout the essay, even though you have considered both sides of the question.

Of course, you could avoid the balancing problem by ignoring one side of the argument entirely. However, your answer would be less convincing and less honest if it merely ignored one viewpoint.

Notice that in all cases it is very unlikely that you will totally agree or totally disagree with the judgement in the question. The approach outlined above should enable you to define clearly, during your essay, the extent to which you agree or disagree.

- *The last couple of paragraphs.* These can be used to summarise your argument, but this may be a little repetitious, since your reasons or line of argument should be clearly stated as the essay unfolds. Rather better is to see if you can use this part of your essay to question the question. Sometimes question setters add in key words that need to be challenged or at least directly addressed in a good essay. Consider the following question: 'Why did Henry VII crush the Simnel conspiracy **so easily**?' Here, a good essay will give the reasons for Henry VII's success and then discuss directly how easy the process was. This in itself might involve a structure similar to the illustration above: i.e. 'It looked easy because ... In fact, it was very long drawn out and difficult because ...' Similar demands are made by the following example: 'Why were the Crown's financial problems **so serious** in the period 1461–85?' Again, the emboldened words need to be addressed directly, probably towards the end of the essay, so that you have given a clear indication of how serious the financial problems were. This may involve considering whether the problems were more or less serious than before or after the period specified and you can see that a good essay might consider, quite relevantly, material from outside the period referred to in the question. In the same way, your essay would be readily enhanced if you could add depth to your argument by comparing the financial problems in this period with those under Henry VII. The last few paragraphs can really widen the scope and depth of your argument. If you can do this, you will impress on the examiner that, at the end of the essay, you are considering and evaluating new perspectives and ideas rather than reiterating those you have just talked about.

Other essay-writing tips

- You will need to define and explain **key terms** or **words**, such as revolution, decline, aggressive foreign policy, rebellion, etc, but you should do so within the framework of your argument, not as an isolated paragraph unlinked to the main ideas.
- **Historiography** (knowledge of different historians' viewpoints on the central topic) can be very helpful and add depth to your answer but only if it used analytically rather than descriptively. Do not write about different views for the sake of it, i.e. to show what you know, but make historiography part of your argument. For example: 'S.B. Chrimes backs up this point clearly when he says ...' or 'Although Alexander Grant plays down the power of the nobility during the reign of Henry VII, they remained a formidable and dangerous force.'
- **Contemporary quotations** are very much appreciated by examiners, but again they must support a relevant idea rather than being brought in descriptively. For example: 'Henry VII's famous remark that the Irish "would crown apes at last" deliberately understated the threat from Simnel.'
- One extra refinement that you might consider in judgement questions is the idea of **change over time**, i.e. the answer to the question changes during the period under review. Consider this question: 'How powerful was English government, 1483–1513?' Rather than giving an overall assessment saying that English government was basically weak or basically strong, you might take the view that it was weak at first, became stronger, especially after the destruction of Warbeck, but then became even stronger in the early years of Henry VIII's reign, when the nobility regained their natural place in the governance of the realm.
- Though this may sound alarming, the most important thing in essay writing is to try to **enjoy the process**! Essay answers develop your analytical skills and help you to think through problems in an organised and logical way. If you do this, you should be able to develop your own individual lines of argument rather than regurgitating the notes you have been given in class. Remember that there is no correct answer to any historical question; the fun lies in the argument!

SELECT BIBLIOGRAPHY

1450–85

Carpenter, C. *The Wars of the Roses – Politics and the Constitution, 1437–1509* (Cambridge University Press, 1997)

Davies, C.S.L. *Peace, Print and Protestantism, 1450–1558* (Fontana, 1977)

Gillingham, J. *The Wars of the Roses* (Weidenfeld & Nicholson, 1981)

Goodman, A. *The Wars of the Roses* (Routledge, 1981)

Griffiths, R.A. *Henry VI* (London, 1981)

Griffiths, R.A. and Thomas, R.S. *The Making of the Tudor Dynasty* (Alan Sutton, 1985)

Hicks, M.A. *False, Fleeting, Perjur'd Clarence* (Alan Sutton, 1980)

Hicks, M.A. *Edward V: The Prince in the Tower* (Tempus Publishing, 2003)

Kendall, P.M. *Warwick the Kingmaker* (George Allen and Unwin, 1957)

Kendall, P.M. *Richard III* (George Allen and Unwin, 1955)

Lander, J.R. *Crown and Nobility, 1450–1509* (London, 1976)

Lander, J.R. *Government and Community – England, 1450–1509* (Edward Arnold, 1980)

Loades, D.M. *Politics and the Nation* (Fontana, 1974)

Pollard, A.J. *The Wars of the Roses* (Macmillan, 1988)

Pollard, A.J. *The Worlds of Richard III* (Tempus Publishing, 2001)

Ross, C. *The Wars of the Roses – A Concise History* (Thames and Hudson, 1976)

Ross, C. *Richard III* (Eyre Methuen, 1981)

Ross, C. *Edward IV* (Eyre Methuen, 1984)

Storey, R.L. *The End of the House of Lancaster* (Sutton Publishing, 1999)

1485–1513

Arthurson, I. *The Perkin Warbeck Conspiracy* (Alan Sutton, 1994)

Bennett, M. *Lambert Simnel and the Battle of Stoke* (Alan Sutton, 1987)

Bevan, B. *Henry VII – The First Tudor King* (Rubicon Press, 2000)

Brigden, S. *New Worlds, Lost Worlds* (Penguin, 2000)

Chrimes, S.B. *Henry VII* (Eyre Methuen, 1972)

Elton, G.R. *Reform and Reformation* (Edward Arnold, 1977)

Grant, A. *Henry VII* (Routledge Lancaster Pamphlets, 1985)

Gunn, S.J. *Early Tudor Government* (Palgrave Macmillan, 1995)

Guy, J. *Tudor England* (Oxford University Press, 1988)

Lockyer, R. *Henry VII* (Longman, 1968)

Starkey, D. *The Reign of Henry VIII* (Collins and Brown, 1991)

Storey, R.L. *The Reign of Henry VII* (Blandford, 1968)

Vickers, B. (ed.), *Francis Bacon – The History of the Reign of Henry VII* (Cambridge University Press, 1998)